AF600364

THE CATHOLIC UNIVERSITY OF AMERICA
CANON LAW STUDIES
No. 132

THE ALIENATION OF CHURCH PROPERTY

IN THE UNITED STATES

AN HISTORICAL SYNOPSIS AND COMMENTARY

A DISSERTATION

Submitted to the Faculty of Canon Law of the Catholic University of America in Partial Fulfillment of the Requirements for the Degree of Doctor of Canon Law

by

REV. EDWARD LOUIS HESTON, C.S.C., PH.D., S.T.D., J.C.L.
Priest of the Congregation of Holy Cross

THE CATHOLIC UNIVERSITY OF AMERICA PRESS
WASHINGTON, D. C.
1941

Nihil Obstat
EDUARDUS G. ROELKER, S.T.D., J.C.D.,
Censor Deputatus.
Washingtonii, die 20 aprilis 1941.

Imprimi Potest
THOMAS A. STEINER, C.S.C.,
Superior Provincialis.

Nostrae Dominae, Ind., die 3 maii 1941.

Imprimatur
✠ MICHAEL J. CURLEY, D.D.
Archiepiscopus Baltimorensis et Washingtoniensis.

Baltimorae, Md., die 5 maii 1941.

Printed By
The Ave Maria Press
Notre Dame, Indiana

TO MY

FATHER FOUNDER

AND

LAWGIVER IN CHRIST

THE VERY REVEREND BASIL ANTHONY MARY MOREAU

FOUNDER OF

THE CONGREGATION OF HOLY CROSS

TABLE OF CONTENTS

PART ONE — HISTORICAL SYNOPSIS OF THE ORIGINS OF CHURCH PROPERTY IN THE UNITED STATES

CHAPTER I

THE PERIOD OF ACQUISITION

CHAPTER II

THE PERIOD OF ORGANIZATION

CHAPTER III

THE PERIOD OF CONSOLIDATION

PART II — COMMENTARY ON CANONS CONCERNING ALIENATION AND SIMILAR CONTRACTS

CHAPTER IV

THE RELATIONSHIP OF CANON LAW WITH AMERICAN CONTRACTUAL LAW

CHAPTER V

THE NATURE OF ALIENATION AND ITS REQUISITE CONDITIONS

CHAPTER VI

THE MANNER OF ALIENATION

CHAPTER VII

THE COMPETENT SUPERIOR FOR ALIENATION

CHAPTER VIII

CONTRACTS RESEMBLING ALIENATION

CHAPTER IX

REMEDIES AGAINST IRREGULAR ALIENATION

CHAPTER X

DONATIONS MADE BY OR TO ECCLESIASTICAL ORGANIZATIONS

CHAPTER XI

MORTGAGES AND DEBTS

CHAPTER XII

THE SALE AND EXCHANGE OF ECCLESIASTICAL GOODS

CHAPTER XIII

THE RENTAL, LEASING, AND LENDING OF ECCLESIASTICAL PROPERTY

CHAPTER XIV

THE DISPOSAL OF CHURCH PROPERTY IN CASE OF THE EXTINCTION OR DISMEMBERMENT OF ECCLESIASTICAL CORPORATIONS

FOREWORD

Temporal administration occupies an important and even essential place in the external life of the Church. More so than in other countries this aspect of ecclesiastical life claims much detailed attention in the United States. Special circumstances make the situation of the Church in America altogether unusual. Her expansion here, on a scale and along lines unknown in most other countries, calls for a tremendous outlay of material means. The construction and maintenance of churches, parochial schools, whether primary or high, with Catholic colleges and universities, Sisters' houses, rectories and parish-halls, requires a familiarity with financial problems which is unparalleled where the Church has long been established and where the passage of centuries of ecclesiastical life has rendered her temporal condition permanent and comparatively static. This remarkable element of growth and expansion in American Catholic life naturally creates new problems, since financial transactions will not affect an organization in the stages of development as they will react on an organization already completely and definitively established.

The present dissertation aims to study, in the light of the special conditions prevailing in the United States, although not in exhaustive civil legal detail, the Canon Law of the Church on the alienation of ecclesiastical property and on contracts resembling alienation. A valuable study of the more general aspects of this same problem, *Canonical Limitations on the Alienation of Church Property,*[1] was published as a doctoral dissertation in the Canon Law School of the Catholic University of America in 1936, by the Reverend Joseph F. Cleary, J.C.D., of the Diocese of Hartford. This excellent work, precisely because it was a pioneer publication in the canonical field of alienation, could hardly be expected to devote its attention to peculiar problems in the United States. This absence of specific application to our own country sufficiently justifies the present work.

In the circumstances a certain amount of repetition of points already discussed competently by Dr. Cleary has been unavoidable. It has been

[1] The Catholic University of America Canon Law Studies, n. 100.

the aim of the present author to reduce such repetition to the absolute minimum required as general background for more detailed explanations. He has endeavored to organize *The Alienation of Church Property in the United States* in such a manner that it will supplement *Canonical Limitations on the Alienation of Church Property*. Let it be remembered, however, that neither work makes any pretense at treating all the civil technicalities involved in these operations; detailed guidance on these points must be sought from competent professional sources.

Nor does the present dissertation aim to offer a detailed discussion of those phases of alienation which affect religious Orders and Congregations. This question has already been adequately handled by the Reverend James E. McManus, C.SS.R., J.C.D., in *The Administration of Temporal Goods in Religious Institutes*.[2] In the course of the subsequent treatment of alienation in the United States observations will be made from time to time to point out the differences in legislation on secular and religious ecclesiastical corporations. More particular information can be found in the above-mentioned thorough work of Dr. McManus.

In the investigation here undertaken particular stress has been laid on the genuine nature of alienation and its influence in determining the true character of those contracts which resemble alienation. Thus relation to stable capital and the possibility of legal jeopardy before the civil courts are established as the basis of the consideration of these two species of contracts. More particular applications of the general principle thus formulated are attempted in the commentary on the canons dealing with mortgages and debts, donations by and to church bodies, and the sale, exchange, rental, leasing and lending of ecclesiastical property. An effort had been made to coordinate the legislation in each instance by putting the different treatments into their proper relationships with the general canons on alienation and on contracts resembling alienation.

* * *

The author wishes here to offer his filial thanks to his Superior General, the Very Reverend Albert F. Cousineau, C.S.C., and to his Provincial Superior, the Reverend Thomas A. Steiner, C.S.C., for the opportunity to complete his Canon Law studies immediately at the

2 The Catholic University of America Canon Law Studies, n. 109.

Catholic University, after conditions made further residence at Rome inadvisable. At the same time he expresses his gratitude to the members of the Faculty of the School of Canon Law at the Catholic University, for their attention and assistance.

He feels himself obliged most especially to the distinguished canonist, his former Superior, the Reverend William J. Doheny, C.S.C., J.U.D., First Assistant Superior General of the Congregation of Holy Cross, first for suggesting the topic here treated, then for invaluable direction, generous assistance and unfailing encouragement during the preparation of the dissertation, and particularly for the special privilege of consulting the manuscript of his recent excellent monograph, *Practical Problems in Church Finance.*

Lastly, he does does not forget his fellow-religious, priests, seminarians, and brothers, of Holy Cross College, Brookland, D.C., and their many kindnesses, too numerous to mention.

PART I.

HISTORICAL SYNOPSIS OF THE ORIGINS OF CHURCH PROPERTY IN THE UNITED STATES

NOTE

The general historical approach to the problem discussed in this present study can be expedited very briefly. Chapter III of *Canonical Limitations on the Alienation of Church Property,*[3] by the Reverend Joseph F. Cleary, J.C.D., and Sections I-III of *Church Property: Modes of Acquisition,*[4] by the Reverend William J. Doheny, C.S.C., J.U.D., offer thorough and scholarly presentations of the general historico-juridical angles of the present question. This study, consequently, can limit itself to a brief introductory consideration of the historical background of the problem in the history of the Church in the United States. It has been deemed advisable not to limit this outline to strict questions of alienation, but rather to offer a general schematic presentation of the origins of ecclesiastical property in the United States, to serve as a background for a clearer understanding of later problems touching upon alienation in the strict sense and other cognate problems.

3 Catholic University of America Canon Law Studies, n. 100; Washington, 1936.

4 Catholic University of America Studies in Canon and Roman Law, n. 41; Washington, 1927.

CHAPTER I.

THE PERIOD OF ACQUISITION

Article 1. The Church in Spanish Territory

The origins of the Church in what is now the United States date back to the beginning of the attempts to colonize Florida. In 1521, two years after his discovery of this peninsula, Ponce de Leon undertook to establish a Spanish settlement in Florida. This enterprise ended in disaster. Two years later, in 1523, the King of Spain granted a patent of exploration[5] and colonization to Lucas Vasquez de Ayllon, a judge of San Domingo. This expedition drew its principal inspiration from motives of Christian zeal. The King himself provided for all the expenses entailed by the transportation and establishment of the missionaries and the subsequent worthy maintenance of divine worship. In 1538 another expedition, this time directed by Hernando de Soto, set out for the same purpose, in virtue of a new royal patent which stipulated the condition that missionaries accompany the party and be supported by its leader. This project ended tragically in the battle of Mauila in 1540, as a result of which even the missionaries lost the little property they had brought along with them or had been able to acquire in the New World.

On September 5, 1565, the erection of a primitive shrine or hermitage dedicated to Nuestra Señora de la Leche marked the beginnings of the present-day city of St. Augustine. To forestall the danger of

5 Part of the text of this patent of exploration reads as follows: ". . . by these presents I empower you to carry to the said land the religious whom you judge necessary, and the vestments and other things useful for the observance of divine worship; and I command that whatever you shall expend in transporting the said religious, as well as in maintaining them and giving them what is needful, and in their support, and for the vestments and other articles required for divine worship, shall be paid entirely from the rents and profits which in any manner shall belong to us in the said land." — Real Cedula que contiene el asiento capitulado con Lucas Vasquez de Ayllon, in Navarrete, *Colecion de Viages y Descubrimientos,* II, 153-156. Quoted by Shea, *The Catholic Church in Colonial Days* (New York, 1886), p. 105.

attack from the French Calvinists at nearby Fort Caroline, the Spanish commander laid siege to this stronghold on September 21, 1565. After subduing it with great slaughter, he changed its name to San Matheo and at once marked out the site for a new chapel to be constructed out of wood which the French had prepared to build a vessel. The third Catholic chapel in Florida was erected on the shores of Charlotte Harbor, on the western side of the peninsula, for Father Rogel, S.J., and his companions, who had been sent to the mission by St. Francis Borgia.

In 1569 Father Rogel established himself at the new post of Santa Helena, on Port Royal Harbor. This made him the first resident priest in the territory now comprised in the State of South Carolina. From there he pushed on with his companions to the Indian town of Orista, where he erected a church and a house for himself and the three young men who assisted him. The following year, however, he destroyed both the house and the church and returned to Santa Helena. That same year, 1570, an attempt was made to land in the territory along the Chesapeake Bay. All preparations were made for the establishment of a permanent mission: vestments, books, furniture, etc. The mission which was founded along the Potomac by these missionaries from Florida was very humble; a poor hut served as both chapel and house. The stubborn hostility of the natives effectively barred the way to any development in that territory, and before long the mission met a tragic end with the massacre of the religious who had undertaken its foundation.

The Franciscans entered the Florida Mission in 1577. By this time parish churches had been erected in the missions of Nombre di Dios and San Sebastian. Meanwhile the Convent of San Francisco had been built by the Friars at St. Augustine. This important establishment was later destroyed by fire in 1599. That the Church in Florida at this time was comparatively well supplied with temporal goods and property is evinced by the fact that after the fire the religious took up their quarters in the Hermitage of Nuestra Señora de la Soledade, which had been hitherto used as a hospital, and that a new hospital, dedicated to Santa Barbara, was opened soon after. Contrary to the express wish of the King, the burned convent was not rebuilt. To provide for its community, the Father Guardian of San Francisco was appointed pastor of the parish and chaplain of the fort. This assured him and his community of some revenue.

As a result of constant progress, both spiritual and temporal, this mission and its dependencies were constituted a custodia of the Franciscan Order in 1609 and later erected into the Province of Santa Helena, about 1613. These two measures bespeak a certain degree of increasing temporal prosperity. In 1616 a pastoral visitation of St. Augustine and the surrounding missions, by the Delegate of the Bishop of Santiago de Cuba, attests that the Church was well supplied with chalices, furniture and other necessary appurtenances. About 1617 the parish of St. Augustine was declared to be a benefice. This shows that it was materially prosperous enough to assure at least the becoming maintenance of the pastor.

On December 4, 1630, the King of Spain provided for the maintenance of the Franciscan missions in Florida by ordering money to be sent from Mexico for clothing and supplies. It is estimated that Bishop de la Torre, who as Bishop of Santiago de Cuba had the Florida missions under his jurisdiction, expended on them much more than his total income of approximately four hundred dollars from that portion of his diocese. Despite the lack of rich and abundant resources, the missions of St. Augustine could boast, even at that early date, of two hospitals, one of which was for the poor, and of the hermitage or chapel of Santa Barbara. The Church in Florida was gradually acquiring those temporal goods which enabled her to carry on her spiritual work for the natives and for the Spanish colonists.

In 1674, Gabriel Diaz Vara Calderon, who had been named to the Diocese of Santiago de Cuba just three years previously, undertook the difficult task of making a pastoral visitation in person to the Florida territory which was subject to him. Records show that he examined carefully the accounts of the hospitals at St. Augustine, founded churches with provisions for the maintenance of the incumbent priests, and supplied others with much-needed vestments. His benefactions to the missions which he visited amounted to approximately eleven thousand dollars. The King later made arrangements to pay the expenses of bringing more missionaries to Florida and of providing them with an annual salary of one hundred and fifteen ducats. This project eventually failed because of the many difficulties raised by the royal officials in Cuba.

On Pentecost Sunday, 1684, Juan Garcia de Palacios, then Bishop of Santiago de Cuba, opened a diocesan Synod. The synodal Constitutions, signed on June 16, 1684, were law for the Florida missions for the whole duration of their subjection to the Spanish jurisdiction. Among other points of interest legislated on by this Synod, the inalienability of church property is explicitly enunciated:

> The goods and property held by churches are dedicated to the divine worship, and to rob them is sacrilege; and in order that no occasion may be given to commit it, and at the same time to attest the goods held by churches, and which cannot be alienated or usurped . . . ,

the Constitutions continue, the Synod legislated that the Dean and the Chapter of the Cathedral, as well as all parish priests, were to keep authentic records. These records were to enumerate specifically all houses, farms and other property belonging to churches, with mention of all vestments and other articles employed in divine service or for the adornment of the altar.[6]

The last years of the seventeenth century and the first years of the following century were a sad and turbulent period for the Spanish missions in the south and southwest of the present United States. Invasions and bloody massacres by the heathen, or sometimes apostate, Indians, often at the instigation of bigoted Protestant neighbors, usually culminated in the destruction and plundering of churches and residences, as well as of any other property which the missionaries might possibly have possessed. In 1702, for instance, the savage Appalachicolas, urged on by the fanaticism and hate of Governor Moore of South Carolina, attacked the settlement of Santa Fé and burned the church. Governor Moore himself was responsible for the firing of three churches and convents on St. Mark's Island. In his retreat to his own colony he burned the town and church of St. Augustine, with the Franciscan convent, the shrine and a precious library already worth about six hundred pounds. In the territory which was now only a heap of smouldering and bloody ruins there had once been thirteen towns, each with a church and a convent for the Friars. With characteristic generosity the King decreed that all the revenues of vacant Sees in Spain, which would ordinarily revert to the Crown, should be applied

6 *Constitutiones Synodales,* Tit. IV, Const. I-IV.

to the reconstruction of the church, convent, and hospital of St. Augustine.

A raiding party from Georgia descended on the mission in 1735 and destroyed Nuestra Señora de la Leche, carrying off all the church plate, votive offerings and other treasures. In the following year, nevertheless, the Bishop was in a position to open a classical school. The King appropriated the equivalent of about forty thousand dollars for the reconstruction of the church at St. Augustine, but the project was never realized, due to the dishonesty then prevalent in official colonial circles.

Spanish attempts at settlement in the territories now known as New Mexico, Arizona, and Texas were never as felicitous as those in Florida. Here again the rapid succession of small foundations, murderous invasions and greedy plundering was an almost insurmountable obstacle to the normal development of the Church and the consequent acquisition of ecclesiastical property. More so than in Florida, royal officers and soldiers misappropriated funds and supplies for themselves. Notwithstanding these great handicaps, the missionaries labored strenuously in the new villages which were established to organize the so-called "reductions" for the social welfare and training of the natives. In 1727 three missions were undertaken in Arizona at royal expense, but up until 1763 no reputable Spanish town had yet been founded. This precluded the possibility of establishing church property in those regions. From the year 1763, due to various influences, Spanish activity in the southwest, which in reality had never been anything but sporadic, was virtually at a standstill. This necessarily curtailed the zeal of the missionaries by depriving them of the armed protection which they needed for entrance into the country of the savages and accounts for the absence of ecclesiastical foundations and possessions.

It is not hard to see, then, how amid such unsettled conditions there was little or no room for canonical difficulties on the alienation of church property. Ecclesiastical Superiors were necessarily too intent on the struggle for bare existence and on maintaining ownership of the little they had been able to acquire, by protecting it against banditry and plunder, to be troubled with worries on the transfer or diminution of ownership through canonical procedure.

Article 2. The Church in French America

The beginnings of the Church in the French colonies of North America were wretchedly poor. There is no record of generous largesses of money and supplies being furnished by the colonizing government, as was the case with the greater number of the Spanish foundations in the New World. For the greater part the missionaries were obliged to share the poor lot of their fellow-countrymen in the colony or the still greater misery of the savages. This probably explains why the Second Diocesan Synod of Quebec, held on February 23, 1698, enacted that the Sacraments were to be refused to all who deliberately neglected to pay regular tithes.The absolute necessity of providing support for the clergy and the churches made lack of compliance with this duty indicative of infidelity to the Church itself.

At that time the jurisdiction of the Bishop of Quebec extended to all the Indian missions in the Mississippi valley down as far as Mobile and New Orleans. In these regions, however, better provisions had been made for the upkeep of the churches and the attendant priests. The parish of Mobile, established on July 20, 1703, was to have been assured by royal grant of one thousand livres a year for the salary of the pastor and six hundred livres yearly for the assistant; steps had already been taken to build a church and a house. About this time Abbé Gervaise, a rich young ecclesiastic in France, desired most ardently to devote his life and a portion of his abundant patrimony to the upkeep of the Louisiana missions, in concert with the Foreign Mission Seminary of Paris. Although his uncle subsequently prevented him by force from coming to labor personally in the missions, the zealous young priest sent out provisions for three years, three workmen to construct a house and chapel, and funds for the support of the mission. The zeal and fearlessness of the missionaries can be gauged by the fact that in 1707 the Governor withheld the salaries of the priests in the missions, in order to show his spite and displeasure at their courageous denunciation of the profligacy of the French colonists.

Nevertheless, the spiritual aspect of colonization was not entirely forgotten in official circles. In August, 1717, Letters Patent were issued in the name of Louis XV, authorizing the formation of "The Company of the West" for work in Louisiana and the adjoining territory. Clause 53 of these Letters Patent reads:

> As in the settlement of the countries granted to the said Com-

> pany by these Presents, we regard especially the glory of God by procuring the salvation of the inhabitants, Indians, and savages and negroes, whom We desire to be instructed in the true religion, the said Company shall be obliged to build at its own expense churches in the places where it forms settlements; as also to maintain there the necessary number of approved ecclesiastics; either with the rank of parish-priests or such others as shall be suitable, in order to preach the Holy Gospel there, perform Divine service and administer the Sacraments.[7]

The city of New Orleans was founded about the year 1718. The first church was constituted by one half of a wretched warehouse; later even this humble chapel had to be transferred to a tent. In 1720, the new Jesuit Superior of the New Orleans mission, Father de Beaubois, decided to seek out Sisters to open a hospital and academy. This project was actually realized in 1727, when the Ursulines opened their house, which remains today as the oldest conventual structure in the United States. This auspicious beginning was not continued, as there are evidences that as early as 1752 religion in Louisiana was in a far from flourishing condition.

Things gradually came to such a pass that in 1763, in the wake of the French Parliaments, which had already followed the ignoble example of Paris, the Superior Council of Louisiana banned the Jesuits. The Council decreed that the vows of the religious were null and void, and ordered that everything they owned, with the exception of strictly personal property, was to be sold at auction; the vestments and other church furnishings were to be handed over to the Capuchin Fathers, and all Jesuit churches and chapels of whatever nature were to be razed to the ground. The execution of this iniquitous order had repercussions even at such remote points as Fort Kaskaskia among the Illinois tribes.

When the French territory in the Mississippi valley was ceded to England, everything seemed lost for the cause of Catholicism in that region. The conduct of English colonial officials in the eastern parts of the continent banished all but the faintest hopes for any encouragement in the spread of the Faith in the lands which fell under their domination. Consequently, at the sight of the French officers in New Orleans warring openly on the Catholic Faith and its zealous missionaries and faced with

[7] Le Page du Pratz, *Histoire de la Louisiane*, I, 77-78. — Cf. Shea, *The Catholic Church in Colonial Days*, p. 562.

the discouraging prospect of English rule, Abbé Duverger, of the Foreign Mission Seminary of Paris, who was then laboring practically alone in the Illinois territory, proceeded without any authorization whatsoever to sell all the property belonging to his Society. This property included a stone house and a seven-acre plot of land, along with mills and implements. Thus the growth of the Church in that territory was brought to an abrupt standstill.

The history of Catholic origins and expansion in Maine and New York can be told even more briefly. Chapels, and sometimes even elegant churches, were built at various forts and at missions among friendly Indians. More often than not, however, these flourishing outposts of religion soon became the object of pillage, plunder and fire at the hands of savages acting at the instigation of officers in the neighboring English colonies, or even of soldiers of these same officers and under their direct leadership. Thus very little property was allowed to remain for any great length of time.

Nothing can be said of the origins of church property in New England, since this portion of the country was closed to the Church entirely. Catholics had no civil rights and, consequently, the acquisition of property by other means than subterfuge which had to be carefully concealed, was altogether out of the question. Accounts of Catholic settlements in Georgia and in the Carolinas are none too reliable, with the result that no information on ecclesiastical property can be sought out there.[8]

[8] Dr. Guilday's remarks on the scarcity of material for the historical background of the First National Synod of the United States in 1791 can be very well applied also to the question of the origins of ecclestiastical property: ". . . the colonial period of the Spanish and French jurisdiction over these parts of the present United States where formerly Spanish, Mexican, French and Canadian bishops ruled has not revealed much information on the problem of the possible influence such legislation might have had on our First National Synod in 1791. This may be due, as regards the Spanish-Mexican Church, to the inaccessibility of source material. The literature on the Church in New Spain is a large one; but the books and collections are rare or scarce and only to be found here and there in Mexican libraries, as Father Cuevas points out in his history of the Mexican Church. The French influence was even less, for the reason that, apart from centers like Detroit, Kaskaskia, Cahokia, and New Orleans, there were few Catholics in the territory governed from Quebec. These little French congregations were swallowed up in the drive toward the West which set in immediately after the American War of Independence."—*A History of the Councils of Baltimore* (New York; Macmillan Co., 1932), p. 36.

Article 3. The Church in the Eastern Colonies

A) In Maryland.

Even more so than in the case of the early Spanish settlers in Florida, the idea of pecuniary profit and material aggrandizement were far from the thoughts of the first Catholic colonists in the eastern part of what is now the United States. In the spirit of true Catholicism they had sacrificed positions of comparative comfort and ease in the homeland, hoping to find opportunities for the free exercise of their Faith in a land not yet vexed by the trying restrictions of Catholic-hating lawmakers. The difference between such colonists and those who set forth to enrich themselves, even at the cost of depredatory tactics against others, is emphasized in the account of one of the first attempts to establish a Catholic colony in America. The chronicler of the enterprise, a certain James Rosier, employs in his narration a religious tone which certainly implies a more exalted aim than a grasping trade or thrilling adventure. He says that they set forth on their hazardous journey "supposing not a little present profit, but a publique and true zeale of promulgating God's holy church by planting Christianity to be the sole interest of the Honorable setters forth of this discovery."[9] This was the comment made on the second attempt to found a refuge for English Catholics in North America in 1605. It failed, as had the first effort, made by Sir George Peckham, in 1583. No further steps were taken in this direction until some years later. In 1627, after much careful preparation, Sir George Calvert, member of the King's Privy Council, Baron of Baltimore in the Kingdom of Ireland, and a convert to Catholicism, obtained from King James a charter empowering him to organize an expedition to promote a new colony in America, and sailed on his perilous enterprise.

His first destination was the province of Avalon in Newfoundland. According to his royal charter he could make whatever laws he pleased, provided that they should "not be repugnant or contrary to those of England," and a special clause was added, "Provided allways that no

[9] *A True Relation of most prosperous voyage made this present yeere, 1605, By Captaine George Weymouth, in the discovery of the land of Virginia . . . Written by James Rosier, a Gentleman employed on the voyage* (Londini; Impensis Geo. Bishop, 1605), p. 34. — Shea, *The Catholic Church in Colonial Days,* p. 25.

interpretation be admitted thereof (of the Charter), whereby God's holy and truly Christian tradition or allegiance due to us, our heires and successors may in any thing suffer any prejudice or diminution."[10] Thus, without the necessity of enacting any special legislation to this effect, the charter implicitly authorized Catholics to hold land, and to own their own churches. In this manner the first days of the Church in northeastern North America were marked by official recognition of her sacred and traditional right to hold and administer property in her own name.

This fundamental principle of religious tolerance was retained when Lord Baltimore, after many reverses, finally succeeded in transferring his Catholic colony from Avalon to what is now Maryland. He did not live to see the actual granting of the royal charter for this latter enterprise. His son secured the promised grant, and inaugurated the new colony under the same auspicious religious beginnings as his father had done in Newfoundland, intending "to convert, not extirpate the natives, and to send the sober, not the lewd, as settlers, looking not to present profit, but future expectation."[11]

Before embarking from England, Lord Baltimore had taken pains to seek out priests for the new settlers in America. He applied to the Jesuits through their Provincial in England and their Father General in Rome. Given the poverty of all those participating in the enterprise, he was obliged to inform the Jesuit Superiors bluntly that he could offer the clergy in the future colony no material support. "The Baron himself," he wrote, "is unable to find support for the Fathers, nor can they expect sustenance from heretics hostile to the Faith, nor from Catholics for the most part poor, nor from the savages who live after the manner of wild beasts."[12]

Nothing daunted, the Jesuits accepted this new mission field, where, in addition to countless other hardships, they could expect no financial help from the head of the colony nor from their own impoverished faithful. Two priests were selected to accompany the colonists; a lay brother was also appointed to go with the missionaries. As for their support on arriving in the new colony, it was understood that they were

[10] Cf. the complete text of this charter in Scharf, *History of Maryland* (Baltimore, 1897), I, 33-40.

[11] Quoted in Shea, *The Catholic Church in Colonial Days*, p. 35.

[12] Quoted in Shea, *op. cit.*, p. 38.

to be classified as "gentlemen adventurers." In other words, they would rank with the leaders or promoters of the party, would receive plots of ground and would then provide for their own upkeep by working this land in the free time that remained after the exercises of the sacred ministry.

After landing safely in the New World, Lord Baltimore saw to the establishment of his colony and the conciliation of the Indians. One of the bark houses evacuated by the savages was quickly converted into a chapel by two Jesuit Fathers and their lay brother. This was the first known piece of church property in the Maryland colony. In 1637 Father Thomas Copley arrived in Maryland to assume the general direction of the mission. He at once set to work to make the religious in the colony self-supporting.

In keeping with their privileged status as "gentlemen adventurers" the Jesuit Fathers in the Maryland mission became landowners like their companions. Father Copley made application for the land owed to him for his fellow-missionaries and others who had preceded them in 1634, and for still others who had come with him in 1637. His claim was duly honored, probably on the same basis as for the other leaders in the colony: two thousand acres for every five men brought over in the original party, and the same for every ten men brought over in the two following years.[13] Since Father Copley claimed to be responsible for the coming of thirty men in the first party and of nineteen in the second, it is evident that he was granted a very extensive allotment of land.

The fact that there were no other available means of support, as Lord Baltimore had warned them beforehand, obliged them to set to work at once. After the tedious work of clearing the land, they were able to cultivate it with excellent results. Their original holdings had been considerably increased by the gift of a very fertile tract of land by the Indian chief, Maquaconen, chief or king of Patuxent. The fruits of their labors were so abundant that, on the authority of John Gilmary Shea, the income from their farms met all the cost of maintaining Catholic worship and its ministers in those portions of Maryland for two centuries.[14] It is worth noting here that Father Copley, who was

[13] According to Lord Baltimore's *Conditions of Plantation,* issued on August 8, 1636.

[14] *The Catholic Church in Colonial Days,* p. 47.

known in the mission as Father Philip Fisher (the reason for the dual name is unknown),[15] took all the land he received in the name of the Jesuit Fathers, but nothing at all for himself personally.

This recognition of ecclesiastics' rights to own property was not to last long. Misunderstandings arose in 1637 between Lord Baltimore and the missionaries. This was most regrettable, especially since the occasion for the unfortunate estrangement had been furnished by an individual who was motivated more by ill-enlightened zeal than by downright malice.[16] Subsequent efforts to appease the founder of Maryland produced the effect desired, but only at the price of severe and unjust conditions which were exacted as indispensable for the further entry and activity of missionaries in the colony. Besides being forced to resign all claim to the land already handed over to them by the Indian king, the Fathers had to promise that they would accept no similar grants in the future. Further conditions enacted in 1648 prohibited all corporations, spiritual as well as temporal, from acquiring or holding land without special license, either in their own name or in the name of any person connected with them. In the following year the conditions forebade any adventurer or planter to transfer lands to any such corporation or in trust for it, without special license.[17]

To these restrictions of a more or less legal nature were soon added

15 Dr. Guilday assigns the frequent use of false names by priests as one of the primary reasons for present-day lack of authentic historical data on this important period of American Catholic Church history. — *The Life and Times of John Carroll* (New York, 1922), I, 69.

16 This individual, John Lewgar, secretary to Lord Baltimore, and formerly a Protestant minister, who was later ordained priest, was a convert of only recent standing. Consequently, he was at this time far from familiar with the spirit and practise of the Church on many matters. When he presented to the first legislative assembly (1637) certain projects of laws, on marriage, for instance, which were at variance with the mind of the Church, he was deeply offended because the missionaries, upon consultation by the Catholics of the Assembly, refused to sanction the proposed measures and declared that no Catholic could in conscience vote for them. His exaggerated accounts of the situation in his letters to Lord Baltimore irritated the patron of the colony and gave rise to an indignation which resulted in coldness and even hostility towards the missionaries.

17 These regulations against devising property to religious corporations without special authorization of the legislature have remained in the Maryland legislation down to the present time. Cf. Murphy v. Dallam, 1 Bland 529.

the scourges of hate and undisguised persecution. The neighboring colony of Virginia, with its head, Clayborne, had never entertained anything but animosity for its Catholic neighbors in Maryland. As a result of this antipathy the "anti-popish" bitterness of the Virginia settlers broke out as soon as a favorable occasion presented itself. Clayborne attacked St. Mary's county in Maryland with an armed force, and then, to vent his spite on the hated Catholics, left them at the mercy of a ruthless former sea-captain and pirate by the name of Ingle. This latter spread destruction wherever he went, driving out the Catholics and pillaging their homes. His reaction against the property of the missionaries is more easily imagined than described. It was only natural that the houses of the Jesuits at Potopaco and St. Inigoes should be wrecked. The same sad story was repeated some years later during an outburst of Puritan spite and hatred against their Catholic neighbors.

In spite of all this uncertainty and even constant danger, the faithful were generous and self-sacrificing in their efforts to compensate the missionaries for these sad losses. In so far as lay within their very limited means, they saw to the support of their priests during these distressing times until the general situation was reestablished on a normal basis. Those who were favored with a greater abundance of temporal goods were mindful of the Church in the disposition of their property and, consequently, many legacies and bequests for the benefit of the Church were made in last wills and testaments. In 1661, to cite but one example of this generosity, William Bretton Esq. and his wife, Temperance, donated a tract of land measuring an acre and a half, to the missionaries for the erection of a chapel. This donation was made "to the greater honor and glory of Almighty God, the ever Immaculate Virgin and all the Saints." [18]

Despite the lowliness of its origins and the slowness of its development in the colonies, the Church was gradually making its influence felt by those outside the fold. Her gradual acquisition of property through the missionaries brought her to the attention of her non-Catholic fellow-colonists. Frightened by evident signs of her increasing power and influence, the non-Catholics of Maryland met "for the defense of the Protestant religion." As the fruit of their deliberations they despatched a protest to William III embodying their grievances against their

[18] Shea, *The Catholic Church in Colonial Days*, p. 78.

"popish" neighbors. One of the items of this protest was framed as follows:

> In the next place Churches and Chapells, which by the said Charter should be built and consecrated according to the Ecclesiastical lawes of the Kingdome of England, to our great regrett and discouragement of our religion, are erected, and converted to the use of popish idolatry and superstition.[19]

An impartial investigation of the foundations of these sinister complaints would have proved them utterly groundless. Years later, in 1696 and 1697, in answer to the Governor's order for a report on Catholic ecclesiastical holdings in the colony, the sheriffs informed him that there was in the colony a total of nine chapels: four in St. Mary's County, four in Charles County, and one in Talbot County. This constant carping on the part of non-Catholics, however, at last produced the desired effect. Just seven years later, in 1704, the Catholics were deprived of their chapel at St. Mary's, the cradle of their religious observances in America since its erection in 1634. To aggravate the difficulty of the situation, a law passed in that same year, 1704, outlawed any one of the Catholic faith from holding any land in the colony. This prohibition naturally affected the missionaries and their property. Notwithstanding this prohibition they were still able to contrive ways and means to conceal their ownership and thus to retain their extensive possessions.

The Catholic colonists, with their missionaries, labored under these legal disabilities until the benign exception from these iniquitous laws which was granted by Queen Anne in 1707. The freedom thus conceded was by no means complete, but it at least permitted the exercise of the Catholic religion in private houses. As a result of this provision no more public chapels were built until the end of British rule. The more well-to-do Catholics availed themselves of the opportunity afforded by the law to build large houses where the faithful of the surrounding country could meet in a chapel built under the roof for private prayer and the celebration of the Holy Sacrifice.

About this time, and perhaps on previous occasions also, although

[19] Hawks, *Contribution to the Ecclesiastical History of the United States*, II, 64.

it was in contradiction to the first official policy of colonial management, Lord Baltimore[20] began to contribute to the support of the missionaries in the localities affected by persecution at the hands of fanatical governors. According to the *Instructions, power and authority to Charles Carroll, dated September 12, 1712,* he ordered eight thousand pounds of tobacco to be given to "Mr. Robert Brooke and the rest of the brethren, being in all eight persons," and an additional one thousand pounds to Mr. James Haddock, a Franciscan friar who was also laboring in the mission at this time. This munificent grant by Lord Baltimore was very different from the "Tobacco Tax" of the Protestants. This latter was a toll of forty pounds of tobacco levied on every parishioner for the support of the missioners. The payment of this tax had exercised such a devastating influence on the Protestant pastors that many of them had already been denounced to their Superiors in England for shiftless and even immoral lives. Because they had become in reality tobacco dealers rather than ministers of the Gospel, they aroused all the jealousies and enmities so frequently encountered in business circles and finally found themselves in disfavor with all classes.

The absence of this tax and of consequent business entanglements was a decided advantage for the Catholic missionaries. While four coadjutor brothers cared for their houses, tilled their lands and thus provided sufficient means to support the little community, the fathers were free to devote all their time and energy to missionary work, unconcerned by business worries. Their efforts met with such success that, even among non-Catholics, a movement of sympathy was inaugurated in regard to Catholics, and the members of the Established Church viewed with genuine alarm the unusual situation thus created.

In 1747, when the severity of the laws on the acquisition of property had been somewhat tempered, at least in practise, the missionaries purchased one hundred and twenty-seven acres of land on Deer Creek, near "Priest's Ford," in Harford County. There are records of the first missionary here in that same year: Reverend Benedict Neale. A combination house-chapel, complying with the restrictions still imposed by the concession of Queen Anne, was erected and soon became known as "Priest Neale's Mass House." A cemetery was attached to this mission, according to the then prevailing custom whereby Catholic cemeteries were established on the private farms of the priests.

20 The third of the name.

A few years later, 1750, an incident took place which gives evidence of the growth of church property in the Maryland colony, notwithstanding the restrictions imposed by the adverse laws. This incident also had disagreeable consequences for the Catholic colonists. Charles Carroll, father of the future signer of the Declaration of Independence, and Dr. Charles Carroll, an apostate Catholic, were co-trustees of an estate which had been willed to priests. Wishing to close the estate, the Catholic Carroll requested his partner in the trust to pay off the sum which he held. When this gentleman offered to compromise with a small amount, his proposition was promptly rejected with a stern reminder that this was a matter of conscience and accounting, not of compromise. To protect himself and escape the insistence of his co-trustee, the renegade threatened to invoke the anti-Catholic penal laws as a guarantee against being obliged to account for his trusteeship in favor of the priests. Through his influence an Act passed the lower House, prohibiting priests from exercising their ministry and providing that all Catholics who did not take the oath of supremacy after attaining their eighteenth year were to be debarred from acquiring property by inheritance. This measure, which was openly directed against the priests in the colony, failed to pass the upper House and to obtain the signature of the Governor. It gave rise, however, to very much bitter feeling and many formal protests were drawn up against the sinister growing influence of Catholics.

Nor was this wave of anti-Catholic feeling only a passing phenomenon. Notwithstanding the attendant bitterness of Protestants, the missionaries continued to hold their property and even to acquire more. The fears of non-Catholics were expressed by a writer in the *Maryland Gazette* of October 17, 1754:

> Does popery increase in this Province? The growing number of popish chapels, and the crowds that resort to them, as well as the great number of their youth sent this year to foreign popish seminaries for education, prove to a demonstration that it does. Moreover, many popish priests and Jesuits hold sundry large tracts of land, manors and other tenements, and in several of them have dwelling houses, where they live in a collegiate manner, having publick Mass houses, where they exercise their religious functions etc., with the greatest industry and without controul.

Lord Baltimore had warned the first missionaries to expect no support from the faithful; this continued to be generally true. In the first report ever sent to Rome on the development of the Church in the colonies, this point was stressed by Bishop Carroll. He states in this account which he prepared for the S. Congregation of the Propaganda:

> Catholics contributed nothing to the support of religion or its ministers; the whole charge of their maintenance, of furnishing the altars, of all travelling expenses, fell on the priests themselves, and no compensation was ever offered for any services performed by them, nor did they require any so long as the produce of the land was sufficient to answer their demand.[21]

Despite all the unjust restrictions which hemmed them in on every side, the Catholic missionaries still succeeded in carrying on and even in expanding their work. This could not escape the eyes of disapproving non-Catholic neighbors. In 1760 a Protestant divine in Delaware referred in a letter to "a very considerable Popish seminary"[22] in the neighboring province of Maryland. The activity of the missionaries had reached the point where they were in a position to establish a circulating library, stocked with standard books from London. This implies a certain prosperity in their general financial situation. It also furnishes some idea, howsoever vague, of the temporal condition of the Church in Maryland on the eve of the American Revolution.

B) In Pennsylvania.

The Charter of Liberties and Privileges, of October 28, 1701, in addition to the freedom already enjoyed according to William Penn's liberal policy of government, made it possible for all "who profess to believe in Jesus Christ, the Saviour of the World . . . (notwithstanding their other persuasions and practises in point of conscience and religion), to serve the government in any capacity. . . ." The only condition stipulated was that of allegiance to the King and fidelity to the

21 Shea, *The Catholic Church in Colonial Days,* p. 364.

22 Perry, *Papers Relating to the Church in Pennsylvania,* p. 313. Cf. Shea, *op. cit.,* p. 404. The minister refers to the Jesuit Academy at Bohemia Manor. At that time the term "seminary" was usually applied to what would today be called an academy or college.

Governor. This generous provision attracted many Catholics from other less-favored regions, with the result that the Church in Pennsylvania grew with comparative rapidity.

Already in 1704 Father Thomas Mansell was established in Cecil County. The acquisition and holding of church property in Pennsylvania followed the same general lines as in Maryland. Two generous Catholic ladies, the O'Daniel sisters, gave Father Mansell lands near the Herman manor. On July 10, 1706, Father Mansell himself added to his mission property by obtaining the deed for four hundred additional acres in the name of St. Xaverius. This land was further enlarged by the subsequent purchase of the St. Inigo tract from a Catholic settler, named James Heath. As had been the case in other settlements, the manor-house became the residence of the missionary and also the chapel for the faithful. In 1729 a chapel was erected in Philadelphia by means of a subscription raised among the faithful.[23]

The contributions of the faithful of Pennsylvania were generously seconded by a munificent foundation made in England. Sir John James, a Knight of the realm, of Heston, Middlesex, had established a fund of four thousand pounds, which was entrusted to the custody of the Vicar Apostolic of London. Out of the income accruing from this fund, forty pounds annually were to be devoted to the care of poor Catholics in London, while the remainder was to be used for the support of Catholics in the Pennsylvania colony. Thus the four missions then existing in Pennsylvania were assured of some twenty pounds yearly.

The general plan for the organization of church property in Pennsylvania resembled closely the main points of the system which had been hitherto followed in Maryland. The priests took the title to lands in their own names. This method seems to have met with success, if evidences of comparatively rapid growth and permanent expansion are of any value. Already in 1742, it is said of the settlement called Lancaster:

> In Lancaster town there is a Priest settled where they have bought some Lotts and are building a Mass-house, and another

23 The caution exercised by the Catholics at this time is shown by the fact that the first inquiries as to the number and residence of Catholics in Philadelphia were made by a priest disguised in Quaker garb. His first visit was to a lady whom he subsequently discovered to be a Catholic herself.

itinerant Priest that goes back in ye country.[24]

And again:

> Popery has gained considerable ground of late years . . . One of that order (the Jesuits) resides in this place and had influence enough last summer to get a very elegant chapel of hewn stone erected in this Town.[25]

About this time a missionary named Father Schneider acquired property at Cushenhopen. He settled there after moving about from various places and purchased the land from a renegade Mennonite, who sold his property to the Catholic priest in order to spite the Brotherhood. Before long Father Schneider had erected a school on this plot of land.

This general freedom was short-lived. Anti-Catholic feeling grew apace within only a few years. The instances of progress which have just been enumerated came about in spite of the severe laws which had been passed some years before in an effort to keep Catholics from gaining further footholds in the colony. In 1730 a law had been passed, providing that none but Protestants could hold lands for the erection of churches, schools and hospitals.

The particular characteristic which differentiated the growth of the Church in Pennsylvania from its development in Maryland was the fact that the Catholics in Pennsylvania habitually contributed to the support of their missionaries. This may, perhaps, be explained by the consideration of the extensive estates owned by the missionaries in Maryland, which they had contrived to retain despite all the hostile provisions of the civil law. The income from these lands supported the missionaries, covered the cost of maintaining divine worship in the chapels either at their residence or in the various mission stations, and even enabled the Superior of the mission to reimburse those in England who had contributed towards defraying the expenses of their passage and support in the first difficult days. In the Pennsylvania missions, however, there are no traces of any such estates. The settlers there were not among the first pioneers arriving in the territory, and thus could

24 Letter of Anglican minister, Reverend Richard Backhouse, June 14, 1742. — Shea, *The Catholic Church in Colonial Days*, p. 391.

25 Thomas Barton to the Secretary, Lancaster, November 8, 1762. — Shea, *loc. cit.*

not be allotted large tracts of land as was the case in Maryland. Whatever property they acquired seems to have been limited to the absolute essentials for constructing churches, schools and residences. This also explains why the faithful were called upon to share in the expenses connected with the upkeep of the mission and the support of the missionaries.

This hasty sketch of the early origins of church temporalities in the eastern part of the future United States furnishes little information that is definitive.[26] This rapid panoramic view, however, verifies the age-old cycle of the Church's use of earthly goods: humble beginnings and modest growth on her part, with clutching envy and pillaging persecution on the part of her enemies. Evidently enough, a pioneer situation such as the one just outlined, leaves little or no room for the rise of serious problems of temporal administration. The Church's greatest concern at such a time is to preserve her modest patrimony in order to be the better equipped to carry on her work of spiritual conquest. Problems will arise as expansion becomes greater and as organization develops along necessarily more complicated lines.

[26] "To sum up the status of the Catholic Church on the eve of the Revolution, it must be admitted that comparatively little has come down to us from the past clothed in the habiliments of historical certitude. Legends there are in abundance, and traditions in every town and city along the Altantic coast, but no secure history can be based upon these uncertain data. The use of *aliases* on the part of priests; the fear of committing historical facts to paper; the insufficient system of keeping records; and the hard missionary life of the day have had the regrettable effect of wrapping these years in a cloak of silence. Only occasionally in old registers that have survived do we catch a glimpse of these years of crypto-Catholicism in the colonies; or, as in old deeds that are recorded, we are enabled to picture the sturdy Catholic life that was veritably hidden in the Lord." — Guilday, *The Life and Times of John Carroll,* I, 69.

CHAPTER II

THE PERIOD OF ORGANIZATION

Article 1. The Post-Revolutionary Period

The period of organization followed hard upon the painful period of acquisition. The unsettled background of early Catholic life in America made the struggle for actual existence the primary end of churchmen. As years went on, however, the missionaries gradually acquired bits of property through purchase or donations. The difficulties attendant upon anti-Catholic hatred and bigotry made it generally necessary to conceal these possessions, as also the actual names and residences of the missionary priests. This enforced secrecy, in some aspects not unlike the *disciplina arcani* of the early Church, makes it impossible to follow the gradual development of American Catholic life with anything like accuracy. Nevertheless there are some few clues which indicate that with the close of the Revolutionary War Catholic ecclesiastical Superiors were feeling the need of more careful and complete religious organization and administration, if they were to profit by the liberty which they enjoyed in the new republic. The question of assuring the Church of the peaceful possession of the temporalities which she had so laboriously acquired was not the least of their concerns.

Although the missionaries at work in the new republic were for the most part Jesuits, the suppression of their Society a few years before[1] made it impossible for them to apply their Constitutions to the situation at hand. With the end of the colonies' political subjection to England, efforts were being made to obtain likewise the cessation of their ecclesiastical dependence on the Vicar Apostolic of the London District. The aim was to constitute them a complete and independent ecclesiastical personality subject, of course, to the supreme authority of the Holy See.

In 1782 Father John Carroll, a native-born Jesuit missionary, whose clear insight and vision coupled with other outstanding qualities were even then designating him as the natural leader of the Church in Amer-

1 They had been expelled from France in 1763, from Spain in 1767, and had been formally suppressed by Pope Clement XIV in 1773.

ica, had already drawn up a *Plan of Organization* for the clergy. He had been motivated in this step by the general dissatisfaction experienced by himself and his fellow-priests with "the rather loose ecclesiastical system"[2] which prevailed at this time. The reader of this *Plan* would surmise that property questions were uppermost in Carroll's mind; nowhere does he touch upon the necessity or even the advisability of centralizing the spiritual administration of the new-born nation. Like most of his fellow-priests he seemed to be primarily concerned with preserving as carefully as possible the property of the suppressed Society of Jesus. He says explicitly in number VI of the *Plan:*

> It has been observed already, that the preservation of the Catholick clergys estates from alienation,[3] waste and misapplication, is to be the object and end of this meeting. But that they, who are deputed to it, may come better prepared for the consideration of this important matter, and that their views may all be drawn more to a center, it will not, 'tis hoped, be deemed impertinent to mark out with more precision the subjects for their deliberation. In the first place, by the present mode of conveying and holding the estates, is sufficient precaution taken to prevent their alienation or their falling into other hands, than those of the clergy? 2ly. Is there any sufficient provision made to prevent the possibility (for not only what has, but what may happen, should be considered) of those persons, who enjoy the legal title to the lands, appropriating the whole income of them to themselves, their friends and relations, or dealing it out partially to their fellow labourers in the mission, more to some and less to others? 3ly. Will it not be proper to devise some sufficient securities, checks and controuls to prevent these mischiefs? 4thly. Should not a mode of application be determined in this meeting, or, as that will be difficult, ought not some general rules to be laid down, whereby they may be directed, who have in their hands the immediate management of the estates?[4]

2 Guilday, "The Appointment of Father John Carroll as Prefect Apostolic of the Church in the New Republic," — *Catholic Historical Review,* VI (1920), 207.

3 "Alienation here means the application of such property to other than pious uses. It does not mean selling and exchanging within the purposes of a pious use." — Hughes, *History of the Society of Jesus in North America Colonial and Federal* (New York, 1906), Document 143, VI, note 6.

4 Hughes, *History of the Society of Jesus in North America,* Document 143, VI.

Then follow proposals for the presentation of annual accounts to someone other than the usual manager of the estate, suggestions as to the provisions to be made for the old and infirm missionaries, and the penalties to be inflicted on those members of the clergy who may fail in their duty by negligence or otherwise.

With a watchful eye on the present and a provident eye on the future, Carroll based his interest in the temporalities of the nascent Church in America on the following very legitimate and commendable motives: "The obligations of justice to the benefactors, who took up or left these estates for pious uses; the sort of consecration which estates from such a destination acquire; the duty of charity to the present and future generations." His preoccupations were heightened by ominous rumors that enemies of the Society of Jesus in Europe, not yet placated by its canonical suppression, were plotting the confiscation of its temporal goods as well. In order, consequently, to preserve their possessions intact for the happy day of restoration, should it ever come, the American Jesuits organized the Clergy Corporation. This was not an exclusively Jesuit organization but was, under certain conditions, open to any priest laboring in the United States. It provided them with whatever legal safeguards were available for the property which they already held and which they perhaps would eventually acquire. Thus the control of all their goods was centralized within the country, and this fact had very great significance for the relations of the Church with non-Catholics who were not infrequently anti-Catholics as well.

In fact, Father Carroll seems to have been almost obsessed by the nightmare of eventual foreign interference in this phase of American church life. He was undoubtedly influenced by the spirit of newfound American independence, jealously and watchfully on its guard against future possible encroachments on its liberty. The situation was aggravated by the mistrust of Protestants towards the Church and the suspicion that spiritual dependence on Rome would also entail temporal subjection to the Holy See. This explains Father Carroll's general stand on these matters.

Praiseworthy as this patriotic spirit was in reality, it led him to unjustifiable exaggerations. He went so far as to write on one occasion, for example, that in the face of the possibility of European interference with the property of the Jesuits, his brethren in England "had rightly distinguished between the spiritual power derived from the bishop, and which must be left in the hands to which he had entrusted it; and the common rights of the missioners to their temporal possessions, to which as the bishop, or Pope himself, have no just claim, so neither can they invest any person or persons with the administration of them."[5] This virtual denial of the papal right of "high domain" over all ecclesiastical property can hardly be reconciled with accepted Catholic juridical principles. This particular phase of Carroll's mentality must not be lost sight of in an attempt to understand the strong and even bitter language which he employs in referring to the S. Congregation of the Propagation of the Faith and its supposed interference with the efforts of the American clergy "to secure an equitable and frugal administration of our temporals."[6] He cannot be countenanced when he implies that the Sacred Congregation will be obliged to change its attitude, because "foreign temporal jurisdiction will never be tolerated here."[7]

In all probability these unfortunate expressions should not be taken at their face-value, especially since they cannot easily be reconciled with Carroll's otherwise well-known devotion and spirit of subjection to the Holy See. Prescinding from whatever relationship they may have had to his subjective viewpoint, they are certainly most regrettable and very likely contributed not a little to the attitude of caution and almost distrust with which the Church in the United States was viewed for quite some time.

In this atmosphere a General Chapter of the American clergy was convoked at Whitemarsh, Maryland. The body of the clergy was to be represented by two delegates from each of the three ecclesiastical districts then existing. Meetings were held at infrequent intervals from June 27, 1783, to October 11, 1784. The deliberations of this Chapter follow closely the lines of the *Plan of Organization* which had been drawn up by Father Carroll in the preceding year. Of the two questions presented to what Dr. Guilday so aptly terms the "Constitutional Assembly of the American Clergy"[8] — that is to say, the maintenance

5 Guilday, "The Appointment, etc." — *Catholic Historical Review,* VI (1920-1921), 208.

6 Guilday, *loc. cit.*

7 Hughes, *The History of the Society of Jesus in North America,* Document 144, A.

8 "The Appointment, etc.", *Catholic Historical Review,* VI (1920-1921), 205.

of ecclesiastical life and discipline and the preservation of ecclesiastical property[9] — only the second calls for treatment here.

In 1782 Carroll had written rather bluntly on the temporal administration of church property in the new republic in a letter to his dear friend, Father Charles Plowden:

> I regret that indolence prevents any form of administration being adopted, which might tend to secure to posterity a succession of Catholic clergymen, and secure to them a comfortable subsistence. I said, that the former system of administration (that is, everything being in the power of a Superior) continued.

Then, recognizing the dangers of such a system, he adds:

> It is happy that the present Superior (Father John Lewis) is a person free from every selfish view and ambition. But his successor may not be.[10]

The Chapter of Whitemarsh passed *Regulations Respecting the Management of Plantations*. These regulations constituted a set of rules embodied in eight sections, to consolidate the administration of the farms and other property which had accrued to the Fathers with the passage of years. The members also pledged themselves to bring about the reestablishment of the Society of Jesus in the United States, with the consequent restoration of all its property.[11]

The results of this solidarity among the missionaries were evident seven years later when one of Carroll's first acts as Bishop of Baltimore

9 Dr. Guilday remarks that by this time the amount of church property in the United States had reached considerable proportions. — "The Appointment, etc.", *Catholic Historical Review, VI* (1920-1921), 205.

10 Hughes, *The History of the Society of Jesus in North America,* Document 142, A.

11 "The Chapter declare for themselves, and as far as they can for their constituents, that they will to the best of their power promote and effect an absolute and entire restoration to the Society of Jesus, if it should please Almighty God to re-establish it in this country, of all property belonging to it; and, if any person, who has done good and faithful service to religion in this country, should not re-enter the Society so re-established, he is nevertheless to receive a comfortable maintenance whilst he continues to render the same services, and to be provided for as others in old age or infirmity." — Guilday, *Life and Times of John Carroll,* II, 529.

was to renounce any claim on the part of his diocese to the old Jesuit estates.[12]

This step is all the more significant when it is recalled that the early missionaries were for the most part members of the suppressed Society of Jesus with no other canonical status for their missionary apostolate than that of secular priests in the Maryland missions. The above-mentioned regulations adopted at Whitemarsh in 1783 continued in force until 1814, when the canonical restoration of the Society of Jesus obliged these regulations to cede their place to the official Constitutions of the Society on the use of temporalities. These were the first steps taken in the United States to safeguard ecclesiastical holdings and prevent their passage into undue or unworthy hands.[13]

In the same year that this General Chapter of the American clergy took place, and altogether independently of it, detailed negotiations were being carried on between the Holy See and Benjamin Franklin, then American Minister to Paris, on the future of the Church in the United States. Prescinding from those aspects of the correspondence which are not relevant here, it may be noted that not a little of the discussion dealt with the question of temporalities. The circle composed of Franklin, the Apostolic Nuncio in Paris, and Cardinal Antonelli, Prefect of the S. Congregation of the Propagation of the Faith, showed great interest in the establishment of a college in France where the future clergy of the United States could be trained. Evidently, the Church in America was quite unequal to the burden of providing means for such a foundation. With ingenuous candor Franklin had suggested that, as a means of surmounting the difficulty, the four monasteries of English Benedictines in France should be suppressed by the Holy See and their revenues devoted to financing the project of the American col-

12 The text of this renunciation is as follows: "To prevent any disagreement or contention hereafter between the Bishop of Baltimore and the Clergy, or any of them, in consequence of any words contained in his Holiness' brief for erecting the See of Baltimore, etc.; I hereby declare that I do not conceive myself entitled by the said brief to claim any right of interference in the management of those estates in Maryland and Pennsylvania, which were heretofore applied to the maintenance of the Jesuit missioners; and since their extinction to the ex-Jesuits, and other Clergymen admitted to partake of their labor, in serving the Congregations, which were before served by he Jesuits."—Guilday, *Life and Times of John Carroll.*

13 Bishop Carroll gives no indication that his action has been authorized by the Holy See.

lege in France. In other words, ecclesiastical property belonging to one religious organization would have been unjustly alienated for the benefit of another having no direct connection with it. It is not surprising that Cardinal Antonelli answered the Nuncio on September 27, 1783: "The proposition of Mr. Franklin, to suppress the four monasteries of English Benedictines existing in France, should be rejected, without further discussion."[14]

In a letter dated February 17, 1785, to his friend Father Thorpe in Rome, Carroll mentions that Rome has manifested active interest in the material prosperity of the Church in America. He mentions receiving a letter from Cardinal Antonelli, who "wishes to know the number of our Clergy, and the amount of their incomes: for tho' the Congregation means not to meddle *in temporalibus,*[15] yet conceiving and believing that there are Church possessions here, it is proper for them to know how many Clergymen can be maintained from them."[16]

It was apparently in response to this request of the Sacred Congregation that Father Carroll drew up his *Relatio pro Emo Cardinali Antonello de statu Religionis in Unitis Foederatae Americae provinciis,* which he forwarded to His Eminence through the Chevalier de la Luzerne, French Minister Plenipotentiary at New York. Regarding the specific question of the means of supporting the clergy and of the Church's property in this country he wrote:

> Presbyteri sustentantur ut plurimum ex fundorum proventibus; alibi vero liberalitate Catholicorum. Nulla hic proprie sunt bona ecclesiastica. Privatorum enim nomine possidentur ea bona ex quibus aluntur Presbyteri; et testamentis transferuntur ad haeredes: ita faciendum suggessit dira necessitas, dum legibus Catholica Religio his arctaretur; neque adhuc inventum est huic incommodo remedium, quamvis a nobis id anno elapso tentaretur.[17]

From his *Relatio* it is clear that the questions connected with church property in America were as yet only in the inchoative stage; nothing

14 Guilday, "The Appointment etc."—*Catholic Historical Review,* VI (1920-1921), 221.

15 This explicit assurance of the Congregation may have been the result of Carroll's misgivings on this score being made known to the Holy See.

16 Guilday, "The Appointment etc."—*Catholic Historical Review,* VI (1920-1921), 235.

17 *Relatio* etc., 3°, in Guilday, "The Appointment etc."—*Catholic Historical Review,* VI (1920–1921), 245.

had yet been firmly established on a good working basis. Guilday remarks that "the administration of Church property was causing quarrels and scandals, which were threatening the unity of the Church in the United States; the Revolution had not amalgamated the races that had fought side by side for liberty, and the spirit of nationalism in Church affairs was looming up as a potent source of antagonism."[18]

Pioneering attempts at precise and official legislation along the lines of temporal administration are found in the Statutes of the First Diocesan Synod of Baltimore, which met on November 7, 1791. From Bishop Carroll's subsequent Pastoral Letter of May 28, 1792, it is clear that the support of the clergy at that time depended largely on the contributions of the faithful,[19] since the number of priests had grown to the point where income from estates and plantations was no longer sufficient. This explains why the Synod of 1791 and the Pastoral of 1792 devote so much time to this point; it was a necessary prerequisite for the smooth functioning of the Church's spiritual activity.

In the first of the Synodal Statutes touching upon the point at hand are found the first official beginnings of the trustee-system which will later be considered more in detail. Decree VI of this first Diocesan Synod reads as follows:

> It is decreed, therefore, that in every congregation, two or three persons of approved virtue and respectability be chosen by the Congregation, or appointed by the pastor, to be Churchwardens or guardians; and that the persons so appointed, on Sundays and other festivals, after the reading of the 1st Gospel at Mass, or after the sermon, shall collect the offerings of the faithful.[20]

Decrees VII, VIII and XXIII likewise deal at great length with the temporal status of the Church at large and of the individual churches in particular:

> VII. The offerings, according to the practise of the Church, are to be divided into three parts; so that one be applied to the maintenance of the pastor; another to the relief of the poor; and a third to the procuring of all things requisite for divine worship,

18 Guilday, "The Appointment etc., *ibidem,* 247.

19 Cf. also the passage from the *Relatio* quoted above, p. 27.

20 Guilday, *The National Pastorals of the American Hierarchy* (Washington, 1923, N.C.W.C.), p. 10.

and for building and repairing the church. But if provision be made otherwise for the maintenance of the pastor and the poor, all offerings are to be appropriated to the fabric of the church, or to furnishing it with proper utensils and ornaments for the more dignified celebration of divine worship.

VIII. The offerings made by the faithful, to render God propitious to themselves or others, through the efficacy of the Holy Sacrifice of Mass, should be accepted by the ministers of the altar in such manner as to afford no room for suspicions of avarice or simony; let them be contented, therefore, with such an acknowledgement of their services as cannot be burthensome to the bestowers of it; nor yet so insignificant, as to render the priestly ministry despicable in the opinion of considerate men.

XXIII. The number of Catholics having increased, and being dispersed through the different States, and at great distance from each other, it is become necessary to have likewise a greater number of spiritual labourers; but these cannot be brought from foreign countries or maintained, unless the faithful concur towards bearing that expense, as they are bound by the law of God, according to the testimony of St. Paul, who says, "If we have sown unto you spiritual things, is it a great matter if we reap your carnal things?" The faithful, therefore, are to be reminded often of this duty, with which, if they neglect to comply, they will omit, through their own fault, hearing Mass on Sundays and festivals, and receiving the Sacraments at these seasons, in which they need them most, the seasons of sickness, of Easter; and when through the prevalence of sinful passion, or long habits of vice a speedy reconciliation with God becomes indispensably necessary. Wherefore, as long as they refuse to contribute for the ministry of salvation, according to the measure of worldly fortune given to them by a beneficent God, and thus violate the divine and ecclesiastical laws, they are to know that they are in a state of sin, unworthy of obtaining forgiveness in the tribunal of confession; and that they will be answerable to God, not only for their own non-compliance with duties so sacred, but likewise for the ignorance and vices of the poor people, who remain destitute of Christian instruction on account of the sordid avarice of those who are more favoured with the gifts of fortune. To begin, then, in this Diocess, that which is practised in other Christian countries, the preceding regulations were formed, relative to the obligations of the faithful; and others will be added hereafter.[21]

These were the first lineaments of ecclesiastical property organization by the newly established hierarchy of the United States. The provisions of church authorities will become more direct and more detailed, in proportion as the problems become more complicated.

Article 2. Trusteeism

It was mentioned in the preceding section that the First Diocesan Synod of Baltimore formulated a decree which gave rise to what afterwards became known as the "trustee-system" in the administration of church property in the United States. Consequently, before entering upon a treatment of the development of property legislation in the various provincial and plenary councils of Baltimore, it will be useful to preface these discussions with a brief synopsis of the origin and evolution of the trustee-system in America. Its influence on the expansion and development of the Church in America in the nineteenth century was so far-reaching that no adequate view of this period can be formed without at least a rapid sketch of this phase of the administration of American church property.

The plan of having laymen participate in the administration of church property was adopted primarily for two reasons: 1) to provide a body of individuals who could obtain incorporation and consequent legal protection for ecclesiastical property; 2) to present to the non-Catholic element of the nation's population a method of administering church goods which would be more in harmony with the democratic tendencies and traditions of the new republic. The first of these reasons was, of course, the more fundamental, and seemed best suited to meet the exigencies of the peculiar situation created for the Church in America by the then existing civil laws. Thus the primary and original aim of the establishment of lay-trustees for church property was the preservation of this property in ecclesiastical hands. Because of this aspect of the problem Bishop Carroll himself was one of trusteeism's most ardent supporters in the first years of its existence, although he found it necessary to modify his viewpoint considerably at a later period. The reasons

21 Guilday, *The National Pastorals*, pp. 10-11.

which induced American church authorities to approve this plan are quoted as follows by Dr. Guilday, from a report to the S. Congregation of the Propagation of the Faith made by the Jesuit, Father Grassi, whose years in America had afforded him abundant first-hand information on the system at work in actuality:

> By virtue of the laws in America, Churches cannot possess, unless they are *incorporated* by the Legislature of the State in which they are, and by means of this act of incorporation all the material value of the church, the presbytery, the cemetery, or other goods belonging to the church is placed under the guardianship of the law, in order that they may be used for their destined purposes. For that reason, an act of incorporation is never in harmony with the law unless there be syndics or administrators for the same church property. These are called *Trustees* or Vestrymen, and they are elected from time to time from the Catholic congregation belonging to the church. The same thing exists also among the Protestants. The advantage which arises from *Incorporation* is, that the property does not run the danger of being lost to the purposes for which it is intended. In many cases, however, instead of incorporation, the property is held in the name of a particular person, as for example, the bishop, or the missionary etc., and these in the eyes of the law are the private owners of the property. In this case, it is clear that if ever the possessor die *intestate,* the heirs could by virtue of the laws claim the property. Or, if the possessor himself should so wish, he might alienate the property and he could have the protection of the law in his favor. I have heard that such a case did arise in Philadelphia, where there were some houses belonging to the Church, but held in the name of a priest. At his death, his nephew claimed the houses, and this was the principal reason why Archbishop Carroll of illustrious memory was not so adverse to the Trustee system.[22]

The objective utility of the system and its apparent harmlessness are reiterated in a letter of Archbishop Hughes of New York. Although he had been through the thick of the long and bitter struggle with the abuses of the trustee-system in practise, still he could write in 1855:

[22] Guilday, *Trusteeism* (New York, United States Catholic Historical Society, 1928), pp. 8-9.

> . . . regarded *a priori,* no system could appear to be less objectionable, or more likely both to secure advantages to those congregations, and at the same time to recommend the Catholic religion to the liberal consideration of the Protestant sentiment of this country. It would, he thought (referring to Bishop Carroll), relieve the priest from the necessity and painfulness of having to appeal from the altar on questions connected with money, touching either the means of his own support, repairs of the church, or other measures essential to the welfare of his congregation. It would at the same time secure the property, by the protection of law, for the perpetual uses to which it had been set apart and consecrated. It would be a bond of union between the priest and the people. It would be a shield to protect the minister of the altar from the very suspicion of being a money seeker, and at the same time a means to provide for his decent maintenance. All these were no doubt the considerations which moved the venerable and patriotic Archbishop (Carroll) to adopt and recommend the system of Lay trustees. On paper and in theory that system was entirely unobjectionable.[23]

As Dr. Guilday remarks in his monograph on Trusteeism, the evils of the system came to the front when unworthy men were placed in the trusteeship of the church or when the pastor lacked that prudence which local circumstances required for harmonious cooperation. By far the greatest of all the ills was the provision of the civil law that, once an organization was duly incorporated in legal form, there was no remedy for any of the acts of the trustees unless they ran afoul of the laws of the land. From being administrators, it was not long before the trustees assumed the rights of actual owners. Since they considered themselves to be in actuality what they were regarded in the eyes of the law, that is, owners of the material property possessed by the parish, the trustees were not slow in asserting their presumed authority in matters pertaining to strictly spiritual administration. And although they were trustees for only one individual church,they did not hesitate to defy in some instances even the authority of the bishop of the diocese.

That these were the abuses into which the usefulness of the trusteesystem unfortunately degenerated, can be gathered from the following

23 Guilday, *Trusteeism,* p. 12.

extract from a letter of Dr. Connolly, Bishop of New York, to Archbishop Maréchal, of Baltimore, on December 30, 1819:

> I return your Grace most sincere thanks for your kind and friendly letter of the 24th inst. But am exceedingly sorry that it is not in my power at this moment to do or suggest anything likely to quiet the minds of the two contending parties here, whereas the major part of the trustees of our church of St. Peter labour to deprive me of my spiritual rights, while the major part of the trustees of our cathedral, and the mass of our numerous congregation are intent on supporting me in the enjoyment of them. The former have, especially since the beginning of the year, insisted that it is their right, as trustees, not only to provide priests for St. Peter's church, but also to dismiss them when they please. The latter acknowledge that affairs of this nature belong exclusively to me. The former insisted in a peremptory manner that I would immediately dismiss Rev. Fr. Ffrench from both said churches. The latter respectfully prayed me that I would not dismiss him. The former threatened me to shut their churchdoor against him. I answered that if I did, they would have no priest in that church. They deprived him of his salary; it was immediately paid by the trustees of the cathedral. One of the trustees of St. Peter's church threatened me that my annual pension might perhaps be withdrawn from me by his colleagues of S. Peter's Church.[24]

For these and other reasons, another adviser of the S. Congregation of the Propagation of the Faith, Father Harold, O.P., who had long been personally acquainted with church administration in the United States, wrote:

> But as this office of Trustee is liable to degenerate into abuse, and will often be abused, notwithstanding the utmost caution and most exemplary conduct of the Pastor, measures should be adopted for its gradual suppression. Such an attempt will require great discretion and considerable influence, but the best Catholics wish for it, and would gladly concur in any prudent plan which might be devised for the purpose.[25]

24 Guilday, *Trusteeism,* p. 57.
25 Guilday, *ibidem,* p. 10.

This recommendation to abolish the trustee-system could not be immediately carried out. It was not until the First Provincial Council of Baltimore, in 1829, that the first national law was drawn up to curb the regrettable abuses of trusteeism. Sensing the gravity of the situation as it then stood, the Fathers of the Council voted to abolish the system entirely. The mind of the Council on this matter and the reasons which motivated this far-reaching and courageous step are well summarized in the following passage from the Council's Pastoral Letter to the clergy and the laity of the United States:

> Yet there have been found amongst you, men who, not fully acquainted with the principles of our church government, either presumed to reform it upon the model of those separate from us, or claimed imaginary rights from the misapprehension of facts and laws with which they were badly, if at all acquainted; they have sometimes been abetted by ignorant or unprincipled priests; and disastrous schisms have occasionally arisen. We have shed bitter tears when we beheld those usurping and frequently immoral delinquents, standing in the holy places, and profaning the services of the living God; we have deplored the delusion of their adherents. But we trust that those evil days have passed away and forever. Still we feel it our duty to declare to you, that in no part of the Catholic Church does the right of instituting or dismissing a clergyman to or from any benefice or mission, with or without the care of souls, exist in any one, save the ordinary prelate of the diocess or district in which such benefice or mission is found. We, of course, consider our holy father the Pope, as the ordinary prelate of the whole church, yet it is not usual for him to interfere, save on very extraordinary occasions; this right never has been conceded by the Church to any other body, nor could it be conceded consistently with our faith and our discipline.[26]

With this firm and straightforward assertion of episcopal rights over all phases, material and spiritual, of church administration, the position of the hierarchy and its legitimate representatives in regard to the trustees became well defined. The trustee-system continued in vogue for

[26] Guilday, *The National Pastorals*, p. 33. These observations are a summary of Pius VII's letter, *Non sine magno*, to Archbishop Maréchal, on August 24, 1822, *Fontes*, n. 480. Cf. also the letter of Gregory XVI, *Dudum*, August 22, 1841, to the Vicar Apostolic of Gibraltar.

many years, but the control of the diocesan bishop was always the predominating element. The appointment of the trustees was subject to episcopal authority;[27] the trustees had no power to determine. diminish or suppress the salary of the pastor;[28] nor, much less, to remove him; candidacy for trusteeship was made dependent on exemplary Catholic life,[29], thus rightly subordinating the material to the spiritual. In a word, it was evident that the hierarchy was tolerating the trustee-system because of necessity rather than for reasons of positive approval.[30]

These instances of ecclesiastical legislation against lamentable abuses prevented the trustee-system from defeating the very purpose for which it was instituted, namely, the proper custody of church property and the prevention of its passage into unworthy hands.

Article 3. The Provincial Councils of Baltimore

In the light of early disorganization and dissension on property matters, it was clearly seen that some kind of stringent and uniform legislation on this vexing problem was a most pressing need. This explains why the First Provincial Council of Baltimore (1829) deliberated on this delicate matter. From the time of this first gathering of the American hierarchy until the last of the Plenary Councils in 1884, there were few meetings of the American bishops which failed to dedicate a goodly portion of their considerations to the question of ecclesiastical temporalities.

The First Provincial Council of Baltimore (1829): Reference has already been made to the deliberations of this Council which resulted in the abolition of the trustee-system. To emphasize still more the complete control of the bishop over all the temporal administration pertaining to the diocese, the fifth decree of this Council enacted that all church property without exception should be deeded over to the bishop. In addition, to insure compliance with this prescription, it was further decreed that no church could be erected, or at least not consecrated, until this step had been taken. In view of the State constitution forbidding

27 *Concilii Plenarii Baltimorensis II Acta et Decreta,* (1866), n. 198.

28 *Ibidem,* n. 201, 4°.

29 *Concilii Provincialis Cincinnaten. IV Acta et Decreta,* (1882), tit. III, cap. 1, n. V; *Synodus Grandormen.* (Big Rapids) *I,* (1903), n. 326.

30 *Conc. Prov. Cincinnaten. IV,* (1882), tit. III. cap. 1.

any such arrangement, the Council allowed a lone exception in favor of the Diocese of Charleston.

The earnest desire of the bishops to surround church property with all necessary and useful legal safeguards was evidenced in an unusual step taken by this Council. The sincerity and practical character of their efforts to be on solid legal ground on this point are shown in the following extract from the *Acta* of the Council describing the proceedings of the ninth public session held on October 13, 1829:

> The prelates and theologians met at four P.M. After the reading of the decrees which had been adopted that morning, the lawyers, Roger B. Taney,[31] John Scott and William G. Read were brought into the council hall and were permitted by the bishops to take their places near the theologians. In the name of his colleagues, the lawyer, William G. Read, read his reply to the questions previously presented in writing by the Fathers. The lawyers also responded to other questions proposed by the Fathers. After they had given satisfaction on all points, they were thanked by the Council and immediately withdrew from the hall.[32]

The decrees of this First Provincial Council of Baltimore were adopted and promulgated as particular diocesan law in three local synods which were convoked shortly after the Council: the First Synod of Charleston, held on November 21, 1831; the First Synod of New Orleans, which met on February 26, 1832; and the First Synod of Philadelphia, which convened on May 13, 1832. This last-mentioned synod devoted special attention to the fifth decree of the First Council of Baltimore, requiring that all church property be deeded over to the bishop.

The Second Provincial Council of Baltimore (1833): Given the short time elapsing between the First and the Second Councils, and the consequent difficulty of promulgating the previous legislation of the First Council in the various dioceses and insisting on its observance, the

31 Then Attorney-General of Maryland, and later Chief Justice of the United States Supreme Court.

32 *Concilia Provincialia Baltimori Habita ab anno 1829 usque ad annum 1849* (*Baltimori*, 1851), p. 47.

Second Council did not formulate any new decrees regarding church property or its administration.

The Third Provincial Council of Baltimore (1837): The fourth decree of this Council was concerned chiefly with providing legal safeguards for eclestiastical property, to prevent it from passing into unauthorized hands.[33] It recommends that bishops make use of all the legal protection at their disposal, and warns clerics who use church goods against the will of the donors that they incur *ipso facto* the penalties decreed by the Council of Trent.[34]

The Fourth Provincial Council of Baltimore (1840): Pastors and rectors were again forbidden to hold property in their own name. Bishops were urged once more to avail themselves of all the civil protection compatible with the free exercise of their episcopal rights. They were to make wills insuring the proper transfer of ecclesiastical goods and, in case they were to be absent from their dioceses for any extended period of time, they were to designate a trustworthy representative with powers of attorney to look after the proper administration of church property.

The Fifth Provincial Council of Baltimore (1843): Between the Fourth and the Fifth Provincial Councils three diocesan Synods had been held. The Second Synod of Philadelphia (1842) promulgated for its territory all the decrees of the preceding Baltimore Councils; it adopted no new particular provisions dealing with church property. The First Synod of Boston (1842) reaffirmed particularly the existing provisions against pastors' holding property in their own names. It enacted also that suspension *a divinis* was the penalty to be inflicted on any priest who abetted the trustee-system. Finally, the First Synod of New York insisted on complete liberty of action for the bishop and pastors in the administration of church goods. A penalty, likewise that of suspension *a divinis,* was adopted also by this Council against any priest who failed to report to the bishop irregularities connected with the functioning of the trustee-system. Thus the decrees of the preceding provincial Councils gained more and more currency with the celebration of subsequent Councils in other parts of the United States.

[33] *Concilia Provincialia,* p. 142.

[34] Sess. XXII, *de ref.* C. II.

The first decree of this present Fifth Council humbly suggests to the Holy See the advisability of introducing some modifications into the rigorous requirements of the Instruction which the Sacred Congregation of the Propagation of the Faith issued on December 15, 1840,[35] in view of the detailed prescriptions enacted in the Conciliar decree for the making of wills by bishops in order to insure the preservation and proper transfer of church property in the event of their death.[36] According to the sixth decree of this Council, precautions were to be taken to forestall the dangers of rash building and the contracting of debts. These precautions consisted in exacting the written permission of the bishop for all building projects and for the contracting of debts, and the obligation of priests to make annual financial reports to the bishop on the status of the church entrusted to their care.[37] Finally, the seventh decree warns against the danger of possible loss to the Church arising from injudicious and indiscriminate mixing of church property and personal property. The Council even goes so far as to forbid pastors or rectors to make gifts to their churches from their personal goods, without the previous approbation of the bishop and the written testimony of trustworthy eyewitnesses. This measure was intended to protect the Church against the depredations of unscrupulous heirs.[38]

The Sixth Provincial Council of Baltimore (1846): This Council has nothing dealing with the problem of church goods or their administration.

The Seventh Provincial Council of Baltimore (1849): To safeguard the interests of the Church, decree number four of this Council adopted the principle that all donations, etc., coming from the faithful were thenceforth to be regarded as the property of the bishop, unless it were definitely established that they had been given expressly for the use of a religious order or congregation.[39]

35 *Collectanea S.C.P.F.*, n. 916.

36 *Concilia Provincialia,* p. 216.

37 *Ibidem*, p. 217.

38 *Ibidem.*

39 Cf. the later provisions of Leo XIII's *Romanos Pontifices* and of the Third Plenary Council of Baltimore, in Chapter X.

CHAPTER III.

THE PERIOD OF CONSOLIDATION

As was pointed out in the preceding chapter, the Provincial Councils of Baltimore laid the first juridical foundations of organized legislation for church property in the United States. The continuous expansion of the Church in this country, however, with subsequent multiplications of dioceses, had already demonstrated the advisability and even the necessity of coordinating and unifying the practise of the various dioceses. This could be accomplished efficiently only through national legislation emanating from a Plenary Council with the approval of the Holy See; Provincial Councils were now unable to cope with problems of national import. The essential points of the law proper to the Church in America had already been at least indicated; it remained now for the Plenary Councils to take up this great and necessary work on a nation-wide scale, and to consolidate what lesser Councils had slowly achieved.

ARTICLE 1. THE PLENARY COUNCILS OF BALTIMORE

A) *The First Plenary Council* (1852)

The second decree of this Council extended to the entire nation all the decrees of the seven Provincial Councils of Baltimore. The establishment of a Council of Administration, such as is now prescribed for every diocese by canon 1520, was recommended by the Fathers, in the seventh decree. Solemn warnings were formulated in the sixteenth decree against jeopardizing the welfare of the Church and her sacred trusts by allowing undue intrusion of laymen into the administration of ecclesiastical temporalities. The seventeenth decree further assured the Church of liberty in this regard by forbidding pastors and rectors to name any lay trustees without previous episcopal approbation. This precaution would provide men who would not be apt to expose the Church to the danger of unscrupulous exploitation.

B) *The Second Plenary Council* (1866)

In this Second Plenary Council, which has justly been styled the greatest of the Baltimore Councils,[1] the problems connected with the efficacious protection of church property are treated with remarkable thoroughness. The one chapter of *Titulus IV* of the conciliar decrees, entitled *De Ecclesiis bonisque Ecclesiasticis tenendis tutandisque,* treats of this entire question in great detail.

Numbers 182-186 of the decrees of the Council contain legislation aimed at curtailing abuses arising from the trustee-system, by prohibiting all interference in church administration.[2] The Council insists, in its acceptance of the decrees of the Third Provincial Council of New York that not even slight portions of church goods (vel minimam bonorum Ecclesiae partem) can be diverted to outside uses "except with the permission of the bishop, in accordance with the apostolic constitutions on the alienation of church property."[3] In No. 187 the Fathers repeat the fourth decree of the Third Provincial Council on the legal safeguards to be obtained in order to keep ecclesiastical property in the proper hands. The fifth decree of the Fourth Provincial Council was also confirmed, urging bishops to obtain all the legal sanctions compatible with their canonical rights, and forbidding priests to hold church property in their own names personally.[4]

[1] This Council realizes in a very particular manner the ideal to which Archbishop Martin J. Spalding, then Archbishop of Baltimore, under whose direction the Council was convoked and held, referred when he wrote: ". . . I have thought, also, of making our approaching Council a complete repertory of our canon law, embracing, in systematic order, all our previous enactments in the Baltimore Councils, together with such canons of provincial and diocesan synods as we may wish to make of general application. In a word, of making it a sort of *corpus juris* for the American Church; throwing into an appendix all Roman rescripts and decisions which have reference to our affairs." And again: "We have very much to do to lay deeply and solidly the foundations of our canon law. Until now we seem not to have advanced far beyond the rudiments." — J. L. Spalding, *Life of the Most Rev. M. J. Spalding, D.D.,* (New York, 1873), pp. 301-302.

[2] *Concilii Plenarii Baltimorensis II Acta et Decreta* (*Baltimorae,* 1868), pp. 111-112.

[3] *Acta et Decreta,* n. 201, 2.

[4] *Ibidem,* n. 188.

The Fathers summarized the prescriptions of the Instruction which the S. Congregation of the Propagation of the Faith had issued on December 15, 1840,[5] and furthermore indicated the procedure to be followed by all bishops in making wills to provide for the proper transfer of diocesan property to their successors,[6] and finally, quoted the Instruction itself as to the manner in which the bishops were to see to its execution by religious communities. The Council also humbly reiterated the suggestions of the Fifth Provincial Council on the modifications which were desirable in the prescriptions of the aforementioned instruction.[7]

"Lest churches be burdened with debts, or their property be badly administered or wasted," as the text of the decree begins, the Fathers confirmed the second decree of the Fifth Provincial Council exacting annual reports to the bishop, and his written permission before contracting any debts in the name of the Church.[8] Then, since a clear title is one of the surest means of preventing the unlawful seizure or sale of property, it was voted to confirm the fourth decree of the Seventh Provincial Council, to the effect that all goods acquired by pious or charitable organizations were to be considered in the eyes of the Church as the property of the bishop, unless there were indubitable proof that they had been donated for the use of a religious order or congregation.[9]

The seventh, sixteenth and seventeenth decrees of the First Plenary Council, touching upon the presentation of annual reports, the exact fulfilment of the intentions of donors of ecclesiastical goods — with a warning against those who might divert these funds from their purpose — and making the appointment of trustees subject entirely to episcopal authority, were adopted officially by the Second Plenary Council.[10]

Another decree pays tribute to the religious freedom guaranteed by the American Constitution, and exhorts both the clergy and the laity to observe faithfully all ecclesiastical provisions on church property since this observance will be sanctioned by the civil courts.[11] The question

5 *Collectanea S.C.P.F.*, n. 916.

6 *Acta et Decreta*, n. 189.

7 *Ibidem*, n. 191.

8 *Ibidem*, n. 192.

9 *Ibidem*, n. 195. Cf. the provisions of Leo XIII's Constitution *Romanos Pontifices*, in Chapter X of the present study.

10 *Ibidem*, nn. 196-198.

11 *Ibidem*, nn. 199-200.

of trusteeism comes up again in number 201, where the Council appropriates the legislation of the Third Provincial Council of New York, "in order that lay trustees may be held within right bounds."[12]

The decrees terminate with a reaffirmation of the bishop's right of complete control over the administration of all church property without exception,[13] and an exhortation that bishops see to the proper transmission of church property by drawing up wills in due form after consultation with lawyers, to insure compliance with legal formalities.[14]

C) *The Third Plenary Council* (1884)

The subject of ecclesiastical temporalities was discussed anew in much detail in the Third Plenary Council of Baltimore. The conclusions reached by the Council Fathers are summed up in *Titulus IX* of the Conciliar decrees, entitled *De Bonis Ecclesiae Temporalibus.* Much of the legislation of this Council is merely a new approbation and promulgation of what had already been decided upon in the Second Plenary Council.

At the time of this Third Plenary Council the Church did not enjoy, as she does today, the legal protection of the civil courts. In many places ecclesiastical societies were not authorized to incorporate; this necessarily deprived them of many legal safeguards and much needed security. Consequently, force of circumstances obliged church authorities to put themselves and their property within the scope of the then existing laws, even though this really implied adopting a procedure at variance with traditional ecclesiastical practise.

The usual manner of possessing church property is for the particular church body (diocese, parish, religious house, etc.) to own goods as a recognized juridical personality. Since this legal incorporation was not forthcoming, it was agreed, not unlike the early days of the Church, that the individual bishops, by virtue of their rights as private citizens, would hold in their own names everything belonging to the various churches under their jurisdiction. To this end, Chapter II of the Conciliar decrees, *De Episcoporum Officiis,* opens by quoting as an exhortation and

12 *Acta et Decreta,* pp. 117-118.

13 *Ibidem,* n. 202.

14 *Ibidem,* n. 204.

fundamental principle the Apostolic Canon 41: *Praecipimus ut in potestate sua Episcopus Ecclesiae res habeat.*[15]

After calling attention to the lamentable hostile attitude of the civil law towards the Church in many States and to the dangers incurred for church property when not handled according to the prescriptions of ecclesiastical law, the Fathers restated the provision of the Second Plenary Council on the necessity of finding such arrangements as would assure the Church of legal protection without jeopardizing the safety of ecclesiastical property.[16]

To make sure that what the Church actually had would always remain in her hands and at her disposal, the Council prescribed that the individual bishops, legally constituted as moral persons in "corporations sole," should officially hold and administer all diocesan property.[17] The second alternative allowed by the Council was that the bishops should be legally authorized to hold all diocesan goods "in trust."[18] Lastly, if neither of the preceding methods were found to be workable in different circumstances, the bishops were empowered to obtain legal recognition as owners and administrators of all church goods in their own names personally, by the juridical institution known as *fee simple.*[19] In all cases, however, no matter what might be the particular nature of the arrangement adopted in different localities, the bishops were to bear in mind at all times that they were not proprietors of what was incorporated in their name, but only stewards or administrators.[20]

15 *Concilii Plenarii Baltimorensis III Acta et Decreta* (Baltimorae, 1886), n. 266.

16 *Ibidem*, n. 266.

17 With the constitution of a *corporation sole* before the civil law each individual bishop became a legally recognized juristic person, with full rights of ownership and administration over all the property included in the establishment of the corporation and all other goods that might accrue to the corporation at a later date.

18 This expedient guaranteed to the church equitable title to the property, although the real legal title was vested in the bishop.

19 In this unsatisfactory and somewhat dangerous system, the bishop as an individual, not as a juridical person, was the real legal owner of all church property in his diocese. Certain sad experiences had already demonstrated the unfeasibility of this arrangement.

20 *Acta et Decreta*, n. 268.

Lest goods once consecrated to divine worship and pious works be diverted from their sacred destination, all bishops were to make careful inventories which would establish clear-cut distinctions between what they owned legally for the Church and what they possessed for themselves personally.[21] The Fathers reiterated the provisions of several Popes and, in particular, of the preceding Councils which required bishops to make proper wills for the legal transfer of diocesan property into the hands of their successors.[22] Special attention was devoted to decreeing that all these documents affecting the possession or the transfer of property should be drawn up in strict legal form, with expert legal advice whenever this would seem advisable.[23]

In order to safeguard church goods against legal seizure for liabilities incurred in imprudent financial transactions, all ecclestiastical persons, whether physical or juridical, were forbidden to organize or direct banks; those already in existence were to be dissolved within five years from the date of the publication of the decrees of the Council.[24] Bishops were also instructed to use canonical penalties against those clerics who would divert funds to their own personal uses or contract debts without previous episcopal approbation.[25] The Fathers fixed upon the sum of five thousand dollars ($5000.00) as a debt-limit not to be exceeded without an indult from Rome.[26]

Likewise, "ad praecavendum omne injustae alienationis periculum," the provisions of number 188 of the decrees of the Second Plenary Council were reenacted against those who violated the long-standing statute against priests holding churches or other ecclesiastical property in their own names.[27] Lastly, as a safeguard for the establishment and maintenance of clear title, all administrators of church property were

21 *Acta et Secreta,* n. 269.

22 *Ibidem,* n. 269.

23 *Ibidem,* n. 270.

24 *Ibidem,* n. 274. It is not unlikely that the Council's insistence and severity on this point were prompted by the memory of the unfortunate incident during the administration of Archbishop Purcell and the consequent financial crisis of the archdiocese of Cincinnati.

25 *Ibidem,* n. 279.

26 *Ibidem,* n. 20.

27 *Ibidem,* n. 282.

ordered to secure deeds for their holdings and then, after certifying their conformity with all the formalities required by the civil law, to present them for episcopal approval and subsequent custody in the diocesan archives.[28] The title on ecclesiastical goods closes with Chapter IV on the question of lay trustees and councillors. It regulates their necessary qualities, their appointment, and the extent of their powers.[29]

The decrees of the Third Plenary Council marked the end of nationwide legislation through Conciliar decrees on ecclesiastical temporalities, as on all other church matters. No Plenary Councils have been held since 1884.

Article 2. Special Indults for the United States

The Third Plenary Council of Baltimore requested the Holy See to grant Ordinaries in the United States special powers in connection with the alienation of church property. The Council asked that, by reason of the peculiar circumstances existing in the dioceses of the United States, American Ordinaries should not be held to compliance with the formalities exacted by Canon Law for the alienation of church property, when there would be question of changing the property and other possessions of the diocese, subjecting them to mortgage, or carrying on other transactions usually considered within the category of alienation.

On September 25, 1885, a decree of the S. Congregation of the Propagation of the Faith granted the desired faculty for a period of ten years, beginning with the date of the promulgation of the Council's decrees. The Holy See, however, imposed the observance of certain conditions in connection with the use of this indult. First, the faculty was to be used only after conferring with the Board of Consultors on the necessity or at least the evident utility of the proposed transaction for the good of the Church. Secondly, the bishops were to report to the S. Congregation every three years the number of times the faculty had been used, with express mention of the respective amounts involved, as also the financial status of the missions in whose favor debts were contracted.[30]

28 *Acta et Decreta,* n. 282.

29 *Ibidem,* nn. 284-287.

30 The text of this decree has been incorporated in the *Concilii Plenarii Baltimorensis III Acta et Decreta,* in the appendix, p. ciii.

This indult in favor of the special conditions prevailing in the United States and their remote distance from the Holy See was renewed by Rome at the request of the Archbishop of Baltimore, petitioning in the name of the entire hierarchy, on February 12, 1896, for ten years. A prolongation for the same period of time was granted on June 12, 1906, and again on July 31, 1916.[31] This last-mentioned renewal, however, did not run its full course. By a decree of April 25, 1918, the S. Consistorial Congregation declared, among other points, that in view of the more generous faculties granted by canon 1532 of the impending Code of Canon Law, all previous indults conferring special powers for alienation were to be considered as revoked from May 18 of the year 1918.[32] This automatically extinguished the special indult renewed in 1916 for the American hierarchy.

On September 7, 1909, the S. Congregation of Religious had issued a decree which fixed the sum of two thousand dollars ($2000.00) as the limit of alienations and debts allowed to religious Institutes without authorization from the Holy See.[33]

Since this provision, especially in a country where the growth and expansion of the Church were very marked, multiplied occasions for recourse to Rome and greatly hampered the proper expediting of many ecclesiastical business transactions,[34] the Archbishops of the United United States, assembled in general meeting, requested the Apostolic Delegate, then Mons. Falconio, to petition the S. Congregation for more liberty of action. On October 11, 1910, the Apostolic Delegate announced that, by virtue of a rescript of the S. Congregation of Religious, of September 1, 1910, he thereby authorized "for a period of ten years, the Ordinaries of the dioceses, of the United States, *onerata tamen*

31 Cf. text of the indult in *AER,* LV (1916), 664.

32 *AAS,* X (1918), 190.

33 Published in the *AAS* as of September 15, 1909 (I [1909], 695), and in the *AER,* XLI (1909), 609. The English text of the decree with a commentary by A. B. Meehan is given in *AER,* LIII (1915), 670-674.

34 The instruction had also fixed the limit of two hundred dollars for local, and one thousand dollars for provinicial administrations, with two thousand dollars as the top-limit for general administrations. At present canon 534, within the limits of six thousand dollars (cf. the exposition of the equivalent of lire and francs, in Chapter VII) leaves further determinations of competence to particular Constitutions.

eorum conscientia, to permit the religious communities in their respective dioceses to contract debts up to the sum of fifty thousand francs ($10,000.00) without the necessity of having recourse to the Holy See.[35] The Ordinaries were at the same time explicitly reminded that this indult affected *only the necessity of recourse to Rome;* all the other formalities then required by ecclesiastical law still remained in force. A question arose in the minds of many as to whether, even with this new indult, bishops were still obliged to ask the advice of their Board of Consultors for sums exceeding five thousand dollars ($5000.00), as prescribed by number 20 of the decrees of the Third Plenary Council of Baltimore.[36]

In the following year the Holy See again evidenced its deep interest in protecting ecclesiastical property in the United States against the danger of loss. On August 8, 1911, the S. Congregation of the Council, after receiving the *vota* of the various Archbishops of the United States, issued a decree on the best manner of assuring a safe and proper title for church goods. The provisions of this decree were as follows:

> 1) Wherever possible, "parish corporations"[37] shall be established, within the limits and with the precautions in force in the State of New York.[38] Where this arrangement is not yet recognized for ecclesiastical organizations, the bishops are to make every effort to bring about its introduction.
>
> 2) Where parish corporations cannot be organized, each bishop shall proceed to have himself erected into a *corporation sole,* on condition that the bishop, while possessing full powers before the law, act only after conferring with his Consultors and, in more serious matters, with their consent.

35 The text can be found in *AER,* LIII (1915), 676.

36 Cf. *supra,* p. 44.

37 The parish corporation was usually composed of the bishop, the vicar general, the pastor, and two laymen designated by ecclesiastical authority. This corporate body was the legal owner of the property vested in its name.

38 These safeguards and precautions embodied in the Civil Code of the State of New York regulated in the light of Catholic principles such important questions as the appointment of trustees, their tenure of office, and the disposal of ecclesiastical property in the event of the division of a parish. The text of these civil provisions is found in *AER,* XLV, (1911), 596.

> 3) The method known as *fee simple,* which had been formerly allowed by the Third Plenary Council of Baltimore as an alternative, is to be abolished altogether.[39]

With the promulgation of the Code of Canon Law and the precise provisions of canons 1529-1543, legislation on the alienation of temporalities took on a more unified tone. The above-mentioned decree of the S. Consistorial Congregation,[40] suppressing all previous special indults in view of the generous faculties accorded by the Code, placed the American hierarchy in a much more disadvantageous position than before the Code; the faculties they enjoyed heretofore were far beyond what the new canons allowed. Consequently, it was not long before further faculties were granted, over and above what the new law authorized. In the Quinquennial Faculties, among those granted by the S. Congregation of the Council, Ordinaries in the United States are empowered "to permit the alienation of ecclesiastical property up to the value of ten thousand dollars ($10,000.00) in the United States . . . provided it be necessary and there is no time to have recourse to the Holy See. After the transaction the Holy See should be immediately notified of it."[41]

This special power of permittting alienations not exceeding ten thousand dollars ($10,000.00) can be used by the Ordinaries only in connection with diocesan transactions. The Quinquennial Faculties granted by the S. Congregation of Religious contain no such authorization in regard to religious Institutes.[42]

The Apostolic Delegate to the United States enjoys, with other Delegates, Nuncios and Internuncios, more liberal faculties than the diocesan Ordinaries for the expediting of ecclesiastical financial transactions. The power contained under n. 20 of Formula II of his Faculties provides that "Whenever there is urgent necessity, evident advantage, and where delay would be dangerous, the faculty is granted to per-

39 The text of this decree is printed in *AER,* XLV (1911), 585.

40 Cf. *supra,* p. 46.

41 *Index Facultatum Quinquennalium, Formula IV,* Faculties from the S. Congregation of the Council.

42 In case of necessity, however, nothing prevents Ordinaries in the United States from applying the provisions of canon 81.

mit alienations of ecclesiastical property or of property belonging to pious causes . . . up to one hundred thousand francs ($20,000.00).[43]

The Holy See still further manifested its readiness to accommodate itself as far as prudently possible to varying special conditions in different countries by granting even more liberal extensions of this faculty. A special indult, dated November 18, 1924,[44] authorized the bishops of the United States, for a period of ten years, to permit the alienation of ecclesiastical property up to the sum of fifty thousand dollars ($50,000.00). This indult was not renewed in 1934.

In more recent years there have been few, if any, documents on the present question emanating from the Holy See. The most recent enactments on the alienation of church property are contained in a letter addressed to all religious Superiors in the United States by the present Apostolic Delegate, on November 13, 1936. In this letter the Apostolic Delegate pointed out that "the Sacred Congregation (of Religious) has considered for some time the necessity of formulating certain definite rules to assist religious Superiors in their grave and difficult obligations in the administration of temporalities. . . . To this end the Sacred Congregation has authorized me to address a communication to all the religious Superiors in the United States in order to bring to their attention again *the obligation which they have in conscience* of fully carrying out the prescriptions of canon 534, §1, of the Code of Canon Law. And this obligation *extends to all religious,* including regulars and *other exempt religious.*"[45]

43 Bouscaren, *Canon Law Digest,* I, 186.

44 S. Congregation of the Council, Prot. N° 4938/24.

45 Cf. Bouscaren, *Canon Law Digest, Supplement* 1938, p. 17. There is a striking similarity between the provisions of this letter and those of the decree *Inter ea* of the S. Congregation of Religious, already mentioned on p. 46. Cf. *AAS,* I (1909), 695.

PART II

COMMENTARY

ON

CANONS CONCERNING ALIENATION

AND

SIMILAR CONTRACTS

CHAPTER IV.

THE RELATIONSHIP OF CANON LAW WITH AMERICAN CONTRACTUAL LAW

Canon 1529

Quae ius civile in territorio statuit de contractibus tam in genere, quam in specie, sive nominatis sive innominatis, et de solutionibus, eadem iure canonico in materia ecclesiastica iisdem cum effectibus serventur, nisi iuri divino contraria sint aut aliud iure canonico caveatur.

Article 1. The Attitude of Canon Law Towards Civil Law

It is in the field of contracts that the Church and its members will have most contact with the civil law. Especially today, when Catholics so often constitute such a small minority in the midst of overwhelming numerical superiority, church organizations enter into countless contracts with those outside the fold. There are, besides, the innumerable contracts in strictly ecclesiastical matters, which are made between various moral persons within the Church or between individual Catholics. It is true that, in order to safeguard the divine law, the Church can and does legislate on some details of contractual jurisprudence, just as she legislates on other points of faith or discipline.

Since, however, contracts can so frequently become matters of dispute before the civil law, the Church does her utmost to avoid conflicts with lay courts. Notwithstanding her inborn and essential superiority over civil power, she has no desire to create the impression of encroaching on state rights. She wishes to live in peace and harmony with the civil authorities, in order to be the better able to execute her divinely given spiritual mission to the world. Consequently, to lessen the danger of harmful opposition between herself and the civil authority, she has always sought out for contracts some common juridical ground whereon all parties can meet on an equal footing.

According to the general principle prevailing before the Code, this common ground was Roman Law.[1] This usage originated in the days when Roman Law was the generally accepted basis of civil law. By the later decades of the last century, however, modern codes had supplanted the ancient body of Roman Law, to the extent that this latter was no longer even the basis of civil law, except in the civil code of Germany. Besides, civil courts were already actually handling many cases which were by right within the competence of the Church tribunals.[2] Traditionally desirous of forestalling all unnecessary conflicts with the secular arm, the legislators of the Church once more applied the principle which had first induced their predecessors to conform to the provisions of Roman Law. They surmounted the difficulty of no longer possessing a common body of laws as the basis of civil law, by adopting the particular provisions of the civil law in force in different localities.[3] This acceptance is not limited to law in force in whole nations, but extends even to particular localities, that is, to states, counties, or even cities: *in territorio.* This is the principle of present-day canonical legislation in regard to the civil law on contracts, as embodied in canon 1529.

This general stand of ecclesiastical adaptation to civil law is closely connected with the United States. The only source quoted by the Code in connection with canon 1529 and its ecclesiastical approbation of civil law is the decree of December 15, 1840, whereby the S. Congregation of the Propagation of the Faith ordered all bishops and religious Superiors in the United States to provide for the proper and legal transmission of church property to their successors by making wills "juxta

1 "Ecclesia enim in huiusmodi rebus temporalibus, quae in suo foro sive ratione *rei* sive ratione *personae* fuerunt definiendae, generatim *adoptaverat ius Romanum.* Quare in libro tertio *universum* ius de rebus ecclesiasticis, contractibus, negotiis legitimis propriam sedem non obtinuit, nisi quid in iure Romano fuit corrigendum vel supplendum."—Wernz, *Ius Decretalium* (Romae, 1908), tom. 3, Pars 1, n. 252.

2 "At nostra aetate causae illae temporales *clericorum* ut personarum privatarum, imo etiam *institutorum ecclesiasticorum* ad forum civile deferri solent, ubi ex concessione vel tolerantia Ecclesiae ad tramites legum *civilium* disceptantur et definiuntur."—Wernz, loc. cit.

3 A somewhat similar principle prevails in civil law: "It is a rule conditioned by imperative necessity that immovable property should be governed, especially in respect of its transmission, by the law of the country in which it is situated."—Woerner, *American Law of Administration* (2 ed. Boston, 1899), I, §168.

legem Status, in quo degunt, quarum accuratam notitiam ex certis fontibus sibi comparabunt."[4]

Article 2. The Attitude of Civil Law Towards Canon Law

The general theoretical attitude of American civil law in regard to church matters is somewhat complex and confusing. Depending on the nature or viewpoint of the particular court rendering the decision, some verdicts have been handed down which are in complete accord with the principles of ecclesiastical law, while others have flagrantly ignored the provisions of church legislation. Perhaps the fundamental reason for this marked inconsistency is the difference prevailing between the theoretical attitude of the law, and the practical mentality of those interpreting the law.

As a matter of fact, the existence of ecclesiastical corporations in general and of Catholic corporate bodies in particular in the United States is set in a very special background. Even in purely business circles they are accorded much consideration and many privileges not required by the bare fact of their corporate existence. The law distinguishes sharply between the Church and the corporation and yet, all this notwithstanding, though they legally deny any influence of the Church on the incorporated society, men recognize that the spiritual aim and background of the Church necessarily exert a very palpable influence on the spirit and dealings of the corporation.

In theory, the emphasis has been laid almost exclusively on the corporation aspects of ecclesiastical organizations. A New York court has declared that American religious corporations "are not to be regarded as ecclesiastical corporations, in the sense of the English law, which were composed entirely of ecclesiastical persons, and subject to the ecclesiastical judicatories; but as belonging to the class of civil corporations to be controlled and managed according to the principles of the common law as administered by the ordinary tribunals of justice."[5]

In the light of this fundamental juridical principle, ecclesiastical corporations will get no legal recognition *in so far as they are ecclesias-*

4 *Collectanea S.C.P.F.*, n. 916.

5 Robertson v. Bullions, 11 N. Y., 243, 251, affirming Barb. 64, 87.—Zollmann, *American Church Law* (St. Paul, West Publishing Co., 1933), §126.

tical.[6] Their legal rights will be on a perfect par with those of any other society which has obtained corporate existence. The accidental element of the society's religious background will not affect it legally as a corporation; nor, vice versa, will the fact of corporate existence modify the religious status of the church. "The corporation can exist without the church, and the church without the corporation. The corporation, created by the state, may continue though the church is dissolved, while the church may continue though its charter has expired or been cancelled by the state. Each is derived from a different source, has different powers, and is absolutely independent of the other."[7]

The explicit banishment of all religious and ecclesiastical considerations from the legal standpoint of church incorporation is further borne out by Zollmann in the conclusion of his chapter on "The Nature of Corporations":

> From the foregoing the sphere of activity of the American religious corporation is clear and well defined. It has no concern with church work proper. It is not created to preach or administer the sacraments. Its work is of a far humbler kind and compares with the work of the church proper as the work of the church janitor compares with that of the clergyman. Its sole purpose is to make contracts, and acquire, hold and dispose of property. It is thus a purely secular agency. It is as much a business corporation, within its limited powers, as the International Harvester Company is within its wider powers. It is the humble handmaid of the church

[6] "Though American Civil Law has failed to recognize completely the plenary claims of the Church as a juristic personality, it has, by statute and judicial decisions, generally recognized the corporation sole, the diocesan or parish corporation, and other religious aggregate entities, their basic rights in the acquisition and disposition of property, and the basic exclusive jurisdiction of the Church to pass finally upon all questions of faith, morals and religious discipline where its communicants are concerned. This legal doctrine, notwithstanding criticism, due in part to an inability to understand a hierarchical church organization, is now firmly imbedded in American jurisprudence."—White, "Certain Aspects of the Legal Status of the Church in the United States,"—*The Jurist,* I (1941), 21.

[7] Zollmann, *American Church Law,* §143. It is not hard to see how these juridical principles aggravated the evils of the trustee system in early American church history. Cf. *supra,* Chapter II.

created by the state for the purpose of conducting the business affairs of the church.

> To sum up: The modern American religious corporation in its relation to the state is, unlike its predecessors, in no sense a public municipal body but a mere private corporation created by the state for the benefit of the corporators and those connected with them. In its relation to the church it is not a spiritual agency with spiritual powers to preach the gospel and administer the sacraments, but a humble secular handmaid whose functions are confined to the creation and enforcement of contracts and the acquisition, management and disposition of property. The corporation thus has neither public nor ecclesiastical functions, being a mere business agent with strictly private secular powers.[8]

Even in the case of an unincorporated ecclesiastical organization civil jurists distinguish between the church and the society. For them the society is not necessarily composed of members of the church, nor vice versa. Given its temporal and visible character, only the society can come into contact with the civil courts. The legal effects of incorporation will not go beyond the purely external and secular element in church organization. The church as such will derive no other benefit from incorporation beyond that of having a legally recognized representative to handle its business affairs. The church *as church* will not be modified in its own proper sphere of activity. "Since the church is thus entirely removed from temporal control it follows that incorporation will not affect it in the least. The spiritual entity created by spiritual means can neither be swallowed up nor affected by a temporal corporation created under temporal statutes."[9]

[8] *American Church Law,* §147. Cf. Brown, *The Canonical Juristic Personality with Special Reference to its Status in the United States of America;* Washington, 1927, pp. 121-130. Brown here quotes the "higher-plane theory" to show that courts do attribute a spiritual quality to church corporations.

[9] Zollmann, *American Church Law,* §143. Cf. also Judge Peackham in Bradford v. Roberts, 175 U. S., 291: "Whether the individuals who compose the corporation under its charter happen to be all Roman Catholics, or all Methodists, or all Presbyterians, or Unitarians, or members of any other religious organization, or of no organization at all, is of not the slightest consequence with reference to the law of its corporation, nor can the individual beliefs upon religious matters of the various incorporators be inquired into."

These brief considerations demonstrate the altogether accidental character with which an incorporated ecclesiastical society is vested in the eyes of civil law. This concept of incorporation as a mere stamp of juridical approval on an accidental adjunct to the Church proper is far removed from the true Catholic ideal. Such a system, as is evident, does not give rise to an *incorporated ecclesiastical body.* On the contrary, it leaves the church intact, while setting up in harmonious cooperation with it another entity called the *corporation.* The church, which is powerless in the temporal order, is assisted by a legal agency, the corporation, which in turn has no authority over the spiritual realm. There is no interaction between these two distinct spheres of activity. The church thus has its authorized representative in the legal world, but is not empowered to act itself as a legal body; the corporation is the agent of the spiritual body. Consequently, there is no strict incorporated ecclesiastical body, but rather a juxtaposition of the ecclesiastical body and the civilly recognized corporation.

Catholic principles of ecclesiastical public law, on the other hand, regard the Universal Church and the Apostolic See as juridical persons in their own right and by their very nature.[10] Legal persons of inferior grade in the Church receive their juristic personality either from a special provision of Canon Law or through a special concession of a competent ecclesiastical superior. Thus the individual units of ecclesiastical life and organization become legal persons *as they are,* precisely in their ecclesiastical character. Once this juridical personality is acquired there is no longer any room for distinction between the ecclesiastical body and the corporation. The church *is* the moral person, with all the rights and privileges accruing to it from the fact of official recognition.

To regard civil juristic personality merely as a distinct and separate legal entity, having no intrinsic connection with the church body proper, cannot be reconciled with the requirements of the foregoing Catholic juridical principles. According to these principles, what is a corporate body in the eyes of the Church, should become a corporate before the civil law, *without forfeiting its essential religious character in the eyes of the courts.* In the light of this genuinely Catholic ideal there is no delineation of separate spheres of activity. On the contrary, *all* the acts of the ecclesiastical body, be they of a spiritual or of a temporal nature, should be recognized by the state, should be endowed with legal bind-

10 Canon 100, §1.

ing force and should claim the protection and cooperation of civil authorities.

The practical consequences of the legal distinction of the civil courts between the church and the corporation are quite evident. If an unincorporated religious society has a case before the court, the civil authority has no means of contact with the society. Consequently, in cases of faith, discipline, or ecclesiastical rule, custom or law, or of dispute between the individual members of such an organization or between its members and its Superiors, the verdict of the court will generally be based on the internal rules of the organization.[11] All its elections and other proceedings, so long as they are not contrary to state laws, will be judged according to the regulations of the church and the rule prevails that the inferior authority must give way to the superior authority in all matters within the limitations of the constitutions and laws of the organization.[12] On this last point, however, not all courts have the same viewpoint.[13]

Should a property dispute arise within an incorporated church body, the case will usually be decided strictly according to the enactments of corporation law. In the light of the preceding considerations on the effects of incorporation for a religious body, the court will usually prescind

[11] "Whenever the questions of discipline, faith, or ecclesiastical rule, custom or law have been decided by the highest of these church judicatories to which the matter has been carried, the legal tribunals must accept these decisions as final, and as binding in their application to the case before them."—Watson v. Jones, 80 U. S. (13 Wall), 679 and 727.

A recent exemplification of the principle just enunciated is that of a schism in the Greek Catholic Parish of the Holy Ghost at Indiana Harbor, Indiana, followed by legal attempts on the part of the seceders to obtain possession of the property. The Court at Laporte, Indiana, under Judge Wirt Worden, ruled that the schismatic group did not represent the real organization since its independent "pastor" could show no evidence of legitimate nomination by the Greek Catholic bishop of Pittsburgh, who alone, according to the laws of the Church, was empowered to make this appointment.

[12] Den. v. Bolton, 12 N.J.L., 206. "It is of the essence of these religious unions and of their right to establish tribunals for the decision of questions arising among themselves, that those decisions should be binding in all cases of ecclesiastical cognizance, subject only to such appeals as the organism itself provides for."—Watson v. Jones, 80 U. S. (13 Wall) 679 and 727.

[13] Bonacum v. Murphy, 65 Neb., 831 and 71 Neb. 463. Watson v. Jones is the outstanding civil legal case vindicating the independence of church courts on purely ecclesiastical matters. It is responsible for the "higher-plane theory."

entirely from the ecclesiastical nature of the corporation. But even in this case there have been courts which upheld that all disputed questions must be settled according to the canons of the religious organization itself, rather than according to the prescriptions of civil corporation law.[14]

Article 3. Limitations on Ecclesiastical Acceptance of Civil Law.

Because she is a perfect society in her own right, independently of any recognition by the civil courts, the Church has an inherent capacity for making laws on all points within the field of her own proper jurisdiction. If, however, she has valid reasons for adapting herself to the civil law in given instances, she is perfectly free to determine both the nature and the extent of this adaptation. Her very nature as a perfect society of the supernatural order forbids her any acceptance of those laws which would entail any renunciation or even diminution of her God-given prerogatives. She must insist on her divine nature and her consequent rights, especially against such civil enactments as positively contradict, limit, or ignore them. This is particularly true when she comes face to face with laws that are imbued with anti-Catholic or anticlerical bias. Consequently, the Church's conformity to civil laws is not absolute and all-embracing. With characteristic prudence she accepts some points the while she rejects others which do not recognize her inborn and inviolable superiority. The reasons for her distinctions and her reservations will be more evident from a schematic enumeration of some of the provisions of contractual American law which she may accept without infringing upon her divine dignity, and from a listing of some examples of statutes to which her supernatural character forbids her to accommodate herself.

Article 4. Acceptable Provisions of American Law on Contracts.

It would appear that there is not much actual danger of conflict between the general provisions of American contractual law and the general spirit or background of Canon Law. American contractual law, particularly as contained in the *Restatement of the Law on Contracts,* to

14 Dockhus v. Lithuanian 206 Pa. 25.; 55 at 779.

which frequent reference will be made in the subsequent pages, evidences a very marked tendency towards conformity with the principles of the natural law and thus is brought into close harmony with the provisions of the law of the Church.[15]

At first sight a conflict may appear inevitable from the different definitions of contracts given in canon and in civil law. For the moralist or the canonist the essential element of every contract is the *consent* of the parties duly expressed: *duorum vel plurium in idem placitum consensus.* This constitutes a *moral* contract. The American civil lawyer, however, while not denying the necessity of consent for the formulation of a valid contract,[16] includes among its essentially constitutive elements the *protection of the civil law:* "A contract is a promise or set of promises for the breach of which the law gives a remedy, or the performance of which the law in some way recognizes as a duty."[17]

This apparent contradiction, however, comes only from the mode of expression, not from the substance of the idea expressed.[18] The general principles of contractual law in American civil courts correspond very closely to the fundamental principles of moral theology and Canon Law.[19]

15 In the subsequent references to the *Restatement of the Law on Contracts* it should be borne in mind that this compilation is not officially binding law. It is a guide drawn up by a body of lawyers for uniform adoption in the various state legislatures.

16 "A manifestation of mutual assent by the parties to an informal contract is essential to its formation and the acts by which such assent is manifested must be done with the intent to do these acts."—*Restatement of the Law on Contracts* (St. Paul, American Law Institute, 1933), §20.

17 *Restatement,* §1.

18 Cf. the detailed treatment of this special point in Chapter VIII, *Contracts Resembling Alienation.*

19 Compare, for instance, the *Restatement,* §18, on the necessity of contractual capacity; §13 on voidable contracts (cf. Canons 1687-1689 on *restitutio in integrum*); §20, on the requirement of mutual assent; §21, on the ways of manifesting assent; §32, on the requirement of certainty in the terms of an offer; §§40-41, on the termination or revocation of an offer, etc. On the specific point of the necessity of legal sanction for contracts, the general tradition of the older canonists is in complete accord with the *Restatement,* as is shown further on in Chapter VIII.

The following are some of the enactments of American contractual law which may be accepted by Canon Law:

A) *On contracts in general:*

1) No one can be bound by contract who has not legal capacity for incurring at least voidable contractual obligations. Contractual incapacity may be total or only partial.[20]

2) To constitute a contract, acceptance of the proposed offer must be unequivocal.[21]

3) A revocable offer is terminated by the offeror's death or such insanity as deprives him of legal capacity to enter into the proposed contract.[22]

4) An acceptance of an offer may be transmitted by any means which the offeror has authorized the offeree to use, and, if so transmitted, is operative and completes the contract as soon as put out of the offeree's possession, without regard to whether it ever reached the offeror, unless the offer provides otherwise.[23]

5) A written revocation, rejection or acceptance is received when the writing comes into the possession of the person addressed, or of some person authorized by him to receive it for him, or when it is deposited in some place which he has authorized as the place for this or similar communications to be deposited for him.[24]

6) A promise is not binding unless the promisor knew or had reason to know the essential facts of the previous transaction to which the promise relates, but his knowledge of the legal effects of the facts is immaterial.[25]

20 *Restatement,* §18. Some few authors, among whom may be mentioned Vermeersch-Creusen (*Epitome Iuris Canonici,* II, n. 850 I, 1.), are hesitant in admitting the validity of such provisions; they are reluctant to admit that the capacity arising from mere natural law can be restricted by civil prescriptions. Against this stand it can be urged that the general language of the Code establishes no limitations. While Vermeersch-Creusen hesitate, Vromant, who formerly defended the validity of these provisions, (*De Bonis Temporalibus,* ed. 1927, n. 275, III) no longer (ed. 1934, n. 275, III) holds the same position.

21 *Restatement,* §58.

22 *Restatement,* §48.

23 *Restatement,* §64.

24 *Restatement,* §69.

7) The law may determine provisions for respective duties and rights where more persons than one are promisors or promisees of the same performance.[26]

8) Civil law establishes rules for the discharge of contracts.[27]

9) Civil legislation may determine judicial remedies for breach of contract.[28]

10) The civil courts may legislate on the influence of duress, violence, and mistakes in the field of contracts.[29]

B) *On contracts in particular:*

The provisions just enumerated will be applicable likewise in their particular relationships to specific contracts of sale, loan, etc. *(contractus nominati)* or to contracts of an undetermined character *(contractus innominati)*.

C) *On payment of contracts:*

The Church accepts as her own the prescriptions of the civil law which deal with determining:

1) The time,[30] manner and place of paying.

2) The nature of the consideration to be conveyed in payment: e.g., cash, checks, securities, etc.

3) The equitable apportionment of expenses incurred in drawing up or executing the contract.

4) The procedure to be followed when the same person becomes both debtor and creditor, e.g., when the debtor becomes the heir of his creditor.[31]

5) The manner in which several creditors are to arrange to receive their *pro rata* portion of the assets of an insolvent debtor, even

25 *Restatement,* §93.

26 *Restatement,* §§111-132.

27 *Restatement,* §§385-483.

28 *Restatement,* §§326-384.

29 Restatement, §§500-511.

30 Cf. the explicit provision of canon 33, §2.

31 *Restatement,* §45, c.

when there is question of pious works that would otherwise benefit.[32]

6) The procedure to be followed when the object of the contract ceases to exist either in whole or in part.

7) The substitution of a new obligation (novation) for one already extinguished.

8) The right of appeal to retrieve a donation, e.g., if the donor becomes the parent of children, or if in giving his donation he acted against the duties of piety, charity, or justice.[33]

Article 5. Inacceptable Provisions of Civil Contractual Law

The following summary of some civil enactments which cannot be accepted in ecclesiastical contractual matters introduces some modifications and exceptions into the list of acceptable civil prescriptions just given:

A) *Provisions contrary to divine law (natural or positive):*

Canon Law would prevail over civil law in case of:

1) Provisions which would sanction contracts having stolen goods as their object: against the natural law respecting the property of of another and his right of ownership;

2) Provisions which would recognize a right acquired by prescription based on bad faith: such prescription is equivalent to theft, which is contrary to the natural law;

3) Provisions depriving regulars of their right to acquire property either for themselves or for their religious Institute: against man's natural capacity to acquire property;[34]

32 This departure from the usual stand of Canon Law on preserving intact all bequests to pious funds is based on the principle that the laws of the Code do not violate a vested right which has been acquired by third parties. Cf. can. 4.

33 Cf. infra, Chapter X, Article 3.

34 No law forbidding religious to receive property by will exists in the United States: "The doctrine that one dedicating himself for life to religious work and taking a vow of poverty thereby becomes civilly dead, never obtained in this country. Such a person is clearly competent to take a devise or a legacy."—Rood, *Wills* (Chicago, 1904), §194.

4) Refusal to recognize bequests to pious cause:[35] against the divine right of the Church to be unhampered by the State in the acquisition of property for religious, educational, or charitable purpose;

5) Refusal to recognize wills in favor of the Church if they are devoid of legal formalities or state permission, or if made within a certain time-limit before the death of the testator: against natural freedom to dispose of one's goods;[36]

6) Refusal to recognize trusts in wills in favor of pious causes: against the divine right of the Church to freedom in acquiring property for purposes connected with her end;

7) Lack of distinction between clerics and layfolk in cases of insolvency: against natural respect due to ministers of religion.

B) *Provisions contrary to formal prescriptions of Canon Law*

Many of the above-mentioned civil enactments, besides being at variance with the principles of the natural law, would also be in conflict with explicit prescriptions of Canon Law. For instance:

1) The denial of the right of regulars to acquire property whether for themselves or for their Institute contradicts the express provision of canon 582.

2) The limitation of the right recognized by ecclesiastical law to dispose of one's property freely, through refusal to recognize donations or bequests to pious causes, is at variance with canon 1513, §1.

3) The denial of legal value in wills in favor of the Church when

35 In Connecticut, for example, any devise to a religious corporation, in order to be valid, must be expressly authorized by statute. (Green v. Dennis, 6 Conn. 293); in Maryland, leave to devise land to a religious society must first be obtained from the legislature if the amount of property exceeds five acres to be used for church, parsonage or cemetery purposes (Murphy v. Dallam, 1 Bland 529); in Alabama, bequests and devises for Masses are void, as superstitious uses (Festorazzi v. St. Joseph's, 104, Ala. 327).

36 This period of time within which wills are held to be invalid varies in the different states from thirty days to two years. Cf. Woerner, *American Law of Administration,* II, §425. In this same category must be placed those laws which invalidate bequests in favor of the clergyman who assists a person in his last illness.

they are devoid of required legal formalities goes against canon 1513, §2.

4) The refusal to acknowledge the legality of trusts for pious causes when included in a will conflicts with the implicit provisions of canon 1516.

5) The lack of distinction between clerics and layfolk when there is question of insolvency is against canon 122.

6) The legal sanction of the withdrawal of a donation to a church on the grounds of the ingratitude of the rector, is disclaimed by canon 1536, §4.

Article 6. The Binding Force of Civil Laws Adopted by the Church

The Church's adoption of acceptable legal provisions for contracts incorporates these civil enactments into her own law: *eadem . . . iure canonico serventur.* Thus the observance of these prescriptions of the civil law becomes matter of ecclesiastical obedience, just as much as provisions explicitly contained in the Code of Canon Law. Hence disobedience to these prescriptions would not be a violation of a purely civil law, but disobedience to ecclesiastical authority as well.

The "canonization" of civil law in contractual matters carries with it the same effects as those provided for in the particular articles of the civil legislation: *iisdem cum effectibus.* Hence, for example, whatever penal action is afforded by the civil law in case of breach of contract remains applicable also in ecclesiastical matters. The reservations enunciated by canon 1529 regarding the acceptance of civil prescriptions apply also their effects. Thus, for example, unless there has been a previous agreement with the proper ecclesiastical authorities, no one may legitimately cite a cleric before a lay court, even for an unjust and harmful violation of contract, though the cleric could certainly be held to repair the damage thus occasioned, within the limits of canon 122.

In regard to the binding force of Canon Law in case of conflict with civil law, two questions are raised on the extent of the phrase: *eadem, iure canonico, in materia ecclesiastica . . . serventur.* The first question asks whether *custom,* legitimately established and observed, takes precedence over the local civil law in case of conflict. Opinion among canonists is divided.[37] The more probable answer would seem to be in the affirmative. In fact, the text of canon 1529 makes no restrictions, but simply enunciates the general principle: *eadem, iure canonico . . . serventur.* Since custom under the requisite conditions is regarded as *particular law,* and is thus considered in the Code,[38] there seems to be no valid reason for not according it precedence in conflict with civil law, as is done for the general prescriptions of church law.[39]

The same line of reasoning solves the second question frequently raised: Is precedence to be granted to *particular* ecclesiastical laws in conflict with the provisions of civil contractual law, e.g. to those prescriptions of the Baltimore Councils which are *praeter codicem* and which may be at variance with the present prescriptions of civil law? Again the absence of any restrictions in the language of the Code calls for an affirmative answer. This is so, *a fortiori,* in the light of the solution of the previous question.

In fact, the Church provides for special local needs by means of appropriate special legislation which may modify in a greater or lesser degree even the prescriptions of her general ecclesiastical laws. The fact that these particular laws have been made to supersede even the universal church law in a given locality suggests that special circumstances make it advisable to hold to these laws against the prescriptions of civil law on contracts in that same locality or in some particular organization whose constitutions conflict with the rulings of civil law. For example, the special provisions of certain religious Constitutions approved by the Holy See in regard to the disposition of goods before profession will have to be observed in preference to the civil law of the territory which happens to forbid such dispositon.

Another question on the binding force of contractual civil law in the eyes of the Church deals with the obligation to be engendered by future laws. In virtue of the principle laid down in canon 1529, any provision of the civil law on contracts, whether actually in force or

37 Authors for both sides are cited by De Meester, *Compendium Iuris Canonici et Iuris Canonico-Civilis;* vol. III, Pars. I, 401, note 3.

38 Canon 25 says: "Consuetudo *vim legis . . . obtinet.*" In addition, authors are agreed that legitimate custom is not outlawed when Canon Law forbids something *salvo iure particulari.*

39 Vermeersch-Creusen, *Epitome Iuris Canonici,* II, n. 850.

subsequently to be enacted, is adopted as the law of the Church, unless it runs counter to divine or explicit ecclesiastical law.

A concluding observation can be made in regard to the legal status of moral persons in the Church. Canon 100, §3, establishes the general principle that all ecclesiastical juridical persons, collegiate or otherwise, are assimilated to minors. As a consequence of this provision, the prescriptions of civil law relating to the contractual dealings of minors will be applied to juristic persons within the Church. In case, however, the civil law of a particular territory should deny to minors all contractual capacity, this provision would have to be considered as having no binding force and as being against a positive prescription of ecclesiastical law. Many sections of the Code, particularly canons 1529-1543, necessarily suppose that ecclesiastical juristic persons have the right to make contracts, even though they are considered as minors before the law.

CHAPTER V

THE NATURE OF ALIENATION AND ITS REQUISITE CONDITIONS

Canon 1530

§1. Salvo praescriptio can. 1281, §1, ad alienandas res ecclesiasticas immobiles aut mobiles, quae servando servari possunt, requiritur:

1° Aestimatio rei a probis peritis scripto facta;

2° Iusta causa, idest urgens necessitas, vel evidens utilitas Ecclesiae, vel pietas;

3° Licentia legitimi Superioris, sine qua alienatio invalida est.

§2. Aliae quoque opportunae cautelae, ab ipsomet Superiore pro diversis adiunctis praescribendae, ne omittantur, ut Ecclesiae damnum vitetur.

Article 1. The Nature of Alienation

In its etymological sense alienation means *making something become the property of another,* or making it a part of *someone else's* goods: *alius, alienare, alienatio.* This consideration gives rise to the term's juridical meaning, which implies "the transfer of the *direct* ownership of an object to another."[1] This transfer of direct ownership may be made in return for some other consideration, as in a *sale;* in return for direct ownership over another object, as in *exchange;* or it may be made gratuitously when one person makes another a free *gift* or *donation* of an object.

In order to understand the full force of the juridical definition of alienation, it must be borne in mind that by its very nature alienation implies a *diminution of property already owned,* or the transfer of an

[1] Ferraris, *Prompta Bibliotheca,* "Alienatio," art. 1, n. 2.

object from the patrimony of one physical or moral person to the patrimony of another.[2]

The term "alienation" admits of an even wider signification. Under this aspect it goes beyond the direct transfer of ownership and comprises every transaction in which dominion is even *diminished* without being given up entirely, or which exposes the Church to the juridical danger of losing or lessening her proprietary rights over goods possessed. Thus the language of the Code applies the term "alienation" to *mortgages,* which confer on another a conditional right and title to church property; to *leases* and *rentals* extending for a period of time longer than nine years, since complete ownership of property is thus hampered by another's legal right to its use; to the negotiation of *loans,* because another party thereby acquires a conditional right to a part of ecclesiastical property corresponding to the amount of the loan; to the allowing of passive *easements* or *servitudes* or the renunciation of active easements and servitudes, since the former bestow on another the right to the use of church property and the latter deprive the church body of a right already acquired.

Under alienation taken in this wide sense are classified also *surety for others,* since this implies an added liability burdening church goods; the *contracting of debts* because ecclesiastical administrators are thereby decidedly restricted in the use of the rights consequent on the ownership of their property; *compromise* and *yielding lawsuits,* whereby the Church consents to a real diminution of her objective rights for the sake of preserving or establishing harmony and concord; *pawning* of ecclesiastical goods, since this puts such goods in the custody and under the partial ownership of the person advancing the money. In a word, alienation understood in this very wide sense, includes any and all contracts whereby the condition of the Church is legally jeopardized.[3]

2 A superior who refuses a legacy, says Schmalzgrueber, harms his Institute, ". . . non tamen patrimonium ejus diminuit, *in qua diminutione consistit alienatio.*"—Lib. III, tit. 15, n. 18. And Pirhing: ". . . quae alienatio) *in diminutione bonorum propriorum* consistit."—*SS. Canonum Doctrina,* Lib. III, tit. 13, n. 4.

3 "Doctores vero omnes conveniunt . . . . quod nomen *alienationis* latissimo sensu accipiendum sit, ut includat quemlibet actum aut contractum, quo onerentur bona ecclesiastica, et ideo emptio venditio, precariae, locatio conductio ultra triennium, emphyteusis, hypotheca, pignus, sequestrum, seu retentio rei ad cautionem, feudum, etc., ut videre est apud Commentatores Decretalium in hunc titulum *De Rebus Eccl. alien. vel non.*"—S. C. Conc. Calatayeronen. *Bonorum,* 25 ian. 1902—*Thesaurus Resolutionum,* CLXI, 60.

This wide interpretation is expressly contained in the Letter sent by the Apostolic Delegate in the United States to all religious Superiors in this country: "The term alienation includes not only purchases or transfers of property, but includes as well any contract, debt or obligation. The Canon Law regards all transactions, which may render the financial condition of the Institute, Province, or religious house, less secure, as alienations."[4] A more detailed treatment of this matter will be undertaken later[5] and the conditions will be pointed out which must be verified before even this wide interpretation is to be employed. For the present it is sufficient to have established the nature of alienation in general, and the meaning which the term will have in canonical literature.

The necessity of stringent regulations on the alienation of church property arises from the obligation of ecclesiastical authorities to protect in all things the best interests of the Church. It will be noticed that those empowered to supervise important alienations are always the higher superiors, whether ecclesiastical or religious. They are in a much better position to evaluate the urgency or the advisability of a given transaction in the light of the common good of the Church. They are thus better enabled to prevent particular private interests from conflicting with the more important welfare of the whole body which they govern. Without the restraining hand of general legislation, as experience has shown, prelates and other ecclesiastical and religious superiors would be too easily and too quickly led into business deals which might easily endanger the security of ecclesiastical interests other than their own.[6]

4 Bouscaren, *Canon Law Digest,* Supplement 1938, p. 18.

5 Cf. the commentary on canon 1533, in Chapter VIII, *Contracts Resembling Alienation.*

6 "Ratio hujus tam multiplicis prohibitionis est necessitas, et utilitas ecclesiarum ac locorum piorum, contra quam praelati, aliique administratores facile alienationes fecissent, nisi hae adeo multiplici, et stricta lege fuissent prohibitae."—Schmalzgrueber, Lib. III, tit. 13, n. 26.—In his *Life and Times of John Carroll* (II, 675-679), Dr. Guilday recounts how the bishops of the United States, in their deliberations on the eligible candidates for the See of Philadelphia, rejected Father Prince Gallitzin despite his many commanding qualities, on the score of the great indebtedness he had incurred in his missions, even though this had been done for good and charitable purposes.

Article 2. The Nature of Stable Capital

Not every transaction involving an outlay of money or other property is to be regarded as alienation. If this were the case, the efficient operation of many ecclesiastical administrators would be very much impaired, while the organization and the development of not a few important church bodies would be completely paralyzed by the constanly recurring need of complying with the formalities prescribed by Canon Law. Consequently, the field of transactions to which the rules on alienation are to be applied is the limited field of what constitutes an ecclesiastical organization's *stable capital.*

Every organization engaged in financial transactions distinguishes carefully between reserve funds and the funds which are received and expended in the course of daily administration. Even in the field of what are called reserve funds, a distinction is to be made between that portion of the reserve which is intended as a means of coping with possible contingencies of an unfavorable nature, and that portion which is, so to speak, removed from circulation, and intended to be a permanent source of regularly accruing income. The traditional language of church law would term this last-mentioned kind of resources as *patrimony.* It is on the greater or lesser security of its stable capital, or patrimony, that the prosperity and surety of an organization chiefly depends. For this reason the Church always manifests great concern over the conservation and, wherever possible, the increase of stable capital for all ecclesiastical and religious bodies.[7] This concern explains the prescription of canon 1531, § 3, requiring that whenever alienation has been legitimately permitted, the proceeds thus derived must be invested "with safety, caution and profit for the benefit of the Church." Thus the stable capital, more or less depleted by alienation, becomes reintegrated through another form of assets, and maintains the ecclesiastical organization in its previous state of security and well-being.

Authors usually define *stable capital* as including all those assets which are not in ordinary circulation, as mediums of barter or exchange, but which constitute *the permanent basis of a church body's financial*

[7] Cf. for example, the provisions on this score made in the Easter Instruction of the S. Congregation of the Propagation of the Faith—*AAS,* XIV (1922), 307—as well as question 49 of the *Elenchus Quaestionum* proposed to all religious Superiors by the S. Congregation of Religious as the matter for their quinquennial report.—*AAS,* XIV (1922), 281.

security. It is that sum which has been legitimately set aside to remain intact and be a source of regular income. This stable capital may consist of actual cash deposited at interest in a bank; in securities which bring in income either in interest or in dividends; or in real estate which is rented or leased, etc., as a means of procuring steady income. All these categories of assets constitute stable capital or patrimony. The general principle, to which reference has already been made is that alienation is had *only when this stable capital or patrimony is diminished*.[8]

The income or possessions of an organization are not automatically incorporated into its stable capital by the simple fact of acquisition. This principle applies even to surplus money. It belongs to the competent Superiors of the organization, within the limits of their Statutes or Constitutions, to determine both the amount and the manner of the incorporation, according to their particular needs.[9] Surplus funds laid aside for explicit future needs, unless it be for the purchase of immovable property or the construction of ecclesiastical buildings, are not

8 "In re temporali administranda, Superiores et oeconomi sedulo distinguere debent *bona frugifera* quae sunt vel tribuuntur ut *capitale* seu *patrimonium unde Institutum reditus percipiat,* et alia bona quae Instituto nondum sunt incorporata. Prioris rationis bona non possunt alienari nisi secundum leges statutas de alienatione. Dum erogatio aliorum bonorum mere regitur Constitutionibus et c. 537 de largitionibus quae fiant ex bonis religionis et quae non permittuntur nisi ratione eleemosynae vel alia iusta de causa."—"Quaesita Varia," n. 18,—*Periodica,* XI (1923), (157). Cf. also the note on p. 130, on the restriction of alienation to the diminution of goods already possessed.

9 This aggregation to the stable capital of the ecclesiastical organization must be done "cum Superioris auctoritate et Clericorum consensu."—Ferraris, *Prompta Bibliotheca,* "Alienatio," art. 1, n. 6. This principle is confirmed for present-day legislation: "Haec (pecunia), usquedum in sortem stabilem legitime redacta non fuit vel alicui fini, item legitime, ad normam juris, alligata, non subjicitur regulis alienationis."—Larraona, "Commentarium Codicis," *CpRM,* XIII (1932), 191.—There would, however, seem to be no valid reason for excluding the possibility of *implicit* aggregation of funds to stable capital, such as would be the case of money belonging to a parish which is completely out of debt, and has no immediate needs to be provided for. The simple fact that this money is deposited at interest in a bank or invested in securities, without any intention of using it for specified needs, would seem to be sufficient assignment of the sum to stable capital, even though this be not explicitly mentioned.

thereby necessarily aggregated to the juridical person's stable capital.[10] The same can be said of money received from such sales as are not regulated by the laws on alienation.[11]

The S. Congregation of the Council has confirmed the same principle in regard to sums derived from wills provided that no obligations remain to be acquitted. It declared expressly that these sums may be alienated without authorization, provided they have *not yet been incorporated into the stable capital* of the church or pious place for which they have been destined.[12] Money set aside for the specific purpose of purchasing immovable property or erecting a church or any other ecclesiastical edifice is to be considered as already belonging at least implicitly to the stable capital of the Institute.[13] Money which has been formally invested, in the strict sense of the term, or placed permanently at interest in a bank, appears by that very fact to have been aggregated

10 "Pecunia ad modicum tempus, donec occasio utilis erogationis habeatur, deposita in argentaria vel conversa in titulos, non ideo rationem boni de quo Superior libere disponat, amittit."—"Quaesita Varia," n. 18, *Periodica,* XI (1923), (158), d).

11 In the case wherein the funds derive from legitimately authorized alienation, canon 1531, §3, prescribes that they be incorporated into the stable capital, unless legimate Superiors have determined otherwise.

12 ". . . intentionem legis ita explanat Ferraris, Bibl. Can. v. *Alienatio,* art. 4, n. 1: 'Quamvis sine solemnitatibus possit fieri alienatio rei ecclesiasticae .... cum talia bona *nondum sunt Ecclesiae seu pio loco incorporata....* Requiritur tamen beneplacitum Apostolicum pro tali alienatione quando bona sunt *jam Ecclesiae vel pio loco incorporata,* ex Decreto S. Congr. Concilii in una *Salutiarum,* 20 sept. 1624, lib. 27 Decr. pag. 103.' "—S. C. Concilii Calatayeronen. *Bonorum* 25 ian. 1902.—*Thesaurus Resolutionum,* CLXI, 61. That this has been the traditional practise of the Holy See is evidenced by another decision of the S. Congregation of the Council, where it is said: "Quoad mobilia pretiosa *Ecclesiae incorporata,* esse necessarium beneplacitum apostolicum."—S. C. Conc. *Ord. S. Franc.* 18 mart. 1719.—*Fontes,* n. 3185, and *Thesaurus,* I, 172. Schmalzgrueber likewise observes: "ad bonorum autem ecclesiis non incorporatorum distractionem solemnitates non exiguntur."—Lib. III, tit. 13, n. 40. On this same principle of preserving intact the funds that have once been incorporated into the stable capital of churches and other ecclesiastical bodies, the III Plenary Council of Baltimore forbade pastors to take their salaries from the fixed capital of their parishes, even when ordinary income did not suffice to complete the salary agreed upon.—*Acta et Decreta,* n. 273.

13 Reiffenstuel, Lib. III, tit. 13, n. 15; Ojetti, *Synopsis,* "Alienatio," n. 300.

to the fixed assets of the organization to which it belongs. If this investment or deposit were made temporarily until, for instance, more favorable building or purchasing conditions could be obtained, the money involved would be more of the nature of surplus funds of which Superiors still retain the free and untrammeled disposition. Funds which pass through the hands of Superiors or administrators for meeting current expenses are certainly not to be considered as belonging to stable capital and, consequently, are not subject to the restrictions affecting alienation.

In case of doubt as to the status of a given amount of money, the presumption would favor not regarding it as part of the fixed capital. The opposite opinion would automatically restrict superiors in their use of this money. Consequently, as it is among the *odiosa* of canonical provisions, it should not be imposed except when the existence of the obligation is altogether certain.

In view of the preceding considerations it will be readily seen that the following categories of money or securities are parts of stable capital and, as such, subject to all the canonical restrictions on alienation:

1) All money that has been explicitly incorporated into the stable capital of an ecclesiastical corporation;[14]

2) Money or investments withdrawn from the fixed capital of the organization;

3) Money or securities received from the sale of property which belongs to the stable capital of an ecclesiastical organization;[15]

4) Money or securities received under annuity agreements, since the principal must remain intact as long as there are regular payments to be made;[16]

5) Money or securities from bequests and pious foundations,

[14] S.C. de Propaganda Fide, *AAS,* XIV (1922), 307; and S. Congregation of Religious, question 49, *ibid.,* 281. Vromant says: "Pecunia numerata quae summae capitali seu sorti stabili frugiferae legitime est adjuncta, formalitatibus alienationis subjicitur."—*De Bonis Ecclesiae Temporalibus,* n. 281, 3, c.

[15] Canon 1531, §3.

[16] Vermeersch-Creusen, *Epitome,* II, n. 861. See the special treatment of this question in Chapter X.

especially is the accompanying obligations have not yet been completely acquitted;[17]

6) Money or securities set aside by legitimate authority for the construction of buildings or for the purchase of other immovable property.[18]

The following list enumerates forms of money or its equivalent which do *not* fall within the scope of the restrictions on alienation:

1) Money employed in meeting current expenses;[19]

2) Money or securities borrowed without explicit contractual obligations, even though a nominal rate of interest be paid;[20]

3) Proceeds from the sale of old church furnishings used for the purpose of purchasing new equipment;[21]

4) Withdrawals from the investments pertaining to stable capital, if the withdrawals are made for the purpose of purchasing or con-

17 So stringent is the legislation on this particular point that it is forbidden to alienate the capital of a bequest, even if there are on hand sufficient funds from other sources to provide for the intention of the benefactor.—*Periodica,* V (1913), (29).

18 "Licet pecunia ex se non sit bonum immobile, vel mobile pretiosum; ut relicta tamen et deputata ad emendum bonum immobile, debet haberi pro bono immobili; et ut relicta, et deputata ad emendum bonum mobile pretiosum, debet haberi pro bono mobili pretioso."—Ferraris, *Prompta Bibliotheca,* "Alientatio," n. 41. It is to be noted that the use of portions of stable capital for these purposes is not regulated by the laws on alienation, because this use is tantamount to a *conversion* of stable assets, rather than an alienation of them. The laws on alienation will apply when money set aside for these purposes is diverted into other channels.

19 Vromant, *De Bonis Ecclesiae Temporalibus,* n. 281, 4.

20 The rules on alienation are not applied to this transaction because, as will be pointed out more in detail in Chapter VIII, the church organization so acting does not jeopardize its financial situation before the civil courts by exposing itself to the danger of legal measures to insure payment. Cf. Vromant, *De Bonis Ecclesiae Temporalibus,* n. 281, 4, and Larraona, "Commentarium Codicis," *CpRM,* XIII (1932), 190.

21 S. C. Conc. 12 iul. 1919, *AAS* (1919), 17. The S. Congregation points out, however, that money received from the lawful sale of church property cannot, without new specific authorization, be expended for the enlargement or repair of an old church or the construction of a new church.

structing buildings which will yield income (schools, hospitals, etc.)[22]

5) Money used for the purchase of construction of buildings when this money is already available;[23]

6) Sums used for the construction of residences for ecclesiastics or religious, particularly if this step will obviate the necessity of renting or leasing other buildings;[24]

7) Sums used for the repair of buildings already constructed;[25]

8) Resources changed from securities to simple bank deposits at interest;[26]

9) Portions of capital transferred to safer investments, which are at least equally lucrative;[27]

10) Money given with the express intention that it be used for specific purposes;[28]

22 This transaction, as is evident, changes only the form of part of the fixed capital; it amounts to conversion, rather than alienation. Cf. Vromant, *De Bonis Ecclesiae Temporalibus,* n. 280, 9°, c. And Larraona says very clearly: "Proinde videretur non quamlibet alienationem *pecuniae stabilis,* i.e., stricte collocatae esse nunc veram alienationem, sed illam tantum *quae ad aliam stabilem collocationem non ordinatur."* — "Commentarium Codicis," *CpRM,* XIII (1932), 192.

23 For the same reason as the preceding transaction, it will make no difference whether this money derives from current resources or from stable capital; this is a case of conversion of assets, not of their alienation.

24 Vermeersch, *De Religiosis Institutis et Personis,* I, n. 439. Vermeersch-Creusen, *Epitome,* II, n. 851; Vromant, *De Bonis Temporalibus,* n. 280, 9, c; and n. 285, c.

25 Vermeersch-Creusen, *Epitome,* II, n. 852.

26 Vermeersch-Creusen, loc. cit.

27 Canon 1539, §2. It would not seem rash to allow these transfers even if the income is slightly less but yet much safer than investments with higher returns. As Wernz remarks: "Superior lex est conservatio bonorum ecclesiasticorum et legitima sufficientium reddituum perceptio."—*Ius Decretalium,* tom. 3, pars 1, n. 153.

28 "De Recenti Quaestione circa Bona Ecclesiastica," *Periodica,* XIII (1925), (14).

11) Money obtained by mortgage contract in order to construct church buildings, with the express understanding that the mortgage is on the *buildings to be constructed, not* on the *actual* stable capital of the Institute;[29]

12) Property bequeathed to an Institute which is incapable of possessing;[30]

13) The refusal of legacies or donations.[31]

29 "Similiter alienare non videtur sed minus perfecte acquirere qui aedificia exstruit vel emit eaque simul gravat obligatione solvendi pretium constitutum ex aere alieno, ita ut ipsa aedificia noviter empta vel exstructa hypotheca speciali graventur."—Vromant, *De Bonis Ecclesiae Temporalibus,* n. 280, §8. Bastien gives a clear exposition of this transaction and of its effect on the financial status of an ecclesiastical corporation: "Un Institut achète une propriété et en même temps prend une hypothèque sur le prix soit total soit partiel, n'ayant pas à sa disposition la somme requise. Ou bien on achète une propriété déjà grêvée d'une hypothèque et l'on garde cette hypothèque. Dans l'un et l'autre cas, à notre avis, il ne faut pas de recours au S. Siège, même si la somme dépasse trente mille francs, le bien n'étant pas encore ecclésiastique, c.a.d. propriété de l'Institut; il ne le sera qu'au complet remboursement de l'hypothèque. Autre chose est de prendre une hypothèque sur un bien propriété de l'Institut, par conséquent ecclésiastique. Dans ce cas il faut la permission du Supérieur compétent, suivant la valeur de l'hypothèque. Ce serait aussi le cas si la première hypothèque ayant été remboursée complètement, on en reprenait une autre sur le même bien."—*Directoire Canonique* (4 ed., Paris, Bloud et Gay, 1933), n. 365. Larrona states the same principle when he says: "Alienatio aestimanda non est emptio vel exstructio aedificiorum, hypotheca speciali ipsis statim imposita." His reason for this conclusion can be drawn from the principle which he enunciates in another connection: ". . . . alienatio necessario *supponit dominium jam adquisitum.*"—"Commentarium Codicis, *CpRM,* XIII (1932), 195.

30 "Est enim communis doctorum sententia, quod lex prohibens alienationem bonorum ecclesiasticorum non obliget quando ea bona quovis titulo acquiruntur alicui loco ecclesiastico, qui lege incapax est ad ea retinenda; tunc enim sine alia licentia, potest ea alienare, cum necessitas alienandi adsit, quae plus est quam mera licentia; nam, licet non omnis qui potest debeat alienare, omnis tamen qui debet potest, et lex obligans dat simul licentiam ad id faciendum quod jubet."—De Lugo, *Responsorum Moralium Libri VI* (Parisiis, 1869), Lib. III, dub. 9, n. 2; *Opera Omnia,* VIII, 129. De Lugo argues that the continued existence of the law forbidding a particular Institute to acquire property for itself constitutes a perpetual order commanding the alienation of whatever it receives and thus accords the authorization necessary to legalize such alienation. Cf. *ibidem,* n. 6.

31 Non-acquisition is not the same as alienation.

With these points well in mind, a list of transactions can now be drawn up which, in the circumstances required by Canon Law, verify the notion of alienation either in the strict or in the broad sense of the term. Within these categories the particular spheres of authority for individual Superiors will be determined by the Code, by special Constitutions, Statutes, Indults, etc.:

1) donations from fixed capital;

2) sales of property belonging to stable capital;

3) long-term leases of property belonging to stable capital;

4) long-term rentals of property pertaining to fixed assets;

5) exchange of property belonging to stable capital, with all due allowance for the faculty given in can. 1539, §2, for the exchange of stocks and bonds;

6) compromise in financial dispute over goods pertaining to stable capital;

7) special mortgages covering property already in the full possession of the church organization;

8) payment of debts with funds taken from fixed capital;

9) surety for others with funds other than those deriving from current resources.

Article 3. The Extent of "*res ecclesiasticae.*"

Canon 1530, §1, applies the rulings on alienation only to *ecclesiastical goods.* Canon 1497, §1, states that "temporal goods, whether immovable or movable corporeal goods, or incorporeal goods which belong either to the Universal Church and the Apostolic See or to some other legal person in the Church, are *ecclesiastical goods.* This definition is traditional with canonists. Very similar in substance to this definition, although more detailed in its expression, is the definition given by the Fourth Provincial Council of New York:

> Ecclesiastical goods are understood to be all those things, movable or immovable, money or income from money, which have been or are given by the faithful, or which accrue to the Church from

goods already possessed which have been given to the Lord for religious purposes, for the carrying out of divine worship, for the acquisition and support of schools, hospitals, orphanages, monasteries, and convents, and are therefore rightly called "ransom from sin," the expression of the prayers of the faithful, and the patrimony of the poor.[32]

Canon 1499, §2, expressly declares that the true ownership of ecclesiastical property is vested in the juristic person which has come into possession of it. Thus the Code rejects the position formerly defended by not a few authors, Suarez among them, who maintained that such goods are owned immediately and directly by God as the patrimony of Christ, and that Superiors in the Church are only administrators, with a degree of power over property proportioned to their dignity.[33]

It should be carefully noted that ecclesiastical authority must intervene in the actual *erection* of an organization in order to bring its goods under the classification of ecclesiastical property. Mere ecclesiastical approbation of a particular religious or charitable society does not constitute this body a juridical person in the eyes of the Church, nor, consequently, does this approbation make its property take on the character of ecclesiastical goods. As Cardinal d'Annibale well remarks: "Ecclesiastical goods are those which are *possessed by ecclesiastical persons* and, therefore, *by ecclesiastical authoriy.*"[34]

In the light of this consideration, the property of religious associations erected by clerics or by laymen, even with previous or at least subsequent ecclesiastical approbation, is not held by an ecclesiastical juristic person nor by ecclesiastical authority. The administration of the goods

32 *Concilii Provincialis Neo-Eboracensis IV Acta et Decreta,* (New York, 1883), c. XVI, *De Bonis Ecclesiasticis,* art. 1, p. 75.

33 Suarez, for example, writes: ". . . . per ecclesiastica autem bona (intelligimus) res omnes sacras, et quae ad usus ecclesiarum, Deo, seu ipsis ecclesiis donata sunt, et sub administratione ejusdem ecclesiae, seu ministrorum ejus perseverant."—*Defensio Fidei Catholicae,* Lib. IV *De Immunitatibus Ecclesiasticis,* cap. XVIII, n. 1; *Opera Omnia,* ed. Vivès, XXIV, 442. In this definition he is in perfect harmony with the present-day canonical viewpoint. But when he says, (*ibidem,* n. 7), that these goods are owned directly by God as the patrimony of Christ "non per metaphoram sed per omnimodam proprietatem" his opinion is at variance with the doctrine of the Code. He refers to this position as being common at his time.

34 *Summula Theologiae Moralis* (5 ed., Romae, 1908), III, n. 77.

of such an association will, of course, be more or less under episcopal control, like everything else pertaining to religious works in the diocese, but it will not fall under the restrictions binding all administrators in the matter of alienation. These conclusions are derived from the principle enunciated by the S. Congregation of the Council in answer to a *dubium* proposed on the juridical status of the "Conferences of St. Vincent de Paul."[35]

For mission fields the meaning and extent of *bona ecclesiastica* have been determined with great precision by the S. Congregation of the Propagation of the Faith. In its Instruction of December 8, 1929, addressed to all Vicars and Prefects Apostolic, as well as to the major Superiors of all religious Institutes caring for foreign missions, it is stated that mission property, or ecclesiastical property, whose administration pertains exclusively to the ecclesiastical Superior of the mission, includes ". . . all the resources and funds of the mission . . . as well as all forms of assistance given to the mission, whether they come from such missionary organizations as the Propagation of the Faith, the Holy Infancy, the work of St. Peter the Apostle for the native clergy, or others of a similar nature, or have been offered by the faithful or even by the Institute in charge of the mission, or have been allotted by the civil government or any other philanthropic or charitable organization."[36]

[35] S. C. Conc. Corrienten, *Iurisdictionis,* 14 nov. 1920. — *A.A.S.*, XIII (1921), 135. Cf. also Bouscaren, *Canon Law Digest,* I, 714, and *Periodica,* X (1922), 293, B.

[36] S. C. de Prop. Fide, *Instructio,* 8 dec. 1929—*AAS*, XXII (1930), 112. Cf. also Bouscaren, *Canon Law Digest,* I, 637-643. This Instruction confirms the traditional practise of the Congregation. An Instruction of May 27, 1881, to the Vicar Apostolic of Norway declared that: "I beni che si acquistano con l'elemosine raccolte per le missioni sono veri beni ecclesiastici, ancorchè non vengano riconosciuti come tali dalla legge civile; quindi 1. Un Missionario non può di sua privata autorità acquistarli in nome proprio per poterne poi liberamente disporre, ma solo potrà farlo, quando ne sia debitamente autorizzato e con le necessarie cautele. 2 Nè può neanche in vantaggio della Missione, alienare o ipotecare senza una precedente autorizzazione i beni che avesse in tal modo acquistati. 3. Il Prefetto Apostolico può esigere dai missionari che facciano riconoscere legalmente simili acquisti quando lo creda espediente, dove la Missione cattolica è considerata come corpo civile avente diritto di possedere; o almeno che tali acquisti si facciano in nome di più comproprietari fiduciari, per non esporre a facili perdute i beni acquistati per la Missione."—*Coll. S.C.P.F.*, n. 1553.

Article 4. Movable and Immovable Goods

Paragraph 1 of canon 1530 applies equally to immovable and to movable goods, provided these latter are not perishable. This is a noteworthy departure from the previously existing law, which restricted the alienation only of immovable goods, and left full liberty for all movable goods.[37] The reason for this change is that at the present time movable as well as immovable goods can be incorporated into the fixed capital of an organization as a source of stable income. In the present law, the only element regulating the alienability of ecclesiastical property it its *value,* not its intrinsic nature.

The traditional examples of each kind of property are as follows:

1) Immovable property *strictly so-called* comprises estates, houses and other buildings, fields, herds of cattle, large libraries, etc. *By extension,* immovable property includes rights, claims on immovable property includes rights, claims on immovable goods, active easements and servitudes, stocks, etc., and yearly income, etc.

2) Movable property is the term applied to produce from land, chattels, machinery, clothing, individual books, furniture, etc.[38]

Aside from movable objects of a precious character, the limitations of this present canon apply to other movable property which is not perishable: *quae servando servari possunt.* Such movable objects of a more or less permanent nature are regarded as pertaining to the fixed capital of an organization, no less than immovable property. An old classification termed as "perishable" all goods which normally do not last more than three years, which wear out with use or which yield no income.[39]

The rules laid down in this canon, consequently, extend to *all immovable property,* even though it be of comparatively small value; and to *all non-perishable movable property,* even though it be not classified

37 As the reason for the exception in favor of movable goods, Schmalzgrueber gives only the silence of the law: ". . . . quod non reperitur prohibitum, regulariter intelligitur concessum." He adds that, since the power of alienating movable property was enjoyed by guardians of minors, whose powers were greatly restricted, that same power should be enjoyed likewise by ecclesiastical and religious Superiors.—Lib. III, tit. 13, n. 38.

38 Cf. Vromant (*De Bonis Temporalibus,* nn. 36-37). Here the author observes that, in all probability, since the Code does not define immovable goods, the specific determinations of civil law must be used.

39 Reiffenstuel, Lib. III, tit. 13, n. 47.

as "precious" in the sense of canon 1280, §1, and with due regard for the prescriptions of canon 1281, §1.

Article 5. The Requisite Conditions of Alienation

A) *Appraisal by experts*

The first condition for the legitimate alienation of church goods is that the property be previously evaluated in writing by expert and reliable appraisers. Professional appraisers need not necessarily be called in; any individuals sufficiently well versed in the technicalities of the matter at hand may be asked to present their written evaluation of the property to be alienated. Business prudence, however, would suggest that the appraising be done by individuals who have no personal interest at stake in the proposed alienation.

The purpose of this prescription is to protect the Church against the unscrupulous bargaining of possible purchasers or renters, and also against the inexperience or even imprudence of ecclesiastical administrators. This provision is of a very ancient usage in the Church.[40]

Since the canon speaks of an appraisal made *a probis peritis* it follows that *at least two* are required. The respective Superior may, in virtue of canon 1530, §2, require the intervention of more than two, and can oblige them to take an oath of fidelity to duty, or impose any other measures which he may deem useful or necessary for the protection of the Church. The appraisal made by these experts is not to be merely mathematical and material. It should be made concretely, according to the actual business value of the property at the time of the proposed transaction. All the elements of the situation must be borne in mind by the appraisers if they are to discharge their duty faithfully, and safeguard the well-being of the Church.

The obligation of securing the services of competent appraisers does

40 "Ut neque ulla circumscriptio in rem ecclesiasticam in talibus fiat, duobus pro tempore primatibus mechanicis aut architectis sive in hac regia et maxima civitate una cum deo amabilibus oeconomis, et quinque reverendissimis presbyteris et duobus diaconis, praesente quoque deo amabili episcopo, sive etiam in provincia duobus insignibus mechanicis aut architectis, aut etiam uno, si unum solum civitas habeat, intervenientibus in illis locis, sacrosanctis evangeliis positis, definiatur ab architectis quantum competat pro hoc solvi sanctissimae ecclesiae."—Nov. VII, cap. III.

not affect the validity of the alienation. It does, however, constitute grave matter in itself, but this does not exclude the possibility of light matter in an individual case.

B) *Just cause*

The second requisite for lawful alienation is a *just cause*. The canon does not require a serious cause for each and every transaction, but only a just cause, that is one whose gravity is in proportion to the importance of the proposed transaction. The estimation of the gravity of a just cause for alienation constitutes a serious matter of conscience for all ecclesiastical Superiors. Even though insincerity in this connection will not invalidate the alienation, nevertheless it may make them guilty of serious sin because of the danger to which they expose the church body entrusted to their care.[41]

The canon declares that this just cause may be one or other of three kinds:

a) *urgent necessity:* the necessity which justifies the alienation must be really urgent.[42] Otherwise it should be provided for by other means. This necessity is verified, for example, when a church or other ecclesiastical building must be repaired after a cyclone or a fire, etc., lest it collapse entirely; when a particular piece of property must be disposed of

41 "Cum in omnibus judiciis sit certitudo justitiae et conscientiae puritas observanda, id multo magis in concessionibus alienationum rerum ecclesiasticarum convenit observari, in quibus de Christi patrimonio, et dispensatione pauperum, non de proprio cujusque peculio agitur, vel tractatur: quapropter oportet, ut in examinandis hujusmodi alienationum causis, quae a Sede Apostolica in forma, *si in evidentem utilitatem cedat,* oneratis ecclesiasticorum judicum conscientiis delegantur, nihil favor usurpet, nihil timor extorqueat, nulla exspectatio praemii justitiam, conscientiamque subvertat. Monemus igitur et sub interminatione divini judicii, omnibus Commissariis, et delegatis hujusmodi districte praecipimus, ut caute et diligenter attendant causis in literis Apost. per supplicationes expressas, illasque solicite examinent, atque discutiant testes, et probationes super narratorum veritate recipiant, et solum Deum prae oculis habentes, omni timore ac favore deposito, Ecclesiarum indemnitatibus consulant, nec in laesionem, aut detrimentum earum decretum quomodolibet interponant."—Paulus II, Const. *Cum in omnibus,* 11 maii 1465—Giraldi, *Expositio Juris Pontificii,* I, 286.

42 ". . . facultas alienandi non magis extenditur quam necessitas."—De Lugo, *Resp. Moralium Libri VI,* Lib. III, dub. 10; *Opera Omnia,* VIII, 131.

immediately to avoid financial loss, or when a mortgage must be paid off without delay to prevent the creditors from foreclosing on ecclesiastical property.

b) *evident utility of the Church:* since the utility accruing to the Church must be "evident," it follows that a merely probable, or, *a fortiori,* a possible advantage is not sufficient to justify alienation. Nor is negative utility enough, in the sense that the Church will not suffer harm from the transaction. Reasonable certainty is required that the ecclesiastical organization engaged in the transaction will be in a better condition financially afterwards than before. Nevertheless, even this necessary condition of alienation does not authorize Superiors to undertake any financial operations or alienation contracts which will run counter to the prescriptions of church law against the *negotiatio* and *mercatura* which is forbidden to clerics and religious.[43]

c) *charity:* that is, the furthering of any work of charity or benevolence, whether it be of a spiritual or a corporal nature: alleviating the sufferings attendant upon famine, pestilence, or earthquake; the construction of necessary schools, hospitals, orphanages, etc. This use of ecclesiastical property has been recognized from the earliest centuries of the Church and was applied even to sacred and consecrated objects. St. Ambrose, for example, remarks that it is most fitting that sacred vessels should redeem men from captivity after having held the Precious Blood which redeemed them from sin.[44] In the interests of charity, even the Emperor Justinian tempered the rigor of his enactments against the alienation of ecclesiastical property.[45] The charitable end to be attained through the alienation of church property must be really urgent and of a nature which calls for extraordinary measures; otherwise, more com-

43 "Alienatio rerum ecclesiae potissimum jure prohibita est ob ecclesiae damnificationem: ergo ob causam evidentis utilitatis ejusdem debuit esse permissa, ne quod in ecclesiae favorem, et utilitatem salubriter est introductum, in ejus editum, et incommodum detorqueatur."—Schmalzgrueber, Lib. III, tit. 13, n. 56.

44 "Ornatus sacramentorum redemptio captivorum est. . . . Tunc vas Dominici sanguinis agnoscitur . . . cum in utroque videret redemptionem ut calix ab hoste redimat, quos sanguis a peccato redimit."—*De Officiis Ministrorum,* II, cap. 28; MPL, XVI, 149 A.

45 ". . . . nisi tamen aliquid tale fiat, quod diximus, circa redemtionem captivorum, ubi animae hominum liberantur a mortibus et vinculis inanimatorum venditione vasorum."—Nov. VII, c. VIII, *Iisdem.*

mon measures should be employed to alleviate the suffering at hand. Most authors do not mention this point, but it seems to follow from the general principles of alienation. If alienation is justified only by urgent necessity on the part of the Church herself, it seems only logical that necessity of at least this same degree should be required before the Church be allowed to despoil herself of property in order to assist others.[46]

Because of the rôle played by a just cause in legitimizing alienation, the permission of the lawful Superior is restricted to the cause specified in the petition; no Superior may change the destination of the sum thus authorized to be expended. Even though some other purpose might be equally, or even more, necessary or advantageous to the welfare of the Church, the money may not be diverted from its original purpose without a new intervention of the Superior who was competent for the first authorization.

Like the appraisal of the experts, a just cause is required only for the lawfulness, not the validity, of the transaction.[47]

C) *The authorization of the legitimate Superior*

The provision contained in canon 1530, §1, 3° is explicitly required for the *validity* of all alienation, of no matter what amount, in the eyes of the Church.[48] Any provision of civil law which would legalize alienation of ecclesiastical property independently of this necessary authorization would be devoid of all binding force in the internal forum of conscience.[49]

The requirement of authorization from a competent Superior is based on a traditional principle of Catholic jurists. Ecclesiastical and religious Superiors are not complete masters of the property of their particular

[46] "Sed ut necessitas pauperum aut aliorum miserabilium personarum sit causa sufficiens alienationis, debet esse extraordinaria, et quodammodo extrema, cui provideri nequeat per communes subventiones."—Manfried, *Juris Canonici Universi. . . . Compendium* (Parisiis, 1863), Pars IV, lib. XII, §II, V; vol. II, 682.

[47] Pre-Code legislation required just causes for the *validity* of all alienation: Reiffenstuel, Lib. III, tit. 13, n. 4; and Schmalzgrueber, Lib. III, tit. 13, nn. 69-70.

[48] On this point the Code adheres to the older legislation: "Pupillus ex omnibus causis solvendo sine tutoris auctoritate nihil agit, quia nullum dominium transferre potest."—D. (26. 8) 9, 2.

[49] Canon 1529.

organization or institute. According as their jurisdiction is more universal, they have greater power in the disposition of temporalities. This power, however, is never absolute. It is subordinated to the control of each one's immediate Superior, to his Rule, to the mind and customs of the Institute, to diocesan provincial statutes, or to the Sovereign Pontiff, the case so requiring. Inferior Superiors must have recourse to at least the presumed will of their major Prelate, or to the will of the Institute, as the case may be.[50]

This necessity of obtaining authorization from a lawful Superior does not interfere with or diminish the property or dominion rights of the owner or owners. This authorization does not confer the *power* to alienate, since this power is inherent in the very fact of ownership, but rather approves and authorizes the *use* of that power in a given instance. The giving of this approval entails for the Superior no financial responsibility in the ensuing transaction.[51] The civil law has recognized this fact by refusing to decide in favor of the plaintiff who sued the bishop and the building committee of the diocese to recover debts contracted by a pastor with their approval.[52] Nor does this approval change or in any way modify the objective terms of the contract.[53]

The need of this authorization is based on the provision of canon 100, §3, which considers ecclesiastical juristic persons as minors. Implicity, therefore, it regards their Superiors as their legal guardians in the eyes of the Church. This does not lessen the intrinsic rights of these

50 These are the considerations which Suarez presents: "(Superior) . . . quo universaliorem habet jurisdictionem, eo etiam in hoc genere majorem solet habere potestatem, *numquam tamen absolutam,* sed subordinatam suo Superiori, si illum habeat, vel suae regulae, ac menti seu consuetudini religionis totius; vel etiam Summo Pontifici quando materia id postulaverit. . . . Recurrere debent semper (Superiores) ad praesumptam voluntatem vel majoris Praelati, vel ipsius religionis, quia numquam expendunt ut domini sed ut ministri."—*De Religione,* Lib. VIII, cap. 15, n. 10; *Opera Omnia,* XV, 648-649.

51 As a measure of precaution, and to avoid misunderstanding with those who are not too familiar with the mind and practice of the Church on these matters, the S. Congregation of Religious now gives its indults for alienation "sine ulla responsabilitate oeconomica."

52 Leahy v. Williams, 141 Mass., 345; Freeport v. Egan, 146 Pa., 106; 23 At. 390.

53 Cf. the observations of the commentator on S. C. Conc. *Fidejussionis,* 27 ian. 1866—*ASS,* II (1866), 569.

juridical persons but rather protects and safeguards them against possible error or imprudence.[54]

The "high domain" which the Sovereign Pontiff enjoys in regard to all property held by ecclesiastical bodies throughout the entire world allows him to restrict certain activities and transactions in connection with these church goods, in order that he may thus provide for the welfare of the Church at large.[55] It is also within his supreme power to delegate inferior prelates and Superiors for the exercise of this prerogative in particular instances and within certain limits. This delegation contained in either general or particular law or given only in individual instances confers on bishops and other duly designated Superiors a specific faculty which further determines the right whereby "as they are placed by divine command over the Church, so they cannot be excluded

[54] "Auctoritas enim tutoris in quibusdam causis necessaria pupillis est, in quibusdam non est necessaria. Ut ecce si quid dari sibi stipuletur, non est necessaria tutoris auctoritas; quod si aliis pupilli promittant, necessaria est: namque placuit meliorem quidem suam condicionem licere eis facere etiam sine tutoris auctoritate, deteriorem vero non aliter quam tutore auctore. Unde in his causis ex quibus mutuae obligationes nascuntur, in emptionibus venditionibus, locationibus conductionibus, mandatis, depositis, si tutoris auctoritas non interveniat, ipsi quidem qui cum his contrahunt obligantur; at invicem pupilli non obligantur."—Inst. I, 21, *de auctoritate tutorum*.

Nevertheless there are essential differences between the relations of a guardian with his ward, and the relations of an ecclesiastical or religious Superior with his community or other church body:

1) the office of a guardian is only temporary, whereas the office of an ecclesiastical Superior is perpetual, because an ecclesiastical juristic person, unlike the minor, never attains its majority;

2) a Superior, unlike a guardian, is, within certain limits, entitled to use the goods which are under his protection;

3) the fact of being a Superior is a *honos,* while being a guardian is an *onus;*

4) ecclesiastical Superiors have much wider fields of action and authority than guardians before the civil law.—*Pirhing,* Lib. III, tit. 13, n. 43.

[55] "Dominium autem quo potiuntur singulae personae morales non prohibet quominus Summus Pontifex libere decernere valeat quoad haec bona, iubens etiam ut eadem de una in aliam personam transferantur; huiusmodi facultas vocari solet *dominium eminens,* ut opponatur dominio *proprio* et *formali* quod competit personis physicis vel moralibus."—S. C. Conc. Bisuntina seu Argentinen. *Iurium,* 26 feb. 1898—*Thesaurus Resolutionum,* CLVII, 210.

from the disposition of these goods nor from solicitude and vigilance over them."[56]

The necessity of this supervision of competent Superiors over the administration and especially the alienation of church property is further borne out in a special response of the S. Congregation of the Propagation of the Faith to the Bishop of Bardstown. Here the S. Congregation reiterated the fundamental principle that bishops are invested with the right of administering and controlling all property acquired by individual churches and other units of ecclesiastical life in their diocese, within the limits fixed by the sacred canons and the intentions of the founders or donors.[57] These general principles of ecclesiastical administration were incorporated into the decrees of the Second[58] and Third[59] Plenary Councils of Baltimore, to provide an efficacious check against the then prevalent abuses of trusteeism.

It will be noticed that canon, 1530, §13°, unlike canon 534, §1, which regulates the same matter for religious, does not require the *written* authorization of the legitimate Superior. This does not, however, dispense from the ordinary rules of business prudence. Because this written authorization is very advisable in case of possible conflict before the courts, many synodal statutes and conciliar decrees of ecclesiastical provinces in the United States have made it a matter of particular law.[60]

56 Letter of Pius VII to the bishops of North America, August 24, 1822 —*Collectanea S. C. P. F.*, n. 773.

57 S. C. de Prop. Fide, Bardstown, 1 apr. 1816,—*Collectanea S. C. P. F.*, n. 709; *Fontes*, n. 4704.

58 "Declaramus enim universalem Catholicae Ecclesiae legem esse, omnes illos qui ecclesiae bona quocumque modo administrant, nonnisi consentiente Sede Apostolica vel episcopo id licite facere, eosque in illorum administratione auctoritati et jurisdictioni eorum, quos Sedes Apostolica designaverit, esse subjectos."—*Concilii Plenarii Baltimorensis II Acta et Decreta*, n. 202.

59 *Concilii Plenarii Baltimorensis III Acta et Decreta*, cap. *De Aedituis vel Curatoribus et Consiliariis Laicis*, where the preceding decree of the Second Plenary Council is reaffirmed and promulgated anew.

60 Cf. among others, the fourth decree of the Third Provincial Council of Cincinnati (1861)—*Acta et Decreta*, p. 122, and n. 279 of the decrees of the Fourth Provincial Council of Cincinnati (1882). The same provision is found in art. 337 of the statutes of the First Synod of Grand Rapids (1903), and in art. X of the decrees of the Fourth Provincial Council of New York (1883).

Article 6. The Alienation of Relics, Etc.

The foregoing provisions, however, are subject to certain well determined modifications dealing with objects more intimately connected with the life of the Church than goods of a purely material value. According to the prescription laid down in canon 1281, §1, to which canon 1530 expressly refers, important relics or precious images, pictures, etc., (precious in the sense of canon 1280) may not be alienated without the permission of the Holy See. The same rule is applied to relics, etc., which, without being ranked as important or precious, are, nevertheless, the object of great veneration by the faithful of a particular locality. Prescinding from their intrinsic material value, objects of such worth for the spiritual welfare of the Church are regarded less as the property of an individual church than as belonging to the patrimony of the Universal Church. This explains the solicitude of the Code in protecting such treasures against passage into improper hands, and in preserving them for the particular place where they are the objects of special honor.[61]

Article 7. Further Precautionary Measures

It is altogether evident that no precautions provided by general law will cover satisfactorily all possible contingencies. Consequently, lest the Church be exposed to harm in these eventualities, §2 of canon 1530 empowers all competent Superiors to lay down other conditions not here

[61] Canon 1281, §1, which canon 1530 recalls, deals, first of all, with the more common case of relics, images, etc. which are the property of the church where they are kept. The canon does not affect such objects which do not belong to a church, but are possessed by private individuals or non-ecclesiastical pious societies. The principle of restrictive interpretation *in odiosis* certainly excludes all private and semi-public oratories from the limitations of the law. Since, however, canon 1280 explicitly mentions public oratories along with churches while canon 1281, in the same context, refers only to churches, there is room for doubt whether canon 1191, §1, extending the legislation on churches to public oratories, is to be strictly applied to the present case.—The second provision prescinds from the question of ownership to consider only the fact of the presence of these objects in a church where they are venerated with special devotion. The law forbids the *perpetual* transfer of these objects to another church and, *a fortiori*, prevents them from being taken from the church where they are to an oratory. Such transfer is, in reality, very much akin to real alienation.—Cf. Larraona, "Commentarium Codicis," *CpRM*, XIII (1932), 353, notes 647 and 648.

provided for in detail, according as prudence and necessity may suggest. All those subject to the Superior in the circumstances will be bound to comply with these prescriptions. The nature of these special regulations will depend on the particular background of individual transactions and on the needs proper to given localities. These regulations may prescribe the manner of asking for the permission, the formalities to be followed in recording the grant of the authorization, special procedure to be followed in a case a building project is under consideration, and in general, any other details which in the judgment of the competent Superior are important for the welfare of the ecclesiastical organization entrusted to his care and vigilance.

In conclusion, it may be remarked that compliance with the requirements of this canon is necessary for *every* act of alienation, even though the same thing be the object of successive contracts. The Code makes no provision for the principle formerly held, namely, that an object once alienated with the proper formalities was thereby rendered perpetually alienable without further restrictions.[62]

62 "Communis DD. conclusio est, ut res semel effecta alienabilis cum solemnitate, efficiatur perpetuo alienabilis sine solemnitate, dummodo semper cum eadem ecclesiae utilitate alienetur."—Schmalzgrueber, Lib. III, tit. 13, n. 41.

CHAPTER VI.

THE MANNER OF ALIENATION

Canon 1531

§1. Res alienari minore pretio non debet quam quod in aestimatione indicatur.

§2. Alienatio fiat per publicam licitationem aut saltem nota reddatur, nisi aliud circumstantiae suadeant; et res ei concedatur qui, omnibus perpensis, plus obtulerit.

§3. Pecunia ex alienatione percepta caute, tuto et utiliter in commodum Ecclesiae collocetur.

Article 1. The Price to Be Exacted in Alienation

The first prescription of this canon forbids the disposal of ecclesiastical property for any consideration lower than that fixed by the appraisers, according to canon 1530, §1, 1°. The reasonableness of this regulation is evident. It would be useless for canon 1530, §1, 1°, to require a written evaluation of the property to be alienated, if this estimate could subsequently be disregarded in the actual transaction; there would be no more than a merely theoretical safeguard thrown around the safety of the Church's financial condition.

It may easily happen, however, that no one will be found ready to pay the price set by the appraisers. Even in this case, if the appraisal has been fixed at a rather high price, a lower price cannot be accepted even though the price thus offered is still just and entails no harm for the ecclesiastical organization. A new appraisal must be called for by the same, or preferably different appraisers, to see if the price offered can be accepted without prejudicing the best interests of the Church. If the experts still maintain the price previously agreed upon, every effort must be made to obtain it in the transaction. If these efforts meet with no success, only extreme and urgent necessity, such as the pressing need of ready money or the danger of loss in the whole transaction if the partial offer is not accepted, will justify a departure from this prescription. A decision as to what procedure should be followed in such instances should not be taken without duly weighing which move will do more harm to the Church: disposing of the property at a price actually below the estimated value, or allowing the Church to suffer for want of ready means.[1]

If the appraisal was established between two sums, it is sufficient for the legitimacy of the transaction that at least the lower of these prices be received.

Article 2. Public Auction in Ecclesiastical Alienation

The usual principle that all alienation must ultimately redound to the benefit of the Church has dictated the provision contained in §2 of canon 1531. Public auction to which all interested parties are invited or to which they are at least free to come, provides assurance that the Church will derive all possible profit from the proposed transaction; the competition of several buyers will be more advantageous than the individual offer of a lone purchaser.

For this reason various rules were imposed even before the Code for all such situations. Many of the formalities required by the pre-Code jurisprudence of the Roman Congregations are abrogated by the silence of the present law; provisions which deal with prescriptions contained in the Code are to be considered as still possessing binding force, within the limitations of canon 6.

Thus, for instance, ecclesiastics and religious were obliged to proceed with their alienations only *praevia edictorum affixione,* in order that an eye might be had exclusively to the good of the Church without any considerations dictated by relationship, friendship, etc.[2] Notice of the impending auction could not be posted without the previous *beneplacitum* of the Holy See.[3] Lest the Church create the harmful impression of trafficking in money and property, the time-limit set by the public notices for the offering of bids could not be extended, even if such

1 This conclusion would seem to be justified by the fundamental principle invoked by Wernz: "Superior lex est conservatio bonorum ecclesiasticorum et legitima sufficientium reddituum perceptio."—*Ius Decretalium,* tom. 3, pars 1, n. 153.

2 S. C. Ep. et Reg. Catacen. *Super edictorum affixione in locationibus bonorum Ecclesiae,* 11 maii 1743—*Collectanea S. C. Ep. et Reg.,* p. 363.

3 Cf. the usual procedure of the Holy See in *Collectanea S. C. Ep. et Reg.,* p. 768, note, and in *S. C. Ep. et Reg. Aquaependen. Super alienationibus,* sept. 1793—*Collectanea S. C. Ep. et Reg.,* p. 42.

extension were to the ultimate benefit of the ecclesiastical organization involved.[4]

The bids offered for ecclesiastical goods in such public auctions must be "certain, explicit, determined and unconditioned."[5] This prescription is intended to ward off from the Church authorities all semblance of collusion in injustice with individuals who might be scheming through captious bids to obtain ecclesiastical property at a price below what is just.[6]

After all the offers have been received from the interested parties, the contract is to be awarded to the highest bidder. The highest bidder, however, is not to be determined merely with an eye to the mathematical amount offered. The addition of the qualifying phrase *omnibus perpensis* demonstrates conclusively that other elements as well are to be taken into consideration. Thus, for example, if it is a question of alienating a portion of property near a religious or ecclesiastical institution where other buildings will ultimately be erected, the *omnibus perpensis* of this paragraph would authorize the giving of the preference to another institute of the same nature rather than to a business or industrial organization, even though this latter may have presented a higher bid. Or again, a lower bid wih the certainty of ready payment could be legitimately

[4] Cf. the decree of the S. C. Ep. et Reg. *De locationibus et alienationibus rerum Ecclesiasticarum,* 18 mart. 1835—*Collectanea S. C. Ep. et Reg.*, p. 62, and likewise S. C. Ep. et Reg. *Romana, Super acceptatione oblationis vulgo Soprassesta,* 24 aug. 1866—*Collectanea S. C. Ep et Reg., p.* 766.

[5] S. C. Ep. et Reg. *Nucerina Alienationis,* iun. 1784—*Collectanea S. C. Ep. et Reg.*, p. 40.

[6] The actual legislation of the Code makes no reference to the former rule of allowing a certain period of time for the offering of the *vicesima* and the *sexta,* i.e., after the highest bid had been announced no action was to be taken until it was ascertained if anyone wished to offer one-twentieth *(vicesima)* more than this bid. Then another delay was required to see if the highest bidder wished to offer one-sixth *(sexta)* more than the total already proposed. This was considered in the form of a *restitutio in integrum* for the Church which was looked upon as having suffered a loss of one-sixth of her goods through the alienation. These complications occasioned almost innumerable disputes and misunderstandings which frequently resulted in lawsuits before civil or ecclesiastical tribunals; a large percentage of the cases given in the *Collectanea* of the S. Congregation of Bishops and Regulars in its decisions on property matters deals with the question of the *vicesima* and the *sexta.* By virtue of canon 1529 the prevailing civil law in particular territories will regulate everything connected with the auctions prescribed by Canon Law.

preferred to a higher offer to be paid only in installments extending over a protracted period of time. Likewise, in a country which may be financially straightened, a person who offers to pay the equivalent of the price in valuable foreign exchange may have the prefreence over another who can furnish only national currency.

In phrasing the terms and the rules of the public auction, those responsible should see to it that the liberty thus accorded to the Superior by the Code is fully safeguarded. Otherwise, by virtue of canon 1529, confirming §27 of the *Restatement of the Law on Contracts,* the Church would be under strict obligation to award the contract to the highest bidder, irrespective of other considerations.[7]

It should be noted that, from the canonical point of view, the fact of having offered the highest bid, even in the light of *omnibus perpensis,* confers on the bidder no strict right to exact from the Church the completion of the contract thus initiated, although it implies on his part an obligation to continue with the transaction. His right is solely a *right of preference* before others, entitling him to first consideration if and when the Church wishes to proceed with the contract. With the permission of the Church he may cede this right of preference to a third party who thereby acquires all the obligations and privileges connected therewith. The obligations consist in completing the transaction by paying the full price offered, or in reimbursing the Church for damages in case of withdrawal. Should a third party to whom this right of preference was ceded fail in his obligations towards the Church, the party who ceded the right may sometimes be held to make this loss good to the ecclesiastical organization involved, particularly if this default brings financial harm upon a *locus pius.*[8] The Church always remains free to break off the negotiations, though she also may be held to compensate for the damages which withdrawal in an advanced stage of the transaction might occasion the other party.[9]

[7] "At an auction the auctioneer merely invites offers from successive bidders which he may accept or reject unless, by announcing that the sale is without reserve or by other means, he indicates that he is making an offer to sell at any price bid by the highest bidder. In that case after a bid has been made the auctioneer cannot withdraw."—*Restatement,* §27.

[8] S. C. Ep. et Reg. *Emptionis Venditionis,* 18 febr. 1870—*ASS,* V (1869-1870), 425.

[9] Cf. the observations of the commentator on S. C. Ep et Reg. *Super Acceptatione oblationis vulgo supra sextam,* 24 aug. 1866—*ASS,* II (1866), p. 423, n. 4.

Although the Code, unlike the Instruction to the Patriarch of the Armenians,[10] which is the main source of this canon, makes no mention of immediate payment in cash as one of the conditions of closing the deal, it is evident that all measures consistent with courtesy and prudence should be taken to insure a speedy settlement of the bargain.

Even though the obligation of disposing of church goods through public auction is *preceptive,* it nevertheless admits of exceptions: *nisi aliud circumstantiae suadeant.* It may happen, for instance, that notice of a public auction would occasion great inconvenience to an ecclesiastical organization by exposing it to the danger of interference by the civil authorities, to possible loss of its good name through suspicions of mismanagement or even of dishonesty in its business affairs, with danger of wonderment or perhaps scandal to the faithful. The same exception from the law can be allowed if the need is too urgent and the time too short to permit compliance with all the civil prescriptions regarding public auctions. In this case the competent Superior may adopt the method of alienation which in his prudent judgment appears best suited for the circumstances.

By virtue of his right and duty of vigilance over all ecclesiastical property in his diocese,[11] the Ordinary is thus constituted competent judge of the circumstances justifying departure from this usual method of procedure by public auction, in all cases within the limits of his jurisdiction. His competence would cease if the Holy See had already made specific regulations or provisions in a particular case. Within certain restricted limits, this same power may be legitimately exercised by the Superior whose consent has authorized the alienation, according to the prescriptions of canon 1532.

Article 3. The Use of the Proceeds of the Alienation

In the treatment of alienation in general it was pointed out that canonical restrictions on this matter are concerned only with subtrac-

10 *Fontes,* n. 4867; cf. also *Collectanea, S.C.P.F.,* n. 1310.

11 Letter of Pius VII to the bishops of North America, 24 aug. 1822—*Collectanea S.C.P.F.,* n. 773.

tions from the stable capital of an ecclesiastical organization.[12] It was also observed that even when it authorizes alienation the Church requires that the fixed capital thus affected be safeguarded as carefully as possible. These observations are based on two fundamental principles of ecclesiastical jurisprudence, or rather on two distinct aspects of one general principle:

1) the money of an ecclesiastical organization must be invested in a manner which is *safe, permanent,* and *income-yielding;*

2) sums belonging to the stable capital may not be converted into non-productive assets without compliance with the usual canonical formalities.[13]

The first of these two basic principles is embodied in §3 of canon 1531. By the terms of this provision, mere permission to alienate does not of itself imply permission to dispose of the proceeds of this transaction. These proceeds must, as far as possible, be used to reintegrate the fixed capital already depleted by the alienation.[14] Authors are not agreed as to the necessity of special and specific authorization to dispose of the proceeds in the case wherein alienation was permitted for the precise purpose of meeting special and urgent needs.[15] The necessity of this additional authorization is not evident. In fact, a request for approval of a proposed alienation in order to meet urgent needs will hardly be complied with by approving only the alienation itself without the desired disposal of the proceeds from the transaction. Such an authorization would really violate the prescription of canon 1530, §1, 2°, which requires a just cause for all transactions involving alienation. In practise the question is of little importance in view of the fact that the Holy

12 Larraona, "Commentarium Codicis"—*CpRM,* XIII (1932), 358, III, c and note 669.

13 *"Quaesita Varia,* III," *Periodica,* II-III (1911), p. 93.

14 Cf. the strict insistence on this rule even in the case of alienation made in the face of urgent necessity—*S.C.P.F. Cocincin.,* 27 aug. 1832, *Collectanea,* n. 821.

15 Creusen, *Periodica,* XI (1923), 66.

See usually provides for the use of the funds thus received, in the formula whereby it authorizes the alienation.[16]

Consequently, for any use aside from the one specified in the indult for alienation, even though this other use be of a religious nature, "there is always needed the authorization of the Holy See, or a dispensation from this obligation [of investing the proceeds], which the law imposes in the aforementioned canon [1531, §3] clearly and explicitly without allowing any exceptions."[17] The legislation on this point is so stringent that even in the case wherein a Vicar Apostolic would alienate church property to preserve it from the fury of persecutors, he would nevertheless be bound to invest the proceeds.[18]

All the investments made in accordance with the prescriptions of canon 1531, §3, are, needless to say, governed strictly by the prohibition contained in canon 142. The twofold obligation of safeguarding the financial status and the good name of the Church in general and of individual ecclasiastical units in particular, as well as avoiding anything which even remotely resembles *negotiatio,* constitutes a strict prohibition against anything like "playing the stock market," in the hope of thereby

[16] The pertinent parts of Formula F. 45ª used by the S. Congregation of Religious are as follows: "Vigore facultatum a SS. mo Domino Nostro concessarum, Sacra Congregatio. . . . audito voto Rev. mi P. Procuratoris Generalis (or Em. mi Protectoris, Rev. mi Ordinarii etc.) eidem (or Rev. mo P. Superiori Generali) benigne concedit. . . . ut constito sibi de necessitate vel utilitate (alienationis). . . . petitam facultatem deveniendi ad enunciatum contractum alienationis non minore pretio. . . . pro suo arbitrio et conscientia concedat; ita tamen ut *pretium ipsum impendatur ad effectum de quo in precibus* (or: caute, tuto et utiliter collocetur favore Instituti), servatisque caeteris quae in cann. 1530-1531 praescribuntur."

[17] S. C. Conc. Dioecesis N. *Donariorum Votivorum,* 12 iul. 1919—*AAS,* XI (1919), 418. The case considered here (i.e., using money for enlarging a church) differs from that mentioned above on p. 145, n. 4 and p. 146, n. 6, in that no conversion is here made into *productive* property or buildings which would economize on rent.

[18] *S.C.P.F. Cocincin.,* 27 aug. 1832, Collectanea, n. 827.

bettering the financial welfare of the Church. The end does not justify the means.[19]

This conclusion is in perfect harmony with the answer sent by the S. Congregation of the Propagation of the Faith on January 10, 1837, to the Vicar Apostolic of Western Tonkin in China. This Vicar Apostolic had requested permission to have money which was sent for the benefit of the Mission converted into merchandise in order to forestall seizure by pirates, the dishonesty of unscrupulous merchants, and molestations on the part of the civil government. The requested permission was granted in the following restricted terms:

> *Dummodo absit omne lucri studium vel propositum,* et necessitas ita agendi perduret, et dummodo lucrum, si quod provenerit, non in alicujus missionarii, *sed in Missionis utilitatem cedat,* et pro hoc tantum peculiari casu, tribuatur petita facultas, ita tamen ut non evadat in exemplum, *quasi negotiari liceat missionariis ob Missionis utilitatem.*[20]

The specific determination of the investments to be made with the proceeds of alienation rests with the Superior who authorized it. In the case of religious the following restrictions are provided for by canon 533:

1) The Superioress of nuns or of a congregation of diocesan approval may not invest any money whatsoever without the previous *consent* of the local Ordinary; if the monastery of nuns is also subject to a Superior regular, his *consent* must likewise be obtained;

2) The permission of the local Ordinary is also required before any

19 "Quidquid igitur sapit ludos bursarum et aleatorias rationes emendi et vendendi . . . cum lucro, sedulo vitandum est."—Vermeesch-Creusen, *Epitome,* n. 861. And Larraona observes: "Ceterum leges pro alienatione fundantur non in periculo quod aliquis actus oeconomicus secumferre ut actus potest, sed in periculo *status,* ad quem reducuntur bona ecclesiastica qui, quia minus stabilis minusque securus, etsi ex actu bona augerentur, tamen deterior habetur."—"Commentarium Codicis," *CpRM,* XIII (1932), 194, note 640. In this same connection he remarks that "Administratio ecclesiastica *tutiorismo* nititur, et despicit profectum oeconomicum qui, periculo juridico, obtineri per negotiationem posset."—*Ibidem,* p. 189, note 625.

20 *Collectanea, S.C.P.F.,* n. 853.

Superioress in a congregation of pontifical approval may invest any money pertaining to the dowries of the religious (cf. can. 549);

3) The Superior or Superioress of a house belonging to a religious congregation must obtain the consent of the local Ordinary for the investment of funds which have been donated or bequeathed in order to be expended on divine worship or works of charity in the place where the house of the congregation is situated;

4) Any religious, even if he be a regular, must have the authorization of the local Ordinary in order to invest money given to a parish or mission, or to the religious by reason of the parish or mission;

These same restrictions apply likewise to any change in investments already made.

CHAPTER VII.

THE COMPETENT SUPERIOR FOR ALIENATION

Canon 1532

§1. Legitimus Superior de quo in can. 1530, n. 3, est Sedes Apostolica, si agatur:

1° De rebus pretiosis;

2° De rebus quae valorem excedunt triginta millium libellarum seu francorum.

§2. Si vero agatur de rebus quae valorem non excedunt mille libellarum seu francorum, est loci Ordinarius, audito administrationis Consilio, nisi res minimi momenti sit, et cum eorum consensu quorum interest.

§3. Si denique de rebus quarum pretium continetur intra mille libellas, et triginta millia libellarum seu francorum, est loci Ordinarius, dummodo accesserit consensus tum Capituli cathedralis, tum Consilii administrationis, tum eorum quorum interest.

§4. Si agatur de alienanda re divisibili, in petenda licentia aut consensu exprimi debent partes antea alienatae; secus licentia irrita est.

Article 1. The Competence of the Holy See

A) *General observations*

This canon determines the particular applications of the general principle enunciated in canon 1530, §1, 3°. There it is stated that one of the requisites of valid alienation is authorization by a lawful Superior. The Code now furnishes explicit declarations on the particular powers of respective Superiors. The prescriptions of this canon apply only to the secular clergy, since canon 534 regulates this same matter for religious communities.

The Holy See, in which is vested the right of eminent domain over all ecclesiastical property in the Church, reserves to itself approval for certain alienations. This has been the constant practise of the Holy See. The Holy Office declared to the Bishop of Regensburg, on December 22, 1880, that the Constitution *Ambitiosae,* which required papal approval for certain alienations, had not been revoked by the subsequent Constitution *Apostolicae Sedis* of Pius IX, but that on the contrary all *general* privileges running counter to the demands of the Constitution *Ambitiosae* had been thereby suppressed.[1] The Code confirms this traditional procedure.

In the light of canon 1530, §1, 2°, the Holy See is always ready to grant this authorization when there is question of evident necessity or utility in the proposed alienation.[2] Very serious reasons, on the contrary, are required to justify acts of alienation performed without the preceding intervention of the Holy See if the amount involved requires it. The S. Congregation of the Propagation of the Faith, for example, informed the Vicar Apostolic of Cochin, China, that the *only* reason legitimating such action was the impossibility of providing otherwise for the welfare of the Church in the face of imminent persecution.[3] These rules are to be understood as applying only to important transactions; the law itself rules out the necessity of apostolic approval for alienations involving sums of smaller moment.[4] When papal authorization is required, it is so essential that all contracts made without it are null and void.[5] Although such contracts cannot oblige of themselves, still they may bind by virtue of long-standing custom or prescription, and may for this reason be confirmed or sanated by the Holy See *ad cautelam*.[6]

In a decision of the S. Congregation of Bishops and Regulars, on February 26, 1864, are found the following provisions on the effect of falsehood in connection with obtaining the approval of the Holy See for a projected alienation:

1 S. C. S. Off. Ratisbonen. 22 dec. 1880—*Collectanea S.C.P.F.*, n. 1554.

2 S. C. Conc. Ianuen. *Transactionis et Iurium circa Abbatiam*, 22 aug. 1908—*Thesaurus Resolutionum*, CLXVII, 563. Cf. also Utinen. *Transactionis*, 22 iun. 1908—*Thesaurus Resolutionum*, CLXVII, 341.

3 "Fundos ecclesiasticos a Vicario Apostolico vendi aut permutari non posse nisi quando, persecutione urgente, alia ratio praesto non sit eos Ecclesiae conservandi ad effectum tutius pretium investiendi."—*S.C.P.F. Cocincin.* 27 aug. 1832, *Collectanea*, n. 827.

4 Canon 1532, §§2, 3. Also cf. S. C. Conc. Cassanen. *Iurium*, 31 ian. 1903—*Thesaurus Resolutionum*, CXII, 207.

5 Canon 1530, §1, 3°.

6 S. C. Conc. 25 iun. 1864—*ASS*, I (1865), 594.

1) papal authorization obtained under false pretenses is invalid;

2) the petition for approval of alienation is vitiated as often as a falsehood is expressed *(obreptio)* or the truth is concealed *(subreptio)*;

3) ignorance or error does not excuse if the false pretenses concern substantial points of the petition.[7]

Since apostolic approval is required for the validity of certain alienations, it follows that contracts made without it are devoid of binding force in the eyes of the Church. Validity requires that these contracts be preceded by the *execution* of the apostolic indult authorizing the alienation.[8] The Holy See has declared that whatever be its speculative merits, the opinion defending the validity of contracts made *sub conditione beneplaciti apostolici* is not sustained by the practise of the Roman Curia.[9]

Consequently, when the nature of the transaction is such as to require it, there is no obligation in conscience of completing a contract which has been initiated without the previous authorization of the Holy See.[10] Either party can withdraw with impunity.[11] If there is question of contracts of long standing, about whose origins nothing or little is known, the presumption is that the necessary approval was duly obtained

7 S. C. Ep. et Reg., 26 febr. 1864—*ASS*, I (1865), 285. These principles are still applicable within the limits set down by canons 40 and 42, which legislate on the dependance of the validity of an indult on the truth of the petition.

8 S. C. Ep. et Reg. *Super acceptatione oblationis vulgo Soprassesta,* 24 aug. 1866—*Collectanea S. C. Ep. et Reg.*, p. 766.

9 S. C. Ep. et Reg. *Emptionis Venditionis* 1868—*ASS*, V (1869), 368.

10 S. C. Conc. Praten. *Transactionis,* 25 ian. 1896—*Thesaurus Resolutionum,* CLV, 76. Cf. also Cremonen. *Iurium Parochialium,* 26 iul. 1879—*Thesaurus Resolutionum,* CXXXVIII, 364.

11 This provision affects both the internal and the external forum in the eyes of the Church. Although unjust, and therefore not accepted by canon 1529, a civil enactment enforcing continuance of the contract would have to be complied with in the external forum of civil legislation. Cf. S. C. Ep. et Reg., Fulginaten. *Recessus a contractu permutationis,* 6 feb. 1852—*Collectanea S. C. Ep. et Reg.*, p. 600.

from Rome, if the contract has continued in force for thirty or a hundred years.[12]

Closely connected with the prohibition of alienating without the approval of the Holy See is the obligation of strict conformity with all the particular conditions and instructions imposed by the apostolic indult.[13] This duty is deduced from the principle that the Superior who approves the use of a power or faculty is free likewise to determine the conditions to be observed in this use. Compliance with these instructions and conditions will affect either the validity or at least the lawfulness of the transaction according to the force of the terms used in the indult, and in keeping with the provisions of canons 39 and 40, where the Code determines the limits within which fidelity to the conditions stipulated in an indult influences its valid or licit execution. In no case may an indult which is obtained for the alienation of one particular object or portion of property be used for the disposal of another, even though the second object may be of the same, or even smaller value.[14]

The respective fields of competence of the various Roman Congregations are well defined in the particular canons on their powers in the Code. Thus, the S. Congregation of Religious will act on all cases of alienation arising in religious Institutes, Third Orders, or societies which are governed *ad instar religiosorum.*[15] The S. Congregation of the Council is competent in all the transactions of the secular clergy.[16] These same powers are exercised by the S. Congregation of the Propagation of the Faith for all territories within its jurisdiction.[17] By virtue of canon 255, the S. Congregation for Extraordinary Ecclesiastical Affairs is competent when questions of temporalities must be taken up with

12 S. C. Conc. Praten. *Transactionis,* 25 ian. 1896—*Thesaurus Resolutionum,* CLV, 77.

13 S. C. Ep. et Reg. Comaclen. *Praelationis,* 18 mart. 1835—*Collectanea* S. C. Ep. et Reg., p. 664.

14 ". . . . deest voluntas concedendi facultatem ad horum (i.e. aliorum non designatorum) alienationem. Regula autem generalis est, ut concessio facultatis non extendatur ad casum sub verbis concessionis non comprehensum, quamvis ad illum etiam casum, si peteretur, aeque facile concessio facta fuisset."—De Lugo, *Responsorum Moralium Libri VI,* Lib. III, dub. XIII, n. 2; *Opera Omnia,* VIII, 139.

15 Canons 251, §1 and 676, §2.

16 Canon 250, §2.

17 Canon 252, §§1, 2.

civil governments, or when these questions give rise to conflicts between canonical prescriptions and civil juridical provisions. The S. Congregation for the Oriental Church grants authorization in all cases which touch the territories or persons subject to it.[18] The S. Consistorial Congregation grants the permission when diocesan property is involved.[19] In case, however, the alienation affects property belonging to the diocesan Seminary, the authorization for alienation must come from the S. Congregation of Seminaries and Universities.[20]

B) *Precious goods*

Since the supreme and exclusive power of government over the whole Church is vested in the Apostolic See, it is evident that the control of the more important ecclesiastical transactions should rest ultimately in its hands. These transactions are more apt to affect the general well-being of the Church at large, either because of the unusual character of the objects or because of the great amounts of money involved. Consequently, the Holy See reserves exclusively to itself the right to approve all alienations of precious goods, as well as all transactions involving sums exceeding thirty thousand lire or francs.

Canon 1280, speaking of sacred pictures, etc., affords a general clue as to the elements which make an object "precious" in the sight of the Church. According to this indication an object is classed as precious when it is "outstanding for reasons of antiquity, art, or public veneration." Canon 1497, §2, in turn, inculcates the same principle when it declares that goods are precious when they have "notable value by reason

18 Canon 257, §1.

19 Canon 248, §3.

20 Cf. the decision of the Special Commission of Cardinals to the question proposed:

> Utrum concessio facultatis alienandi bona, quae spectant ad seminaria dioecesana, pertineat ad Sacram Congregationem de Seminariis et Studiorum Universitatibus an ad Sacram Congregationem Concilii.
>
> "Resp. Pertinere ad Sacram Congregationem de Seminariis et Studiorum Universitatibus."—27 nov. 1922, *AAS*, XV (1922), 40.

of art or history, or because of the material out of which they are made."[21]

Before an object can be considered as precious it must, according to canon 1497, §2, have a value which can be classed as *notabilis*. In solving a case of alienation the S. Congregation of the Council calls attention to the many conflicting opinions of canonists on what constitutes *notable* value.[22] After enumerating the various opinions the conclusion is reached that in practise no object is to be considered as precious unless it can be evaluated at a minimum of about one thousand *libellae*.[23] Hence it would follow from this that local Ordinaries may licitly and validly authorize the alienation of objects whose value does not attain this sum, even though artistic or historical considerations might make them appear as precious.[24]

C) *Votive offerings*

In the very same case in which the principles governing the alienation of precious goods were discussed so much in detail, a specific application was made to a particular category of church goods. This was in favor of votive offerings left as lasting pledges of gratitude at shrines or altars in particular churches.[25] By drawing a parallel between these offerings and images, etc., precious or otherwise, which enjoy great veneration in churches, the S. Congregation applies to them the absolute prohibition of alienation contained in canon 1281, §1. The worth of

[21] This definition sums up that of Schmalzgrueber, who says that precious objects are "vasa aurea, vel argentea, torques, tapetes, et similiter templorum ornamenta, auro, gemmis, etc. intextata, uti et reliqua magnae aestimationis supellex, quae est de thesauro Ecclesiae, eique propter materiae pretium, artem, vel antiquitatem singularem splendorem confert."—Lib. III, tit. 13, n. 27.

[22] S. C. Conc. Dioecesis N. *Donariorum Votivorum*, 12 iul. 1919—*AAS*, XI (1919), 416.

[23] Cf. Article 7, E) of this present chapter, pp. 110-112.

[24] Although not explicitly stated in so many words, this conclusion is very openly hinted at in the solution of the case as given by the S. Congregation. When, however, this point was proposed directly as an explicit *dubium* on January 14, 1922, the S. Congregation of the Council declined to answer, but referred the question to the Pontifical Commission for the Interpretation of the Code (*AAS*, XIV [1922], 160). As yet no authentic interpretation of the *dubium* has been given by the Commission.

[25] S. C. Conc. Dioecesis N. *Donariorum Votivorum*, 12 iul. 1919—*AAS*, XI (1919), 416-419.

these objects, it says, is to be estimated less according to their intrinsic value than according to the affection and love of which they are the standing expression, and which connects them almost indissolubly with the statue, picture, or altar which they honor. Consequently, inferior ecclesiastical Superiors of whatever rank are to regard themselves more as the guardians than the owners of these objects, with no power whatsoever to divert them to other uses. The whole line of argument is then summed up as follows:

> Aliis verbis et planius: observandae profecto sunt condiciones a donante fortasse donationi appositae: atqui ex natura rei et negotii in casu praesumi debet omnino donationem factam esse *sub ea conditione ut sit inalienabilis.* Ergo si semper, in alienandis ipsis rebus ecclesiasticis (quibus ceterum non facile ipsa donaria accensentur), cautum est ut obtineatur "eorum consensus quorum interest" (cf. can. 1532, §§ 2, 3), id multo magis in alienatione donariorum votivorum difficultatem facessere videtur, quum iste consensus in alienationem non facile praesupponi possit, imo, aliquo sensu, impossibilis factus sit vel ex parte donantis, qui proprietate rei donatae sese omnino exspoliavit et quidem non in favorem personae humanae, sed potius in obsequium personae beatae aut divinae, cui rem donatam, interposita voti religione, sacravit. Prout igitur "ultimarum voluntatum . . . commutatio, quae fieri ex iusta tantum et necessaria causa debent, Sedi Apostolicae reservantur" (can. 1517, §1), quum eius solius sit necessarium interpretari aut supplere interesse habentium consensum, ita etiam voluntatis, quae in ordine ad obiecta voto donata ultima iure censentur, interpretatio, vel potius commutatio uni Sedi Apostolicae, cuius est solvere ligata in coelo et in terra, iure reservatur.[26]

On the strength of this argumentation and in view of the longstanding practise of the Roman Curia, the S. Congregation of the Council later declared in a response to the Bishop of Lodi (Italy), that the local Ordinary has no power to alienate votive offerings or to authorize their alienation by others, *even within the limits of his ordinary competence.* Still more, the Congregation stated that this restriction was binding on the Ordinary even though the donors themselves freely

26 S. C. Conc. Dioecesis N. *Donariorum Votivorum,* 12 iul. 1919—*AAS,* XI (1919), 419.

consented to the alienation of their offerings.[27] Finally, in the interests of public worship and the devotion of the faithful the principle was established that when an offering has been made at an altar or before a statue or a picture, the presumption is always that this offering is the expression of a vow, and always remains subject to the stringent regulations mentioned above for all votive offerings.[28]

D) *Memorial offerings*

Because of the comparatively small number of shrines, sanctuaries, miraculous statues and the like in the United States this important decision of the S. Congregation of the Council will have little direct practical import in this country. Nevertheless, a study of the principles so clearly enunciated in the erudite *votum* of the Consultor reveals a very wide and important field of application to local conditions. Though not explicitly so stated in the resolution of the S. Congregation, the conclusions of this case would seem to apply with at least equal force to such offerings as those which in memory of departed persons are made for chapels, altars, chalices, vestments, statues, windows and the like offered in memory of departed persons.

It is true that such offerings are not votive offerings in the strict sense of the term.[29] In many cases they will not even be of such monetary or artistic value as to be classed as precious property. In either case, however, the principles underlying the decision of the S. Congregation can be applied:

> Praeter causam itaque pretiositatis etiam causa *cultus, devotionis*

[27] S. C. Conc. Lauden. *Circa donaria votiva et alienationes,* 14 ian. 1922—*AAS,* XIV (1922), 160.

[28] Cf. the preceding remarks (p. 208) on the transfer of ownership to a saint or a divine person. Thus the person in whose honor such offerings are made becomes one of those "quorum interest," whose consent, consequently, would be required for alienation—which it is obviously impossible to obtain.

[29] A search through many authors, old and modern, fails to reveal a satisfactory definition of votive offerings, whereby they may be clearly and definitely differentiated from memorial offerings. Most authors mention votive offerings, but appear to take the definition for granted. The S. Congregation of the Council, however, seems to imply that the term "votive offerings" refers in the strict sense, mainly to such objects as gold or silver hearts, plaques and the like which usually surround famous statues or altars, and to other objects donated as expressions of gratitude for favors received.

aut pietatis obstare potest, quominus huiusmodi donariorum valida sit alienatio: aliis verbis, ut hodie dici solet, non solum valor aestimationis, sed etiam *affectionis* attendendus est.[30]

The case is undoubtedly very clear if these memorial offerings have at the same time been made in honor of the Persons of the Trinity or of one of the saints. This makes them real votive offerings, with consequent inalienability except with the formalities and authorization prescribed by the Holy See. Not even the consent of the donor is sufficient to legalize such alienations, because, as the S. Congregation points out in the citation given on page 107, the donor no longer has any right to dispose of the goods which he has consecrated to purposes of religion.

In the light of these considerations it seems legitimate to conclude that all such memorial offerings are inalienable without recourse to the Holy See. Some will be inalienable because of their intrinsic value as precious objects. Others, without being precious, will be governed by the traditionally strict viewpoint of the Roman Curia on the question of votive offerings for purposes of religion.[31] Consequently, no pastor or other ecclesiastical administrator inferior to the Sovereign Pontiff would be within his powers if he removed, replaced, sold or destroyed any such memorials. Once they have been accepted by the Church they acquire a very special character in her eyes, regardless of even their crying lack of artistic or liturgical value. Hence, they cannot be disposed of without the consent of the Holy See which alone has the supreme power on earth of changing or setting aside completely the intentions of pious donors. If it be a question of remodeling, enlarging, or redecorating a church, or even of adapting it more perfectly to the exigencies of liturgical law or the requirements of good taste, the special character of such gifts prevents them from being disposed of without previous consulta-

30 *AAS*, XI (1919), 418.

31 "Hisce rationum momentis adiicitur etiam positivum argumentum quod petitur ex stylo et observantia perpetua S. Congregationis, quippe quae semper sibi reservavit, et quidem sub religiosissimis clausulis, concedere licentiam huiusmodi alienationem peragendi, quam imo veniam numquam per modum facultatis, sed semper in modum indulti in singulis particularibus casibus, causa necessitatis apprime cognita, concessit. Nec est profecto praesumendum datum Codicem huiusmodi observantiam, rationibus publici boni evidenter subnixam, in posterum tacite abolitam voluisse."—*AAS*, XI (1919), 419.

tion with the Holy See, which in its wisdom and prudence will decide on the advisability of the proposed alienation.[32]

These conclusions in regard to the inalienability of memorial offerings made in favor of religious purposes are logical deductions from the general principles enunciated by the S. Congregation of the Council on votive offerings in particular. They are, besides, corroborated by the provisions of canon 20 whereby, when an explicit prescription of law is lacking in a particular case, the norm to be followed is to be taken "from laws covering similar cases," from the "general principles of law," and from "the practise of the Roman Curia." All these considerations would seem to bear out the application of the law on votive offerings to the case of memorial offerings, votive or not.

E) *The equivalent of thirty thousand lire or francs*

In §1, 2°, of canon 1532, thirty thousand lire or francs are given as the limit which ecclesiastical Superiors may not exceed in alienating church property without explicit apostolic authorization. In order to insure the proper functioning of ecclesiastical organizations with all due dependence on the supreme authority of the Holy See, it is of evident importance to determine for each individual country the equivalent of thirty thousand lire or francs in its own proper money.

Although there has been no explicit declaration to this effect, it is now a commonly accepted opinion,[33] confirmed by the practise of the Holy See,[34] that the sums fixing the limits of competence for various ecclesiastical Superiors are calculated on the basis of the gold value of money. It is only on this basis that a non-fluctuating standard can rest. It follows naturally that, if the gold unit of exchange is to be adopted as the norm for establishing the comparative value of various currencies,

32 "Interest igitur bono publico, seu integritati et profectui sacri cultus, fidelis conservatio donariorum in eo statu iisque terminis in quibus a voluntate donantis ponuntur, adeo ut non sit fortasse nimium quod dicitur, ecclesiam eiusque rectores non tam in proprietate quam potius in custodia donaria ipsa habere, de quibus igitur nullo modo in alium usum disponere possunt."—*AAS,* XI (1919), 419.

33 Doheny, "Church Finance and Problems of Alienation"—*The Jurist,* I, (1941), p. 101, who refers to the Letter of the Apostolic Delegate in the United States, of November 13, 1936.

34 This practice is stated in the classic case on votive offerings (AAS, XI [1919], 418 ff.,) and also in S. R. Rotae Dec. XXII, (1930), p. 124.

this gold unit must be employed in both terms of the comparison. Hence, if thirty thousand lire or francs are to be understood as meaning thirty thousand *gold* francs or lire, their corresponding equivalent in dollars must likewise be taken as representing gold dollars.

Shortly after the promulgation of the Code, the equivalent of thirty thousand lire or francs was fixed at six thousand dollars for the United States. Since that time, however, many radical changes have profoundly altered the world's financial systems, with the result that fluctuations in money value have been of constant occurrence.[35] In view of the fact that the S. Congregation of the Council, although, it is true, in another connection, has stated explicitly that money is to be considered in its *real* rather than its *nominal* value, especially when the nominal value is higher than the real value,[36] it would appear advisable that some readjustment be made in the actual equivalent of "triginta millia libellarum seu francorum." This is true especially at the present time, when even the value of gold has undergone various radical changes.[37] Just as thirty thousand present-day lire or francs do not represent in actual value the sum indicated by the same figures in currency of the immediate post-war period, so, in the same way, six thousand dollars are not in 1941 the exact equivalent of what they were in 1918. This seems incontrovertible, especially in view of the official devaluation of the United States dollar in 1934. Consequently, the power of alienating up to the sum of six thousand dollars at the time of the Code will extend now to what represents this amount today on the basis of the actual gold value of the United States dollar. Since this gold value is fixed by an official act of legitimate authority, it affords the permanent basis necessary for the establishment of a juridical standard of values.[38]

35 Sédillot, *Le Drame des Monnaies* (Paris, 1937-1938).

36 S. C. Conc. *Resolutio,* 23 ian. 1923—*AAS,* XV (1923), 513. Cf. also *Periodica,* XII (1924), 151, and *Jus Pontificium,* III, (1923), 179.

37 ". . . . probati vero scriptores nostrae aetatis monent attendi posse ad mutatum valorem pecuniae."—*AAS,* XI (1919), 418. The *votum* here cited quotes Wernz to the effect that "minime vero extendenda est Constitutio *(Ambitiosae)* ad alienationem rerum mobilium vel immobilium, quae pro diversitate *regionum* iuxta *praesentem* valorem pecuniae (nunc saltem duplo vel triplo minorem) *pretiosae non amplius* dici possunt."—*Ius Decretalium,* tom. 3, pars 1, n. 165.

38 This basis is the official value of gold considered as money, and not merely as a purchasable commodity, as proposed in *AER,* CI (1939), 559.

For these reasons Father Adam Ellis, S.J., who was at that time Professor of Canon Law in the Pontifical Gregorian University in Rome, and Consultor of the S. Congregation of Religious, published in 1938, after a long and careful study of the value of various currencies on the international market, a list of the equivalents of thirty thousand lire or francs in the money of sixty-three different countries. The results of his research fix this sum at *ten thousand dollars* for the United States and Canada.[39] This amount would be the approximate equivalent today of six thousand dollars according to the official standard of 1918.[40]

To avoid confusion no change will be made in the course of this dissertation in regard to the sums which have been set up as fixing the limits of competence for various Superiors. But whenever these sums are mentioned, they should always be understood as susceptible of the proportionate increase which comes from the changed value of the dollar. Thus, quinquennial and other faculties for certain fixed amounts, whether the faculties are stated in dollars or in *libellae,* will be subject to the same principle of interpretation on the basis of the gold unit of exchange, and will admit of proportionate increase.

It may easily happen, especially if alienation takes place through public auction, that the price offered for goods is in excess of the price fixed previously by the appraisers. In this case the price which determines the limits of competence of respective ecclesiastical Superiors is the sum fixed by the appraisers.[41] Thus, for example, if competent appraisal has set the value of a piece of property at six thousand dollars and the ecclesiastical organization is offered eight thousand dollars, the transaction may be completed without recourse to the Holy See.

39 Ellis, "Triginta Millia Libellarum seu Francorum"—*Periodica,* XXVII (1938), 348-349.

40 In view of the fact that Father Ellis drew up and published his list at a time when, as one of its Consultors, he was thoroughly conversant with the procedure and attitude of the S. Congregation of Religious on financial matters, and since he proposes his list as *pro praxi tutum* (the italics are his), his conclusions would seem to deserve very weighty consideration. They seem to constitute a safe norm which can be followed in practise, at least until the question is definitively settled by an authentic declaration of the Holy See.

41 PCI, 24 nov. 1920—*AAS,* XII (1920), 577.

F) *The coalescence of contracts*

Distinct contracts of alienation made on different occasions for sums within the law, but which surpass in the aggregate the limit allowed by the law, will not be subjected to the regulations of this canon unless they verify the rules of moral theology on coalescence. To be affected by the law, these contracts would have to be bound together by some sort of unity.[42]

A Superior, for example, who wishes to sell land worth twenty thousand dollars and who proceeds to dispose of it in four plots valued at five thousands dollars each, certainly violates the prescriptions of this canon. If, however, he alienates one section and then, later on, on different occasions disposes of the three others without there ever having been unity of intention to alienate the entire estate, his transactions would be perfectly legitimate and in complete accord with the provisions of this canon.[43]

By requiring that those portions of divisible property which have already been alienated be specifically mentioned when asking authorization for further alienation, canon 1532, §4, forestalls in some measure the danger of fraud in this matter. The canon obliges also if there is alienation by the same contract of several distinct objects belonging to the same juridical person, provided the global value exceeds the competence of individual Superiors.[44]

42 "*Quaeres* utrum summa 30.000 francorum seu libellarum, pro cujus alienatione requiritur beneplacitum Apostolicum computanda sit attentis singulis contractibus, an simul additis pactionibus?

"*Resp.* Dummodo vere sint distinctae pactiones, et non agatur in fraudem legis, solus separatus valor singularum pactionum vel susceptarum obligationum considerari debet."—"Quaesita Varia, n. 18," *Periodica,* XI (1923), (158).

43 On the practise of splitting up property to bring it within the limits allowed by the old canon *Terrulas* or below the sum fixed by the law, Ferraris makes this comment: "Hoc enim esset aperte agere in fraudem legis et absque solemnitate alienare, quae ipsa sunt inalienabilia.... Et ideo esset totaliter illicita et invalida talis fraudulenta alienatio ratione malae fidei, tam alienantis quam emptoris fraudi scienter consentientis."—*Prompta Bibliotheca,* "Alienatio," art. IV, n. 19.

44 PCI, 20 iul. 1929, V—*AAS,* XXI (1929), 574.

Article 2. The Competence of Local Ordinaries

It is evident that all administrators of ecclesiastical property, as well as of all other property, must be allowed a certain degree of initiative to be used according to their own prudence and on their own responsiblity. Their freedom of action is to be curtailed only in more important cases which may have more direct repercussions on the common good. Consequently, §2, of canon 1532 empowers the local Ordinary to authorize alienations when the amount involved does not go beyond one thousand lire or francs, or about two hundred dollars.[45] A safeguard against arbitrary action is provided in the obligation of consulting the Council of Administration. Even this consultation can be omitted if the object in question is of very little value.

In all cases, however, consent should be asked from any and all parties whose best interests may in any way be compromised by the transaction. Such interested parties would be for instance, the pastor, the rector, the administrator, or the members of a collegiate juristic person if the property is vested in their name. The purpose of this prescription is to safeguard the ownership rights of those who are direct proprietors of the object in question.

Below two hundred dollars the local Ordinary has the power to authorize alienations, although under certain minor restrictions. Above six thousand dollars[46] he enjoys no faculties whatsoever in virtue of common law. Between these two extremes, he is the competent Superior for giving the requisite authorization, provided he employes the precautionary measures laid down for these transactions in §3 of canon 1532. The exercise of these powers is, first of all, dependent upon the *consent* of other bodies. The seriousness with which the Church regards even these minor alienations is evidenced by the fact that she requires the consent of three separate bodies before the authorization of the local Ordinary can become operative. The consent of these three bodies must be *cumulative,* not *disjunctive.* In other words, it is not sufficient to have the agreement of one or the other of these three bodies, but it is required that all three concur in giving their approval. These three bodies are the Board of Consultors (replacing the Cathedral Chapter), the Diocesan Council of Administration, and, before all others, the parties

[45] Cf. observations on this calculation, on page 112.

[46] Cf. pages 110-112.

interested. If any one of these three bodies declines to consent to the proposed alienation, the local Ordinary may not proceed further without acting invalidily.[47]

By the very nature of the case and particularly in view of the end of the law, the Ordinary has no authority to supply the consent which is not forthcoming from any one of these three bodies which must concur in approving the project of alienation. Since the threefold consent called for by this canon is a *conditio sine qua non* of valid procedure on the part of the local Ordinary, for the purpose of exercising prudent and reasonable control over church finances, the whole purpose of the legislation would be frustrated if the Ordinary could override the opposition of any unit whose consent is required. This is the import of the decision of the S. Congregation of the Council, on January 14, 1922.[48] In case the opposition of any particular body becomes unreasonable and evidently prejudices the best interests of the Church, the Ordinary is always free to refer the matter to the judgment of he Holy See.[49]

Like canon 1530, §1, 3°, and unlike canon 534, §1, which regulates alienation by religious, this canon does not require the *written* permission of the competent Superior for the alienation. Obtaining this permission in writing, however, particularly if there is question of a transaction of considerable importance, is always highly advisable for purposes of security in case of subsequent difficulties.

When the legitimate Superior for alienation is the Holy See, the Code does not require the previous consent of other bodies, as it does in §3 of canon 1532 when the authorization for the alienation must come from the local Ordinary. The absolute supremacy of the Holy See in all matters of ecclesiastical administration forbids the restricting of its powers by making their exercise dependent upon others. Nevertheless, nothing prevents the Holy See from requiring such consent as a necessary condition for the execution of the apostolic indult.

In conclusion it should be noted that the limitations thus established for the exercise of authority in alienations by different ecclesiastical Superiors will have the sanction of the civil law. This sanction is not based on the canonical character of the provisions, but rather on the principle that no board of administrators may validly exceed the limits

47 Canon 105, §1.

48 *AAS*, XIV (1922), 160.

49 *Periodica*, XI (1923), 11, and *Jus Pontificium*, II (1922), 56.

placed upon them by their charter of incorporation or by their particular statutes. This has been explicitly upheld by American courts:

> The first inquiry in any case . . . must be whether any proposed action is within the powers of the trustees under their particular statutes and corporate instruments applicable to it. Only if they are within the powers so outlined will they be able to escape personal liability. If they go outside them the result achieved as far as it concerns the corporation will be void as an unconstitutional statute passed by Congress or a state legislature. Where, therefore, the trustees are by by-laws limited in their expenditures, they cannot bind the church beyond the limit so imposed.[50]

Article 3. The Alienation of Divisible Property.

Canon 1532, §4, provides that no petition to alienate a part of divisible property will be valid unless the request specifies what parts of the property have already been alienated. The wisdom of this provision is evident. Since the competent Superior for alienation must have in view only the common welfare of the ecclesiastical body under his jurisdiction, he must be acquainted with the complete background of the case before passing judgment on the necessity or utility of a particular transaction. He must know what specific parts of divisible property have already been disposed of before he can be in a position to decide if it be advisable to deprive the Church of a further portion of these belongings. This last provision of canon 1532 presupposes compliance with all the rules laid down in the first three paragraphs of the present canon.[51]

50 Zollmann, *American Church Law,* §515, referring to Wyncoop and Watkins v. Bellvue Congregational Society, 10 Iowa, 185.

51 Coronata, *Institutiones Iuris Canonici,* n. 1071, c, proposes what seems to be an unjustifiable interpretation of this regulation when he says that it does not apply to an act of alienation in which "eiusdem rei pars, multis ante annis, ab alio forte administratore alienata legitime fuit." The text of §4 of canon 1532 offers no grounds for this liberal interpretation but is rather at variance with it. The case presented by Coronata would seem to be exactly the situation for which the canon wishes to provide.

CHAPTER VIII.

CONTRACTS RESEMBLING ALIENATION

Canon 1533

Solemnitates ad normam can. 1530-1532 requiruntur non solum in alienatione proprie dicta, sed etiam in quolibet contractu quo conditio Ecclesiae peior fieri possit.

Article 1. The Canon Affects Only Legally Recognized Contracts

A) *Preliminary observations*

Canons 1530-1532 treat of the requisites for alienation as understood in the strict sense, that is, as an act whereby ownership rights are completely relinquished: *actus quo dominium rei transfertur.*[1] In her solicitude to preserve intact the sacred patrimony of all the juristic persons subject to her jurisdiction, the Church has forbidden them unlimited and uncontrolled renunciation of their property.[2] This is a precautionary measure intended to safeguard the best interests of individual churches and the welfare of the Church at large.

Despite their severity and their wide field of application, these stringent measures are not sufficient to cover all possible contingencies. The Church can suffer harm not only from contracts which deprive her entirely of property rights, but also from contracts which, while not

[1] ". . . . requiruntur solemnitates jure praescriptae, quando fit vera ac proprie dicta alienatio, cum scilicet rei acquisitae dominium vel jus in re transfertur."—Pirhing, Lib. III, tit. 13, n. 41.

[2] What Van Espen says of beneficiaries in particular can be easily applied to all ecclesiastical Superiors in general: ". . . . potest quidem Beneficiarius rebus sui Beneficii uti, atque ex proventibus vivere; sed res ipsas integras conservare debet, et ad successores transmittere; ut et ipsi earum proventus libere et plene percipere queant: ut sicut ipsa Religio perpetua est, ita et ejus patrimonium jugiter servetur illaesum, uti loquitur Leo Imperator."—*Ius Ecclesiasticum Universum,* Pars II, Sect. IV, tit. V, cap. III, n. 27; III, 623.

suppressing her ownership completely and radically, nevertheless diminish or restrict the rights attendant upon ownership. Consequently, canon 1533 extends the limitations of the three preceding canons to cases which otherwise would not fall within the scope of their legislation. According to this present canon all the regulations provided for alienation in the strict sense of the term are to be transferred to those contracts whereby *conditio Ecclesiae peior fieri possit.* Such contracts, for example, would be those implied in the contracting of debts, mortgages, or annuity obligations, compromise or arbitration in financial matters, in the renunciation of active easements or in the allowing of passive easements, in the acting as security for others, and in other contracts of a similar nature. All these contracts will be governed by the prescriptions of canons 1530-1532, on condition that they verify the conditions which will be set down in the subsequent pages.

It should be carefully noted at the very outset of the discussion that the law embodied in canon 1533 does not deal merely with the general financial condition of the Church. It is concerned more especially with her *juridical* financial condition, that is to say, with her financial situation as it appears in the eyes of a court of law. The canon considers solely the legal and juridical aspects of the question. A situation in which the Church finds herself burdened with new financial liabilities is outside the field of this canon, when the new condition thus arising is based only on a moral obligation, without any danger of *legal* proceedings against a *specifically determined* portion of ecclesiastical property. Since this point is of cardinal importance for a right understanding of canon 1533, it merits special discussion, with a presentation of the proofs of the above assertions from both canonical and civil legal jurisprudence.

B) *Demonstration from the Principles and Sources of Canon Law*

This aspect of the problem is stressed very strongly by Larraona in his commentary on canon 534.[3] His definition of alienation insists repeatedly on the legal elements involved: alienation is an act with *juridical efficacy;* it affects the property of the Church *before the law;* it extends to acts which expose church goods to the danger of being lost or which jeopardize their security *in the eyes of the court.* Possible or even very probable financial profit cannot counter-balance the *juridical danger*

[3] *CpRM,* XIII (1932), 189.

involved in certain transactions. Then he concludes by insisting that the provisions of the law are not to be extended to cases not comprised in the letter of the law or in which the requirements of the law are not duly verified:

> Sensu *magis proprio,* de quo in Can. 534 et in Can. 1533, *obligatio* ab alienatione distinguenda est et ad illos actus, contractus, negotia restringenda videtur, quae cum imponant Ecclesiae in favorem alterius personae, *onus oeconomicum* ex quo ipsius Ecclesiae conditio peior redditur, tamen alienationem proprie dictam non continent. Obligationes huiusmodi *simplices, i.e.* absque alienatione, quoad plura alienationibus aequiparantur, et sensu lato *alienationes* dici possunt et non raro dicuntur, tamen nec sunt proprie dictae alienationes, nec nomine *alienationis veniunt,* non solum *in poenalibus,* sed nec in aliis ad quae aequiparatio ex lege non extenditur.[4]

This same conclusion is corroborated by an examination of the sources indicated for canon 1533:

1) The Instruction of the S. Congregation of the Propagation of the Faith to the Vicar Apostolic of Norway, on May 27, 1881, expressly forbids the alienation or mortgaging of goods belonging to the Mission.[5] Both these transactions would fall within the law: alienation, because it deprives an ecclesiastical body of ownership rights; mortgaging, because it is a contract which lessens the dominion of the Church over her property.

b) The Instruction of the same Congregation to the Patriarch of the Armenians refers evidently only to legally recognized contracts, since it requires that they be duly registered in the court offices according to the approved custom of the country.[6]

c) The decision of the S. Congregation of the Council, in *Faventina* (May 14, June 11, and September 3, 1825 and June 26, 1860),

4 *CpRM,* XIII (1932), 189.

5 *Collectanea S.C.P.F.*, n. 1553.

6 July 30, 1867—*Collectanea S.C.P.F.*, n. 1319, 5°.

speaks exclusively of formal contracts in the transaction under discussion: ". . . probandum esse *contractum* pro ecclesia ineundum."[7]

d) This point is stressed even more forcibly and explicitly by Gregory IX, who emphasizes the formal juridical character that is required to bring transactions within reach of the law. In the exposition of the case it is said that certain discontented prelates, with more zeal for their own welfare and convenience than for the Church entrusted to them,

> . . . ecclesias enormiter dilapidant et dilacerant dum novo alienationis et dilapidationis genere adinvento eas praesumant alienis debitis onerare: *sigilla sua seu literas sigillatas* de contrahendo mutuo quibusdam amicis suis clericis et laicis concedendo.

In his legislation against this abuse the same Pontiff declares:

> Firmiter inhibemus, ne quis praesumat *(de cetero)* ecclesiam sibi commissam pro alienis gravare debitis, aut *literas alicui seu sigilla concedere, quibus possent Ecclesiae obligari.*[8]

e) The all-important Constitution *Ambitiosae* of Pope Paul II prohibits "omnem rerum et bonorum ecclesiasticorum alienationem, *omneque pactum* per quod ipsorum dominium transfertur." Then he adds as examples of this formal agreement or *pactum,* "concessionem, hypothecam, locationem et conductionem ultra triennium, nec non infeudationem vel contractum emphyteuticum, praeterquam in casibus a iure permissis."[9]

Lastly, the Code would hardly include under its title *De Contractibus* transactions not arising from formal contract. This seems to be confirmed by the opening canon of *Titulus XXIX* which adopts for the ensuing canons the particular civil law on contracts in force in various countries.

[7] *Fontes,* nn. 3995, 3998, 4032; *Thesaurus Resolutionum,* LXXXV, 111-114, 121, 204, and XC, 189-192.

[8] C. 2, X, *de solutionibus,* III, 23.

[9] C. un. *de rebus ecclesiae non alienandis,* III, 4, in Extrav. Com.

The element of legal sanction is absolutely essential to bring any transaction within reach of the prescriptions of canon 1533. Merely private agreements which are not supported by the protection of the courts will always retain their moral binding force, but will not suffice to bring the regulation of canon 1533 into play. The canon applies only to contracts in the strict sense of the term.[10]

C) *Demonstration from the Principles of American Civil Law*

An examination of the sources of canon 1533 shows that this canon applies only to contracts in the strict sense of the term. This is implied in the very text of the law: "Sollemnitates . . . requiruntur . . . *in quolibet contractu, quo conditio Ecclesiae peior fieri possi.*" No non-contractual transactions of any kind will fall within the scope of this present canon. Since this canon restricts the free exercise of rights, that is, of the rights of ownership, it is to be interpreted *strictly* as is required by the text of canon 19.[11] Canon 1529, in turn, canonizes, so to speak, the civil law on contracts, provided it is not against divine law or at variance with positive prescriptions of Canon Law. Hence the strict meaning of *contract* in canon 1533 will be drawn from the provisions of American civil law.

As has already been mentioned in Chapter IV, American civil law regards the protection of the civil court as one of the essential constitutive elements of every contract: "A contract is a promise or a set of promises for the breach of which the law provides a remedy, or the performance of which the law in some way recognizes as a duty.[12] It is precisely this element of legal protection and security which differentiates a *contract* from an *agreement*. An agreement ". . . . is a manifestation

10 Larraona cites the absence of legal sanction as one of the two main reasons why the older authors and also modern writers allow "general mortgages": ". . . . quia tantum haec (hypotheca specialis) quae gravat determinata bona et *non a lege* imponitur sed a partibus constituitur, ex opinione recepta, in censu venit relate ad beneplacitum apostolicum." —"Commentarium Codicis," *CpRM*, XIII (1932), 188, note 623.

11 "Leges quae . . . . liberum iurium exercitium coarctant. . . . strictae subsunt interpretationi."

12 *Restatement*, §1.

of mutual assent by two or more persons to another."[13] The commentary which follows this definition declares: "Agreement has a wider meaning than contract, bargain or promise. The word contains no implication that legal consequences are or are not produced."[14] This bears out the definition of a contract as a promise or agreement involving the production of *legal consequences* as one of its essential elements.

The presence or absence of court sanction does not modify the objective mutual obligations of the agreeing parties. It leaves intact the question of moral obligation. At the same time, however, it furnishes an added extrinsic assurance that this moral obligation will produce all the desired effects. In the moral order all agreements of whatever kind engender obligation, in proportion to the gravity of the matter involved and the will of the consenting parties. In the juridical order, however, it is only in well-defined instances that the civil law will add the binding force of its own particular sanction to the obligation already existing and binding in the moral order. Before bringing the agreement into its field of competence the court requires that certain precise details and formalities be complied with. Some regulations must be observed or at least legal proof of the contract must be adduced, in order that the right of the law to intervene and assert its authority may be clearly established in individual instances.

When these prescriptions have been carried out, the civil law acknowledges the existence of a valid contract. When they are lacking, there are no grounds for invoking the protection of the court. Consequently, in view of the place of legal sanction, either coactive or punitive, in the essential structure of a contract in the eyes of American civil law, it may be said that no agreement has any founded claim for legal protection unless the prescribed juridical formalities, if any, have been complied with, and that when the element of juridical sanction is wanting, there is no valid contract before the civil law.

This introduction of the element of legal sanction into the essential structure of a contract has been little stressed by canonists and moral theologians; they have been satisfied generally with emphasizing only the element of mutual consent. Still, an examination of some of the

[13] *Restatement,* §3.

[14] *Restatement,* commentary on §3.

older authors shows that this concept of the essential nature of contracts was not unknown to canonists.[15]

From the place accorded it by the canonical authors just referred to, it is evident that the addition of the legal aspect of court protection into the nature of a contract is not at variance with divine law. Neither does it conflict with any positive prescription of Canon Law. On the contrary, it has been, on the testimony of the canonists just mentioned, incorporated into the body of the traditional doctrine of ecclesiastical jurisprudence. The same must be said of the particular legal formalities which the civil law of individual localities may require for the recognition of a valid legal instrument. These formalities generally extend only to the extrinsic determinations of the time, place and manner of signing the documents, etc. Consequently, the requirement of a legal sanction for the validity of a contract and the establishment of certain formalities to be complied with in order to obtain this legal protection are adopted by canon 1529. They thus become the basis for the canonical interpretation of the term *contract* in canon 1533.

15 "Conventiones omnes pariunt obligationem, ad quam urgendam quasdam jus civile designavit actiones, non pro omnibus tamen conventionibus; hac de re factum est, ut conventiones receptae *veluti sub tutela juris civilis* dicerentur contractus, reliquae venirent nomine pactorum. Unde *contractus* sunt conventiones, vel pacta, *actionis praesidio communita.*"—Sebastianelli, *Praelectiones Juris Canonici, De Rebus,* (Romae 1905), p. 341.

"Praeter hanc differentiam *generis* et *speciei* inter pactum et contractum etiam illud discrimen intercedit quod *contractus* specifice sumpti dicantur pacta (vel conventiones) *legum auctoritate ita ordinata et munita, ut etiam in foro externo civiles pariant obligationes atque actiones.* At *pactis* specifice sumptis adcensentur omnes aliae conventiones, quae in sua forma et obligatione *naturali* relinquuntur nec ex juris dispositione in foro externo adnexam habent civilem obligationem et actionem."—Wernz, *Ius Decretalium,* tom. III, pars 1, n. 228, II, note 2.

". . . . prius pactum (i.e. nudum) solo contrahentium consensu extrinsecus manifestato et naturali aequitati nititur naturalemque producit obligationem; sed nec proprium habet *nomen* in jure nec certam solemnitatem nec causam, ex qua oriatur obligatio et actio civilis; alterum vero ultra consensum naturalem obtinuit proprium nomen, in legibus vel certam verborum solemnitatem habet adjectam, vel causam, *qua nitatur obligatio et actio civilis, ad singularem legis assistentiam;* cui divisioni nostra aetate melius substituitur illa in pacta quae *etiam in foro externo obligationem naturalem et civilem producunt atque actionem et tutelam judicialem concedunt,* et in pacta quae in solo foro *conscientiae* pariunt obligationem naturalem, et per actionem civilem judicis ministerio non possunt exsecutioni mandari."—Wernz, *ibidem,* n. 6.

The whole of the preceding argumentation might be summed up as follows: canon 1533 applies only to contracts. Canon 19 requires that the prescriptions of this canon be understood in their strict sense, since they restrict the free exercise of rights. Canon 1529, in turn, accepts the civil law on contracts, with the reservations there specified. Therefore, the strict meaning of contract in this canon must be drawn from the provisions of American civil law. Now the *Restatement of the Law on Contracts* makes legal sanction an essential element of every valid contract. Consequently, without legal sanction, either urging the observance of the agreement or at least punishing its breach, there is no contract. This concept of a contract is not in conflict with the divine law nor with any particular provisions of Canon Law. The conclusion, then, must be that canon 1533 does not apply to any and all transactions which involve financial responsibility, but only to those contractual obligations which, while not being alienations in the strict sense of the term, nevertheless jeopardize the legal status of the Church before the civil law. This second element of "jeopardy before the civil law" must now be considered.

Article 2. Meaning of "Jeopardy Before the Civil Law"

The next step in the interpretation of this canon is to determine just what contracts will be affected by the provisions of the law. The extent of the law is comprised in the phrase: *in quolibet contractu quo conditio Ecclesiae peior fieri possit.* This general expression is not easy to elucidate. The vagueness of its signifiance can give rise to many misunderstandings, which widen unduly the field of application of this canon. For this reason it is of the utmost importance to study the context and background of this phrase in order to grasp its full force.

Except in compliance with all the prescriptions of canons 1530-1532, canon 1533 forbids all contracts which resemble alienation. As can be seen from an examination of the texts of the classical authors indicated later on, resemblance to alienation consists precisely in this, that the Church is thereby *exposed to the proximate danger of alienation in the strict sense.* The following text from Wernz sums up very concisely the traditional viewpoint of canonists on this matter:

> Porro alienationi adnumerantur alii actus, qui alienationem *praeparare* et inchoare censentur velut pignus (cfr. cp. I,X, de pign.

III, 21), hypotheca specialis (cfr. cp. 5, X de Reb. III, 13), aut transferunt dominium saltem utile v.g. infeudatio (cfr. cp. 2, X, de feud. III, 20), emphyteusis, locatio diuturna, i.e. ultra triennium frugiferum (cfr. cp. 2, 4, X de loc. et cond. III, 18) aut generatim in perpetuum vel ad longius tempus bona ecclesiastica gravibus *oneribus* subjiciunt v.g. per concessionem *servitutis* vel juris advocaticii. Cfr, cp. 2, X, de reb. Eccl. III, 9 in Sext.[16]

From the consideration that, without conformity with all the prescribed canonical formalities, certain contracts are unlawful because of their close resemblance to alienation,[17] there flows a consequence of great practical importance. A study of canon 1530 has shown that there is no question of alienation unless a particular transaction involves a church body's stable capital. Consequently, contracts which are forbidden because they lead to the proximate danger of alienation will be forbidden *only in the degree in which they expose the Church to the danger of depleting its fixed capital or patrimony.* In the light of the juridi-

16 *Ius Decretalium,* tom. III, pars 1, n. 154.

17 "Imo quia finis vetitae alienationis est, ut res Ecclesiae perpetuo integrae conserventur; ut ex earum proventibus Ministri vivere, aliaque ad cultum divinum necessaria semper haberi queant: consequens est, alienationis nomine hic comprehendi omnem illum actum, per quem *res ipsa quocumque modo Ecclesiae adimatur,* aut impeditur quominus Ecclesia hac re ulterius plene et libere uti, aut ejus emolumentum, aut proventum, percipere queat."—Van Espen, *Ius Ecclesiasticum Universum,* pars II, sect. IV, tit. V, cap. III, n. 22.

". . . . cum res talis specialiter hypothecata, *probabili periculo alienationis exponatur,* non tamen si in genere tantum bona ecclesiastica hypothecentur." —Pirhing, *SS. Canonum Doctrina,* Lib. III, tit. 13, 1.

". . . . late tamen sumitur (alienatio) pro contractu, in quo *partialis dominii translatio tantum fit,* scilicet utilis, vel perpetui, vel ad tempus. . . . itaut etiam simplicis dominii utilis alienatio sub hac prohibitione veniat."—Petra, *Commentaria in Constitutiones Apostolicas, In Const. V* Pauli II, tom. V, 205.

". . . . sed etiam comprehendit illos actus legitimos, quibus bona ecclesiastica retento dominio directo quoad dominium utile vel usumfructum transferuntur aut aliis juribus in illa concessis *periculo amissionis exponantur* aut ad longius tempus directae possessioni Ecclesiae subtrahuntur, aut generatim *pejoris conditionis fiunt.*" Wernz, *Ius Decretalium,* tom. III, pars 1, n. 154. Wernz would seem to have been among the first to use the terms which are now embodied in the Code: *quo conditio Ecclesiae pejor fieri possit.*

". . . . pro alienatione, quod tendit *ad pejorem reddendam Ecclesiae conditionem.*" Sebastianelli, *Praelectiones Juris Canonici, De Rebus,* p. 386.

cal aphorism that *accessorium sequitur principale,* the accessory restriction on contracts which resemble alienation will have the same field of influence as the principal restriction on strict alienation. This is the field of stable capital.

In fact, it is only this consideration of permanent assets which reveals the genuine *conditio* of any organization, whether ecclesiastical or otherwise. The very term *conditio* implies a permanent or solid status. This status is independent of the fluctuations attendant upon the constant rise and fall of current resources. Since such resources may vary considerably from one financial period to another, they cannot be a sure gauge of the economic security of any juristic person, whatever its particular nature. Consequently, contracts resembling alienation are forbidden only in so far as they expose the Church to the danger of diminishing its stable capital: *in qua diminutione consistit alienatio.*

For this reason the Church has always placed strict restrictions on every contract which conferred on another a direct right against ecclesiastical property. The classical authors refer to this right as a *ius in re,* or real right,[18] whereby the creditor can really claim an object *as his*

18 ". . . . prohibeturque creditoribus rem Ecclesiae specialis hypothecae titulo obligare: quia licet per pignoris constitutionem non mutetur causa dominii, tamen *jus in re* tribuitur, vi cujus creditor ad ejus distractionem procedere aliquando possit; neque res ipsa pignori aut hypothecae supposita amplius libera manet penes Ecclesiam, sed ob *jus in re* in alium translatum, *jam quodammodo aliena censetur.*"—Van Espen, *Ius Ecclesiasticum Universum,* pars II, sect. IV, tit. V, cap. III, n. 25.

"Non tamen prohibita est constitutio hypothecae generalis, ac proinde Praelatus *ad firmandum contractum legitime institutum, bona Ecclesiae obligare potest sub hypotheca generali,* etiam absque consensu superioris, vel alia solemnitate Canonica, ut colligitur ex cit. c. *Nulli.* . . . . Ratio disparitatis est, quia per hypothecam generalem *non ita facile deveniri potest ad alienationem* seu venditionem rei generaliter solum obligatae, seu oppignoratae, quam per hypothecam specialem, per quam plus juris in rem transfertur in creditorem, *cum periculo eam alienandi.* . . . . per illam (hypothecam specialem) magis praejudicatur, cum acquiratur jus in re; per generalem vero minus, quia acquiritur jus ad rem tantum."—Pirhing, Lib. III, tit. 13, n. 5.

"Hypotheca vero consistit fere in immobilibus, quae penes debitorem manent, jure tamen praetorio *creditori obligata obligatione reali.*"—Baumgartner, *Conclusiones ex V Libris Decretalium* (Romae 1759), Lib. III, tit. 21, concl. 1.

own.[19] As Van Espen says so pointedly in the citation given in the footnote: ". . . res ipsa . . . ob jus in re in alium translatum, *jam quodammodo aliena censetur.*" Because the holder of such a right can lay claim to the *object itself,* irrespective of any other ecclesiastical assets at his disposal, this very fact exposes the Church to the proximate and probable danger of seeing herself despoiled of the property thus obligated. Thus not a few authors make a *jus in re* the equivalent of *dominium.*[20]

Many conclusions of great practical value can thus be drawn from a study of the teaching of the old authors on the reason why general mortgages are permitted on ecclesiastical goods without canonical formalities while special mortgages fall under the restrictions of the law.[21]

19 "Aliud est *ius in re* quod actionem realem—aliud *ius ad rem* quod actionem tantum personalem tribuit. Ius in re etiam *dominium* vocatur."—Arregui, *Summarium Theologiae Moralis,* ed. 13, n. 277.

Still more clearly Cathrein: "Ius ad rem sibi obligatam et devinctam *non ipsam rem,* sed solum personam, a qua quis potest rem sibi postulare; *ius vero in re immediate sibi subjectam et obligatam habet ipsam rem, ita ut eam ubique sibi vindicare ut suam possit.*"—*Philosophia Moralis,* ed. 17, n. 313.

And Reiffenstuel: "Nam primo habet creditor (ex hypotheca speciali) jus in re, vi cujus actione hypothecaria prosequi potest pignus aut hypothecam, ubicunque tandem etiam apud tertium existat."—Lib. III, tit. 21, n. 66.

Actio hypothecaria is defined by Schmalzgrueber as ". . . . jus rem sibi oppignoratam a quovis possessore petendi, si solutionem debiti non possit consequi creditor."—Lib. III, tit. 21, n. 3.

20 Pirhing, Lib. III, tit. 13, n. 41; Arregui, *Summarium,* ed. 13, n. 277.

21 ". . . . (hypotheca generalis) . . . . quae directe et principaliter *non ordinatur ad alienandum* nec per eam transfertur jus aliquod in re, prout in hypotheca speciali. . . . quod ex ipsa (hypotheca generali) nullum jus in re concedatur Creditori super proprietate bonorum."—Petra, *Commentaria in Constitutiones Apostolicas,* In Const. VI Ben. XII; tom. IV, n. 29.

"Nam juxta communem non est prohibitum Praelatis etiam sine solemnitatibus, modo adsit justa causa, constituere hypothecam generalem in rebus Ecclesiasticis. Et ratio disparitatis est, quia per hypothecam generalem *non venitur ad alienationem rei determinatae* sicuti fit in hypotheca speciali."—Baumgartner, *Conclusiones ex V Libris Decretalium,* Lib. III, tit. 21, concl. 3.

". . . . cum per generalem hypothecam *non sit tam propinquum periculum rei ecclesiasticae vendendae,* quale est, si specialiter res aliqua certa obligetur."—Pirhing, Lib. III, tit. 21, §IV.

"Res universali hypotheca jam uni obligata, potest adhuc cuidam alteri

They go on the principle that there is no prohibition against conceding to another a *ius ad rem* over ecclesiastical property. Such a concession establishes no direct claim on a particular piece of property, nor even on any portion of it. It simply accepts as security for the debt the general sound financial situation of the ecclesiastical organization engaged in the transaction; it does not give the mortgagee a real right to a specified piece of church property.

A debt which has been contracted on the strength of such a mortgage, which corresponds to what is called "general credit," will be paid,

---

obligari universali, imo etiam speciali hypotheca; non item 2. res particulari hypotheca jam uni obligata, nisi eadem res utrique debito expungendo par sit, aut alteruter Creditor consentiat. Ratio primae partis (quam tenent Molina *de justit. Disp.* 532, Lopez, 1.10, tit. 13, pars 5 et alii) est: quia haec facultas (scilicet rem universali hypotheca uni jam obligatam alteri obligandi) humano commercio reputatur summopere utilis, immo necessaria; tum ut Creditores de solutione suorum debitorum magis securi maneant; tum etiam ut ex hac majori securitate ad dandum mutuum, vel alios contractus celebrandos, magis alliciantur. Ratio autem 2ae partis (quam tenent Lugo *disp. 20, sect. 6, n. 106,* Molina *disp. 328* et alii plures) est: quia si res particulari hypotheca jam uni obligata, sit insufficiens ad expungendum simul aliud debitum, et nihilominus alteri particulari hypotheca obligetur, necessario debet alteri fieri praejudicium; quia alteruter debebit subire jacturam debiti, sin minus in toto, saltem in parte: secus est si utrique debito sufficiat, vel si uterque, aut saltem alteruter consentiat: *scienti enim et consentienti non fit injuria, neque dolus,* ut habetur Reg. 27 Jur. in 6to."—Elbel, *Theologia Moralis Decalogalis* (Augustae Vindelicorum, 1743), VI, n. 722.

"Quare licet Praelatus contrahens debita, nomine Ecclesiae, bona ejusdem per generalem hypothecam obliget, nihil agit contra prohibitionem SS. Canonum de rebus Ecclesiae immobilibus non alienandis; nam in exsecutione seu reali apprehensione bonorum, ob moram in solvendo factam, prius distrahi debent bona mobila debitoris, ad solvenda debita; si autem mobilia non sufficiant ad ea solvenda, tum etiam immobilia bona, ob pignoris causam, vendere . . . . quia lex naturalis, quae obligat ad solvenda debita, praevalet juri positivo de non oppignorandis aut alienandis rebus Ecclesiae."—Pirhing, Lib. III, tit. 21, §1, n. 16.

"Est insuper circa distractionem pignorum notandum quod si creditori aliqua specialiter, et aliqua generaliter sint oppignorata, creditor prius specialiter obligata vendere debeat (si vendere pignora vult) et illis non sufficientibus generaliter obligata demum vendere possit, *1. Quae specialiter, 9 c. de Distract. pignor.* ibi: 'Quae specialiter vobis obligata sunt, debitoribus detrectantibus solutionem, bona fide debetis ei solemniter vendere etc. Quod si quid deerit, non prohibemini caetera etiam bona jure conventionis consequi.' "—Reiffenstuel, Lib. III, tit. 21, n. 75.

interest and amortization, out of current assets. Only in case these are insufficient will there be any question of seizure of immovable property, as Pirhing remarks so appositely in the note just cited. Consequently, there is no objection to contracting several debts on the strength of the same general mortgage provided this be done within the bounds of prudent business administration. In this connection both Reiffenstuel[22] and Schmalzgrueber[23] remark that a general mortgage is always to be understood as not extending to those goods which the mortgagor has not the right to alienate, i.e. the stable capital or precious property of an ecclesiastical juridical person.[24]

These observations show why one author goes so far as to say that "haec facultas (rem scilicet universali hypotheca uni jam obligatam alteri obligandi) *humano commercio reputatur summopere utilis immo et necessaria;* tum ut Creditores de solutione suorum debitorum magis securi maneant; tum etiam ut ex hac majori securitate ad dandum mutuum, vel alios contractus celebrandos magis alliciantur."

In this background of traditional classical opinion, it is now possible to see more clearly the genuine meaning of the phrase: *in quolibet contractu quo conditio Ecclesiae perior fieri possit.* This expression cannot be taken as applying to any and all new financial burdens assumed by ecclesiastical organizations. Were this the case, every financial transaction involving indebtedness would fall under the regulations of canon 1533, because all these operations make the general condition *peior* from a financial viewpoint by subjecting it to new obligations. They do not, however, except in very well-defined circumstances, jeopardize the general condition of the Church from the *juridical* angle, nor do they touch upon the field of stable capital, as the background of the canon requires. This conclusion is borne out by the consistent opinion of competent canonists, old and modern. Since canon 1533 embodies in one phrase the general principles enunciated under various forms by the jurists of the past, their stand on the matter is a safe indication of the meaning of this present canon.

22 Lib. III, tit. 21, n. 12.

23 Lib. III, tit. 21, n. 17.

24 In accordance with this principle a division bench of the High Court of Travancore (India) has recently "decreed that a site occupied by a Catholic church, rectory, and cemetery cannot be sold in satisfaction of a debt. The two Hindu judges, Justices Madhaven Pillay and Sankarasubha Iyer quoted profusely from Canon Law in their decision."—*The Jurist,* I (1941), 78.

This observation is well brought out by comparing the text of the actual legislation of canon 1533 with the teaching of no less celebrated an author than Fagnanus. After enumerating the various acts which actually deprive the Church of direct dominion over her property, and pointing out how they are forbidden by the law, he continues:

> . . . et generaliter *omne pactum, per quod bonorum dominium transfertur*. . . . Et dominium intelligas tam directum quam utile.[25]

The phrase of Fagnanus: ". . . et generaliter omne pactum per quod bonorum dominium transfertur" expresses what the Code has summed up in ". . . in quolibet contractu quo conditio Ecclesiae peior fieri possit." Interpreting this clause of the Code in the light of the preceding legislation, as commanded by canon 6, 2°, one may regard the conclusion as warranted that canon 1533 does not apply to every financial operation implying a new financial burden for the Church, but *only to legally recognized contracts which jeopardize the legal status of the Church by exposing it to the proximate danger of losing dominion over any portion of its stable capital.*[26]

The substance of the preceding lengthy argumentation can be summed up in the following recapitulation: Since canons 1530-1532 affect only the field of alienation strictly so-called, they apply only to transactions implying a diminution of stable capital. Since canon 1533 aims to forestall the danger of what is forbidden in canons 1530-1532, the conclusion must be that canon 1533 intends to legislate only for the danger of subtractions from the stable capital of an ecclesiastical corporation. Since not all financial transactions involve this danger, not all of them will fall under the limitations of the canon. Now the only contracts which involve this danger of depleting the patrimony of a church body are those which confer on a third party some direct or immediate right to a determined portion of ecclesiastical property. These contracts are known as those which give another a *ius in re* against property *which is actually in the hands of the Church.* Consequently, there is no limitation, beyond that required by administrative prudence, governing those contracts which give another only a *ius ad rem,* that is, a right to claim

25 *Comment. in III Librum Decretalium,* cap. V, p. 225.

26 Dom Bastien (Directoire Canonique, n. 352) states very explicitly that canonical regulations affect only those debts and other obligations *which burden the patrimony of the Institute.*

settlement against the juristic person *(actio personalis)*, with no accompanying right to seize its property *(actio realis)*.

Article 3. Application of This Conclusion to the United States

A) *In general*

It would not be exaggerated to say that very many ecclesiastical financial operations in the United States are carried on outside the field of contractual obligations. There are, of course, certain financial transactions which are executed on the plane of formal and legally recognized contracts. Such instances will undoubtedly be subject to all the restrictions laid down by canons 1530-1533, provided that the other requisite conditions are verified. In addition to such formal contracts, however, there are many other financial operations which are not executed on the basis of strict juridical procedure. Such transactions are mere *agreements*, in the sense of §3 of the *Restatement of the Law on Contracts*.

It may also be said that a large percentage of church financial transactions in this country do not even remotely contact the field of stable capital. When money is borrowed, or other transactions are undertaken, the intention is almost always to meet the interest and pay off the regular amortization through current assets, that is, through collections, or through revenues accruing from social events of various kinds. Such means will either bring in the money as it is needed, or may sometimes permit the administrators to lay up a reserve fund (which is not necessarily fixed capital) against the danger of bad times. The case would be different if a parish already completely established and equipped, were to draw on its endowment fund or stable assets to meet expenses. This would fall squarely within all the regulations laid down in canons 1530-1533. In the ordinary situation, however, there is never any question of drawing on the stable capital of the Church. In fact, and in most cases, there is no stable capital to draw on, outside of what is gradually being acquired by repaying the debt already contracted or by paying off the mortgage on the buildings being constructed. There will be no stable capital until the debts or mortgages have been completely cleared and the property passes permanently and unconditionally into the patrimony of the Church. Since experience has shown that, barring unforeseen complications, Church organizations are always equal to their financial burdens, these transactions are carried out often without contracts and without any security beyond the equivalent of a general mortgage, understood in the sense given the term by the older authors.

This special and happy state of affairs arises from the fact that, as was mentioned in connection with canon 1529,[27] on the status of church corporations in the United States, the absolute separation of the spiritual and material aspects which characterizes the letter of the law on these corporate bodies is not carried out in practise. Businessmen in general are influenced very noticeably by the religious background of church bodies. Catholic organizations in the United States enjoy unique respect and almost unlimited confidence in the financial world. For this reason they experience little or no difficulty in negotiating necessary financial transactions with an absolute minimum of legal formality.

The integrity of the American Catholic clergy in its business deals, coupled with the proverbial unstinting generosity of the Catholic laity of the United States, affords a security which at least equals in value and trustworthiness the financial guarantees which might be exacted. Needless to say, bankers and others require some sort of assurance and security in their business dealings with ecclesiastical organizations. This is most generally afforded by the church body's general credit rating as a reliable business organization. The older authors called this kind of security a *general mortgage*. All of them place this sort of transaction outside the reach of the laws on alienation and on contracts which jeopordize the condition of the Church, as has been abundantly demonstrated in the preceding pages. Thus in their dealings with the Church and her various units of organization, financiers, at least not infrequently, readily waive many of the complex legal technicalities which would mark such negotiations in the world of strict business. The Church in this country is thus privileged to obtain money in various ways, many of which do not fall within the field of canonical restrictions on alienation and on those contracts which resemble it. Even if alienation be understood in the widest sense, as enunciated in canon 1533, many of these transactions, while implying new moral and financial obligations, do not burden the Church with new legal responsibilities. They do not hold over her the ominous threat of legal prosecution or vexing judicial procedure in regard to a determined portion of ecclesiastical property, which conditions must be verified in order to jeopardize the permanent possession and use of her stable capital or patrimony.

[27] Cf. *supra*, pages 55-60.

From all these observations it is evident that canonical limitations apply to only a very limited field of financial operations. This is the field of formal and legally recognized contracts, involving juridical responsibilities before the civil law and touching upon the ownership or use of permanent assets. An erroneous impression has unduly widened the application of canon 1533 by invoking it for all financial transactions of whatever kind, contractual or non-contractual, in which an outlay of money or property is involved. Canon 19, calling for the strict interpretation of any law which restricts the free exercise of rights, has been forgotten. This wrong viewpoint has multiplied unnecessarily the necessity of having recourse to higher Superiors. The result has been that these regulations have been applied to many ordinary acts of administration, whereas the Code aims in this matter to legislate only for extraordinary administration.[28]

Particular provisions in the constitutions or charters of individual organizations may exact such recourse as well as impose other formalities over and above the requirements of the Code.[29]

The purpose of the preceding pages has been to discuss only the strict interpretation of the Code on this matter, starting with the juridical principle that *odiosa in iure sunt restringenda.* The conclusions to which the application of fundamental principles has led do not in any way relax the reins of prudence and honesty in business transactions. On the contrary, the confidence which the Church enjoys in its ability to carry on financial transactions without obligating itself legally before the civil courts should be an incentive to church administrators to be more than circumspect in their financial operations, lest they give the impression of wishing to abuse the unusual confidence which the integrity and prudence of their forebears have acquired.

B) *Application to Certain Particular Transactions in the United States*[30]

a) *Furnishing collateral for loans:* It often happens that an ecclesiastical organization in need of ready cash, for a project of construction

28 "Il est à remarquer que le Code ne s'occupe que de l'administration extraordinaire."—Bastien, *Directoire Canonique,* n. 334, note. 2.

29 Canon 1530, §2.

30 Not all possible transactions will be treated here. Some will find their proper place in connexion with the treatment of canon 1538, on *Mortgages and Debts.*

or for necessary repairs, at a time when receipts are normally suspended, will negotiate a short-term loan, without formal contract, merely on the basis of a general credit obligation. This method is preferable to drawing from the fixed assets to meet a need which is only temporary, especially since the loan can be repaid within a short time, as, for example, when receipts are forthcoming at the beginning of the school year, or at the time of the next special collection, etc. Meanwhile, the organization deposits in the bank an amount in bearer bonds equivalent to the total of the loan with an additional percentage for margin. These securities continue in the interim to bear interest for the church organization which owns them, while at the same time they furnish security for the loan. When the loan is completely repaid, these securities are withdrawn from the bank and deposited as before to the credit of the ecclesiastical juristic person which is their proprietor.

This particular means of furnishing collateral for loans does not appear to be comprised under any form of canonical restrictions on financial operations. Since it does not deprive the Church of any of her stable capital, it is automatically excluded from alienation strictly so called. Because it does not jeopardize the condition of the Church before the civil law, but rather improves this condition by enabling her to increase her property and to make it more useful, it is not included among the contracts which are regulated by canon 1533.[31] The very nature of the circumstances, however, renders it most difficult to formulate a general principle applicable to all cases. In order to arrive at a sound decision careful consideration must be given to every individual case.

b) *Consolidated borrowing:* In the financial operation known as "consolidated borrowing" one person, the bishop, for example, borrows a large sum of money from a banking concern. He, in turn, reloans portions of this sum to individual parishes at a slightly higher rate of interest to cover incidental overhead expenses and, perhaps, to realize a small profit for the diocese. The parishes are thus enabled to profit by their participation in the advantages accruing from a large-scale financial operation, and are saved from the higher interest rates which would be required for their own individual and necessarily smaller loans.

There are two distinct aspects to be considered in this transaction.

31 Bastien (*Directoire Canonique* n. 355) offers this same solution for a case which is practically identical.

It seems safe to say that the transaction between the bishop and the individual parishes will not fall within the law of the Code unless the bishop exacts a mortgage on the parish property or requires some other equivalent security affecting its stable capital. Unless this is so, it will be only a case of borrowing money without contractual obligations, even though a slight rate of interest be paid. This is a transaction which all authors generally hold to be outside the law.[32]

Although it may not be forbidden by the law of the Code, this procedure would, nevertheless, seem to be prohibited by number 274 of the decrees of the Third Plenary Council of Baltimore, which strictly enjoins all ecclesiastical persons without exception from organizing or directing banks. Since this special provision of the Third Baltimore Council is *praeter Codicem,* it still retains its binding force and particularizes an obligation which the Code does not specify.

Another question might be raised as to the inclusion of this transaction under the *negotiatio* which is forbidden by canon 142. Even though it be done with the laudable intention of bettering the general financial condition of the diocese, the exacting of even a small rate of interest beyond what is reasonably necessary to meet overhead expenses will certainly be outlawed by canon 142. It will also run afoul of the above-mentioned decree 274 of the Third Plenary Council of Baltimore as well as of the decree of the S. Consistorial Congregation which explicitly forbids all those in sacred orders from occupying any position of authority in connection with banks, even though they may have been organized for the promotion of charitable or social aims. No exception is made for the running of banks which will bring financial profit to the diocese.[33]

[32] Cf. *supra,* page 78.

[33] "Quapropter SSmus Dominus Noster Pius PP. X, dum hortatur quidem praecipitque ut clerus in hisce institutis condendis, tuendis augendisque operam et consilium impendat, praesenti decreto prohibet omnino ne sacri ordinis viri, sive saeculares sive regulares, munia illa exercenda suscipiant retineantve suscepta, quae administrationis curas, obligationes, in se recepta pericula secumferant, qualia sunt officia praesidis, moderatoris, a secretis, arcarii, horumque similium. Statuit itaque ac decernit SSmus Dominus Noster, ut clerici omnes quicumque in praesens in his muneribus versantur, infra quatuor menses ab hoc edito decreto, nuntium illis mittant, utque in posterum nemo e clero quodvis id genus munus suscipere atque exercere queat, nisi ante ab Apostolica Sede peculiarem ad id licentiam sit consequutus."—S.C. Cons., 18 nov. 1910; *AAS,* II (1910), 910.

The second aspect of the problem concerns the bishop and the banking company. The relation of this phase of the question to the canonical regulations on the contracting of debts will be determined by the specific character of the bishop's arrangements with the banking firm. If he must mortgage diocesan property or furnish collateral drawn from the fixed assets of the diocese or the individual parishes, the financial operation will undoubtedly be subject to all the regulations provided by the law. If, on the contrary, the sound financial condition of the diocese enables the bishop to borrow on his unsecured note, the restrictions of legally recognized contracts which juridically jeopardize a portion of ecclesiastical patrimony will not apply.[34]

Closely allied with this point is the practise of loans by one parish to another. Judgment on this usage will be formed in the light of the previous explanation of the nature of stable capital. The law of the Code does not affect loans from surplus funds, not yet incorporated into the fixed capital of the organization concerned. The case will be evidently different if the patrimony of one parish is depleted, even temporarily, in order to assist another. The second alternative will be governed by canons 1532 and 1538; the first will follow whatever special provisions may have been established by particular local statutes.

c) *Refinancing:* It sometimes happens, particularly in times of financial stress, that a church organization finds itself incapable of meeting financial obligations (e.g. of interest or amortization) which it formerly assumed with the moral certainty of being able to meet them in due time. In these cases, either because there is little or no utility in taking over church property, or because of the certainty of ultimate, though belated, payment, banks and other financial companies usually agree to "refinancing."

The details of refinancing are a matter of negotiation between creditor and debtor, in order to reach agreements which will be mutually satisfactory. These agreements may involve lowering the rate of interest, extending the maturity by reducing the amortization payments with or without change in the interest rates ,etc. Any measures which are within the provisions of civil law and which are mutually satisfactory to the interested parties can be accepted.

34 Cf. commentary on canon 1530.

In judging of the relationship between this procedure and the provisions of the Code, much will depend on the nature of the specific agreements reached in individual cases. But, since according to the general principles already explained in the preceding pages, the situation of the ecclesiastical organization is not thereby imperilled before the civil courts, it seems safe to say that the process of refinancing does not fall within the scope of canon 1533. In fact, the usual reason for refinancing is, on the contrary, to assist the Church and to afford an opportunity to avoid total loss of its property through foreclosure in case of default.

d) *Compromise on financial disputes or rights:* In general a compromise is an agreement whereby both parties to a dispute concede something to the other for the sake of harmony. In the strict sense, Vermeersch-Creusen define it as "an onerous bilateral contract for the purpose of preventing or ending a lawsuit."[35] When this mutual concession is concerned with financial matters or with rights, which are considered among the immovable assets of an organization, it falls strictly within the legislation on alienation, if the sums involved are connected with the stable capital of the juristic person or persons engaged in the compromise.[36] Such cession necessarily implies a renunciation and consequent diminution of the ecclesiastical patrimony of a church body. The total of the amount involved will determine what Superior is competent to authorize the compromise, according to the norms set down in canon 1532.[37]

Because of its great similarity with compromise, *arbitration,* or an agreement whereby the decision on a controverted issue is left to the judgment of one or several persons, will be governed by the same prin-

35 *Epitome,* III, 255.

36 For this reason, Vermeersch-Creusen, *(Epitome, loc. cit.)* explicitly require for compromise: ". . . tum subjectum contrahendi et alienandi capax, tum res dubia et arbitrio alienantis permissa."

37 §418 of the *Restatement* recognizes the right to compromise by drawing up a new contract: "A subsequent contract may itself be accepted as immediate satisfaction and discharge of a pre-existing contractual duty, or duty to make compensation; and if so accepted the pre-existing duty is discharged and is not revived by the debtor's breach of the subsequent contract."

ciples as compromise, if it is a question of financial matters or rights.[38]

e) *Surety for others:* Surety, or guarantee, is a contract to pay some debt or to fulfill some obligation in the event of non-payment or non-fufilment on the part of another person who is obligated to do so. This contract is realized when one party endorses a note for another, furnishes bail fo someone detained in arrest, guarantees the security of an investment, etc.

The juridical danger of contracts of surety or guarantee lies in the fact that the surety becomes liable before the law for the payment of the debt, even without the debtor's default.[39] Independently of all circumstances, the creditor can force the surety to settlement according to the terms of the guarantee. If there are several co-sureties, only one of whom is able to meet the obligation, he will be responsible for the entire guarantee, unless explicit contrary provisions were agreed upon in the drawing up of the contract. The surety satisfying the obligation has, of course, justifiable claims to redress against his co-sureties or against the defaulting debtor. This, however, does not influence the objective fact that furnishing guarantee for another entails legal and financial risks which careful administrators will more prudently avoid except in unusual circumstances.

Contracts of surety, guarantee, or of indemnity, have nothing in common with the grant of authorization to proceed in a financial transaction. This authorization is only an official judgment on the advisability of acting, but does not make the Superior so acting responsible for the success of the transaction which he allows to be carried on.

Considered in their canonical aspects, contracts of surety are equivalent to alienation if the surety furnished comes from the church body's stable capital. Besides, it will be necessary that the surety contract be drawn up in due legal form, with the possibility of juridical risk for the ecclesiastical organization thus obligating itself. As in the question of

[38] The difference between these two acts is that in compromise *(transactio)* the parties themselves come to an agreement, whereas in arbitration *(compromissum)* the decision is left in the hand of another or others. — As for the viewpoint of civil law on this matter, §550 of the *Restatement* declares that arbitration is not illegal, but that it will not be specifically enforced nor will it allow for any more than nominal damages. The award made by the arbitrator is binding.

[39] If he becomes responsible for the debt only in case of the debtor's default, he is *guarantor* rather than surety.

compromise, the competent Superior will be determined by the amount of money involved in the contract. Although the resemblance to alienation would not be verified if the guarantee furnished came from the current assets of a church corporation, this type of transaction has little to recommend it in view of the great risk of inflicting harm on the Church in case the surety has to be actually paid according to the contract.

f) *Renunciation of active, or allowing of passive easements:* Easement is the modern juridical term for the *servitus* of the classical jurists. It consists, actively, in the acquisition of a limited right of use over land belonging to another. It implies a share in the convenience of another's property with no participation in actual ownership of the land itself, nor in the profits accruing therefrom. It might be called an *extrinsic* right over another's goods. Between an easement and a *license* to use the land of another, there is this difference that an easement does not arise from the explicit consent and authorization of the owner, but is founded implicitly and in the sanction of the law arising from long-standing and undisputed use or from other circumstances. The mere fact of use unobstructed by the owner is not sufficient to establish the basis of an easement.[40] The use must be such as to imply an act of dominion on the part of the user: e.g. if he were to use a certain path through another's land and protect that path by building a fence along it. In addition, in order to establish a strictly personal easement, the use must be exclusive. If it is exercised conjointly with others, the easement thus acquired against the property will be in favor of the public at large.

The acquisition of easements by lapse of time is known as *prescription*. It gives rise to a presumption of title which is so conclusive as to be a matter of law. The period of time required for the acquisition of a right through prescription depends on the matter involved and on the legislation of the various states. The provisions of canon 1511 will determine the time-limits if the prescription takes place between two ecclesiastical juridical persons. A civil regulation derogating from this canon will have no binding force in the forum of conscience, but will have to be followed in the external forum before the court.

40 An easement may be either personal or appurtenant to dominant land. In the latter case anyone owning the dominant land may claim the servitude in the other servient land. The law implies an easement where an owner sells to another a piece of land which has no exit to a road except over the land of the seller.

Easements are extinguished by an express grant of the owner of the "dominant tenement" to the owner of the "servient tenement"; they cease also by the merger of both tenements under one owner. Justification for the lawful acquisition of active easements, which are really diminutions of another's rights of ownership, is based on the presumption that the proprietor who does not prevent the factual use of his property at the proper time is not adverse to the constitution of an actual right in those who use it. Thus the *passive* easement which is a lessening of his property rights is a kind of juridical sanction against him for his neglect or carelessness. The most common kinds of easements are those resulting in the acquisition of a right of way through another's property, the right to a flow of water from that or other property, etc. American law, unlike English law, does not recognize easements consisting in rights to air or light through another's property. Since debts can also be prescribed within a certain period, care must be taken to collect all debts owed to an ecclesiastical organization. Such debts can be subject to prescription within a comparatively short time.

By renouncing an easement which it has legitimately acquired against another organization, the Church would be abdicating a legally obtained right. Since rights and privileges are considered part of a church body's stable capital, being assimilated to immovable property, such renunciation is tantamount to a diminution of patrimony. It thus falls within the scope of the rules on alienation.

The same principle applies, *mutatis mutandis,* to passive easements, that is to allowing another to acquire a right of use, passage, etc., against ecclesiastical property.

In themselves, easements can rarely, if ever, be evaluated in terms of money, since they usually consist merely in the use of another's property. The only norm for calculating the value of these servitudes for active easements is to determine the financial outlay required to provide for the substitution of these rights in other ways: e.g., the cost of providing a new road or path for one which has been acquired by easement. As for passive easements, the same principle can be applied, to compute the value of the rights thus permitted the other organization or individual. These calculations will constitute a working-basis for determining the competence of various ecclesiastical Superiors in authorizing the renunciation or the allowing of the easement.

CHAPTER IX.

REMEDIES AGAINST IRREGULAR ALIENATION

Canon 1534

§1. Ecclesiae competit actio personalis contra eum qui sine debitis solemnitatibus bona ecclesiastica alienaverit et contra eius haeredes; realis vero, si alienatio nulla fuerit, contra quemlibet possessorem, salvo iure emptoris contra male alienantem.

§2. Contra invalidam rerum ecclesiasticarum alienationem agere possunt, qui rem alienavit, eius superior, utriusque successor in officio, tandem quilibet clericus illi ecclesiae adscriptus, quae damnum passa sit.

Article 1. Remedies for Illicit Alienation

From the very beginning of laws against alienation of church property provisions have been made to cope with the problem of irregular disposal of ecclesiastical goods.[1] A perusal of the sources cited for canon 1534 shows that the Code embodies the traditional general legislation of the Church on the matter of irregular alienation. As can be seen by a comparision of canon 2347 with the laws in force prior to the Code, the legislation of this latter modifies rather substantially the rigorous

[1] Thus, for example, in his Constitution, *Iniunctum nobis* (14 July, 1555), Pope Paul IV reaffirms his intention of safeguarding church property by enforcing the provisions already made in this matter by Pope Symmachus: ". . . Apostolicae servitutis officium mentem nostram continua pulsat instantia, ut bona Ecclesiastica . . . ad ius et proprietatem eorum, quorum antea erant omnino reducantur .. . licet alias fel. rec. Symmachus Papa Praedecessor Noster praedium Ecclesiae . . . quovis modo alienari . . . prohibuerit, et lege huiusmodi omnes Custodes astringi, ac donatorem, ac censuratorem, et venditorem honorem perdere, et qui praemissis subscriberet, anathema esse, cum eo qui daret, sive reciperet, nisi restituerentur . . . voluerit."—*Fontes,* n. 88.

penalties formerly incurred by offenders against the law.[2]

For a complete understanding of canon 1534 it is necessary to establish a distinction between invalid and illicit alienation. Different procedure is called for in both cases. Invalid alienation produces no effect whatsoever; it cannot effect a real transfer of ownership; after the complete transaction the object of the contract remains in the eyes of the law exactly as it was before. An illicit alienation, on the contrary, is not voided of its natural effect. Consequently, the object in question really becomes the property of the other party. There can be no redress against *what* was done, although steps may be taken to remedy the irregularity arising from the *manner* in which the transaction was carried out.

In determining whether a particular act of alienation is invalid or only illicit, it should be remembered that, for the older authors, the absence of any one of the required formalities nullified the attempted transaction. According to canon 1530, §1, 3°, the permission of the legitimate Superior is the only requisite now necessary under pain of invalidity. Likewise, authors before the Code restricted the penalty of invalidity only to those contracts which resulted in harm to the Church. The Code makes no distinction. Whether a transaction is to the benefit of the Church or to her detriment, it is invalid if the necessary authorization is lacking. The Holy See, however, will much more readily sanate such transactions, if it is shown that the Church did not thereby suffer any harm, provided also that no injustice or other harm was inflicted on third parties.[3] Since there is question here of a provision most favorable to

[2] Canon 2347 does not inflict censures on all irregular alienations but only on those which have been entered into without proper authorization from the competent ecclesiastical Superior. It deals *only* with alienation *strictly so called,* since it is explicitly the penal sanction attached to canon 1532. The severity of the censure incurred varies according as the authorization deliberately omitted should have come from the local Ordinary or from the Holy See. Given the very general terms of canon 2347, it applies to all those who have in any way whatsoever cooperated or had a part in the transaction: *omnes quovis modo reos sive dando, sive recipiendo, sive consensum praebendo.*

[3] S.C. Conc. Piscien. *Emphyteusis,* 2 iun. 1736 — *Thesaurus Resolutionem, VIII* (1736), 243.

". . . censuit (Apostolica Sedes) . . . absolvendum esse . . . a censuris, remissis caeteris poenis, et quatenus compererit contractus fuisse, et esse utiles Ecclesiae, illos confirmandos esse, sin minus revocandos."—S.C.Ep. et Reg. 11 ian. 1692, *Troprein.*—Giraldi, Expositio *Juris Pontificii,* I, 288.

the Church, the term alienation, for invalidity, is to be understood in the widest possible sense, as comprising all transactions covered by canons 1530-1533.

An illicit act of alienation, as was remarked before, does not impede the transfer of ownership. Consequently, the former owner, even though an ecclesiastical juridical person, no longer has any valid claim over the object alienated. It has become the property of another. This fact precludes the possibility of the first proprietor's pursuing the object as his own. His only remedy against the harm suffered in the transaction is recourse against the person, physical or juristic, who was responsible for the act. This recourse can oblige the alienator to compensate the Church for the damages ensuing from the illicit contract, and thus to reestablish her in the favorable condition which she enjoyed before the alienation.

The canon provides for the permanence of this right in the Church by extending the possibility of instituting personal action at law against the heirs of the person responsible for the illicit alienation. Since they enjoy the fruits of an unlawful transaction, they have an obligation to see that the Church is fittingly reimbursed for the loss from which they are benefiting. This moral continuity of illicit alienation in the permanence of its effects explains Schmalzgrueber's observation that proceedings can be instituted against the heirs because by a fiction of law they are regarded as being one person with the deceased.[4] This remedy is so closely bound up with the person of the illicit alienator that it cannot be pressed against the owner of the object itself. He has merely used his natural right of acquisition, and ownership has been actually transferred to him even though illicitly.

ARTICLE 2. REMEDIES AGAINST INVALID ALIENATION

The case is different for invalid alienation. Here the Church is still the legitimate proprietor of the object which has been alienated. Therefore whosoever holds this object as his own against the right of the Church is an unjust possessor. No matter through how many hands the object may have passed successively, it is still the property of the Church and can always be exacted from whoever actually holds it. The good

4 ". . . vel si iste (male alienans) defunctus jam sit, adversus haeredes ejus, quippe qui eadem persona cum defuncto juris fictione censentur." *Ius Ecclesiasticum Universum,* I, *Dissertatio Prooemialis,* §1, n. 24.

faith of the actual possessor does not modify the objective situation at all.[5] It can, however, give the purchaser a right to claim damages against the person who sold him the object, especially if the restitution to which he himself is obliged will occasion him considerable loss or other harm. The purchaser is thus entitled to full compensation from the seller for all loss which he suffers from the fact that the Church reclaims an object of which she has been unjustly despoiled. This right of personal action against the seller implies no right of court action against the Church, which cannot be made to suffer harm for insisting on one of her natural rights.[6]

Article 3. Competence to Act Against Irregular Alienation

After §1, which establishes the right of the Church to redress against the irregular alienation of her property, §2 of canon 1534 states who is empowered to insist on this right. The Code gives this right, first of all, to the person responsible for the irregular alienation. Although he acted wrongly, in disposing of church property irregularly, he is not to be deprived of the possibility of rectifying his error as far as possible.

His Superior is likewise authorized to take action, either against the alienator himself *(actio personalis)*, or to recover the property invalidly alienated *(actio realis)*. This right of the Superior flows necessarily from his sacred duty of vigilance for the welfare of the church body entrusted to him and his consequent obligation of preventing or at least of remedying whatever harm may affect the stability or security of its patrimony.

It should be carefully noted, however, that the Superior who is em-

5 ". . . [res] quae propterea, ad quemcumque deveniat, transit cum isto onere ut is qui jus in ea habet, eam persequi, repetere, et vindicare possit, . . . nam a quocumque illa [res male empta] detineatur, vindicare illam potest [proprietarius]."—Schmalzgrueber, *Ius Ecclesiasticum Universum,* I, *Dissertatio Prooemialis,* §1, n. 23.

6 In connexion with the obligation of restitution, it might be noted that the more common opinion of canonists regards as valid *in the forum of conscience* all alienations which are in keeping with the principles of natural law, even though some canonical formalities may be wanting. Hence such contracts would retain their natural binding force and would engender no obligation of restitution, in case of invalidity, until a decree of nullity has been legitimately passed by a competent judge. — Cf. Cleary, *Canonical Restrictions on the Alienation of Church Property,* p. 102.

powered by the Code to institute court action, if this is necessary in order to safeguard the interests of the Church, may not undertake to sanate the invalid alienation. This is beyond his competence, even if the invalidity has arisen from lack of his own authorization. The invalidity is based on a lack of compliance with a prescription of universal ecclesiastical law. A dispensation from this prescription, especially in the nature of a sanation which remands the effect of the dispensation to the moment of the completion of the invalidly entered contract, can come only from the Supreme Legislator in the Church. No other ecclesiastical Superior is endowed with the right of eminent domain over ecclesiastical property, nor with that superiority over the law which enables him to waive its prescriptions as he sees fit according to the exigencies of circumstances.[7]

The same reasons which empower the *male alienans* and his Superior to act against invalid alienation call for this same right in their respective successors in office. The welfare of the Church is vested with a character of permanence which requires that it be protected at all times and in all circumstances. Since the juridical guilt of the alienator perdures until satisfaction has been made, legal proceedings to remedy the effects of this guilt are always within the power of any competent Superior, who has succeeded him in office.[9]

The solicitude of the law for the best interests of the Church goes even a step farther. The property of even a particular church is so inviolable that it can be vindicated by any cleric attached to the church. He can rightly consider himself wronged by invalid alienation, since the patrimony of the church is intended, partially at least, for the sustenance of its clergy. Cleary observes that the right would not be extended to any priest in the diocese who knew of irregular disposition of diocesan goods.[10] One may wonder at this restriction. Certainly a priest of one

7 S. C. Conc. Albiganen. et aliarum *Sanationis Alienationum,* 17 maii, 1919 — *AAS,* XI (1919), 382. Cf. also *Periodica,* X (1922), 66.

8 Even if he had bound himself by oath not to revoke his act; such an oath is illicit. — Reiffenstuel, Lib. III, tit. 13, n. 59.

9 Cf. *the nisi restituerentur* of Pau lIV, in his Constitution *Iniunctum nobis.* — *Fontes,* n. 88.

10 *Canonical Restrictions on the Alienation of Church Property,* p. 108.

parish would not be entitled, by virtue of the present provision, to take action against invalid alienation of property belonging to another parish. He cannot be considered as pertaining to that church. But when there is question of *diocesan* goods the case is not so clear. By the fact of his incardination a priest evidently belongs to the diocese where he works; he is *adscriptus Ecclesiae N.;* he is thus part of the diocesan clergy and this makes diocesan interests partly his own. There would be somewhat of a parallel between a secular priest in a diocese and a religious priest in relation to a province of his Institute or to his Institute at large. Since Vromant extends the right of legal action to religious in connection with their province or their institute,[11] there would seem to be grounds for the same extension to a secular priest in relation to his diocese.

Article 4. Choice of Available Actions at Law Against Irregular Alienation

All the persons mentioned in §2 of canon 1534 are entitled to all the legal actions which are made available for contravening the effects of an irregular alienation. That is to say, they may either institute legal proceedings against the alienator himself by personal action at law, or they may assert their right over the property alienated. It should be noted, however, that if the Church recovers the invalidly alienated property, personal action against the alienator is extinguished, though he may be condemned to defray the court costs, etc., which were made necessary by his irregular transaction. Such a condemnation is not, strictly speaking, personal action against the alienator.[12].

Similarly to Canon Law, civil law does not allow in its own field of competence cumulative action for both restitution *and* damages, but

11 "Quilibet clericus ecclesiae seu personae morali laesae adscriptus: nempe quilibet clericus pertinens ad Institutum, provinciam vel Communitatem quae propter alienationem *invalidam* damnum passa est." — *De Bonis Ecclesiae Temporalibus,* n. 298, 4°.

12 ". . . si Ecclesia obtinendo contra unum v.g. contra possessorem rem suam reciperet, tunc cessaret actio contra alterum, puta contra praelatum male alienantem: quia bona fides non patitur ut bis idem exigatur." — Reiffenstuel, Lib. III, tit. 13, n. 64.

only for one *or* the other.[13] Nevertheless the simple fact of having instituted one species of legal action, to obtain either damages from the alienator or the actual restitution of the object alienated, does not preclude the possibility of changing to the other. Good reasons must motivate this change, since it will have repercussions on the defendant. Chief among the motives justifying the change in procedure would be the probability of failure in the action already undertaken. The civil law recognizes this right of change for good reasons.[14]

Article 5. Disposal of Proceeds of Invalid Alienation

In an invalid alienation, as has been pointed out, there is no actual transfer of property rights. Consequently, there are no legal or moral grounds for the conveyance of a consideration. If such consideration has been actually received by him who alienated invalidly he is bound to restore the fruits of the transaction from the day the invalid contract was completed. The reason for this obligation is that he really gave nothing in return for the consideration which he received.[15] Even though the ecclesiastical organization may seem to have profited by the operation, restitution of the price received must be made when the property

[13] The *Restatement* has the following provision:

§384. (1) Damages and restitution are alternative remedies, only one of which will be given as a remedy for a breach of contract.

(2) Specific performance and compensation in money are not alternative remedies, and both forms of relief may be given in the same proceeding; but the compensation will not be awarded for an injury that an existing decree is intended to prevent, and specific performance will not be decreed for the prevention of an injury for which there is an existing award of compensation.

[14] §381 of the *Restatement* declares: " (1) When the alternative remedies of damages and restitution are available to a party injured by a breach, his manifested choice of one of them by bringing suit or otherwise, followed by a material change of position by the other party in reliance thereon, is a bar to the other alternative remedy. (2) The bringing of an action for one of these remedies is a bar to the alternative one unless the plaintiff shows reasonable gtounds for making the change of remedy.

[15] S. C. Conc. *Nullius seu Asculana,* 6 mart. 1723 — *Thesaurus Resolutionum,* I, 291.

is reclaimed, lest the Church be maligned for collusion in spoliation.[16]

Article 6. Invalid Alienation and Prescription

Invalid alienation accompanied by good faith from the beginning can furnish a lawful foundation for prescription, provided there be verified the other conditions required by canons 1508-1509.[17] This conclusion tempers the rigor of the provision of Roman Law that no legitimate claim to prescription could be founded on disposition of property belonging to a ward without the proper authorization of his guardian; this principle would ordinarily have to be applied to the alienation of ecclesiastical property without lawful permission, according to canon 100, §1.[18]

16 "Summae quae proveniunt ex alienationibus jure canonico invalidis, nec ecclesiae vindicari possunt, quia secus dici deberet expilationem ab ecclesia esse recognitam." — S. C. Conc. Andrien. *Iurium,* 27 aug. 1904. — *Thesaurus Resolutionum,* CLXIII, 914.

Reiffenstuel expresses the same idea when he says: "Tenetur tamen Ecclesia in integrum restituta alteri, v.g. emptori, rerum suarum reddere pretium, quod ab eo accepit, aliasque expensas in ipsius Ecclesiae utilitatem factas refundere. . . . Et merito: ne videlicet Ecclesia contra naturalem aequitatem cum aliena jactura locupletior fiat." — Lib. III, tit. 13, n. 57.

17 In his observations on the decision of the S. Congregation of the Council in a case *Iurium et Privilegiorum* (December 5, 1863 and June 25, 1864), the commentator in the *Acta Sanctae Sedis* (I, 594) remarks: "Ex iis colliges: . . . III. Ejusmodi conventiones non legitime confirmatas (the *dubium* is really concerned with an abstract right, but a parallel is drawn between the necessity of apostolic approval for such cases and the need of this same approval for transactions involving temporal goods), quamvis, si antiquae sint, interdum possint gignere quosdam juridicos effectus, puta consuetudinis vel praescriptionis, vel etiam causam exhibere possint ob jugem observantiam, cur a S. Sede confirmentur; attamen *in se consideratas vim obligandi non habere.*"

18 "Eum qui a pupillo sine tutoris auctoritate distrahente comparavit, longi temporis spatium non defendet." — C(5. 59)3.

"Contractus enim omnes etiam iuramenti, poenae vel alterius cuiuslibet firmitatis, adiectione vallatis, quos de talibus alienationibus sine huiusmodi licentia et consensu contigerit celebrari et quicquid ex eis secutum fuerit decernimus adeo viribus carere, ut nec ius aliquod tribuant, nec prescribendi etiam causam parent."—C. 1, *de testamentis et ultimis voluntatibus,* III, II, in VI°.

CHAPTER X.

DONATIONS MADE BY OR TO ECCLESIASTICAL ORGANIZATIONS

Canon 1535

Praelati et rectores de bonis mobilibus suarum ecclesiarum donationes, praeterquam parvas et modicas secundum legitimam loci consuetudinem, facere ne praesumant, nisi iusta interveniente causa remunerationis aut pietatis aut christianae caritatis; secus donatis a successoribus revocari poterit.

Article 1. Gifts Made by Churches

A gift, or donation, in the strict sense, is the giving of a *lawful*[1] object out of mere liberality, without any compulsion of law. A gift is motivated by no other reason than the desire to show liberality or munificence.[2] This definition would seem to exclude the possibility of gifts being made out of gratitude for favors received or expected. Still the Code, following the traditional legislation,[3] expressly provides for gifts made out of gratitude, as can be seen from a study of the text: *nisi iusta interveniente causa remunerationis aut pietatis*. Such offerings are gifts or donations improperly so called, since they go beyond the motive of pure liberality.

The giving of moderate donations is considered as part of the normal administration of temporal goods. Showing gratitude for benefits already received, and winning the good will of a prospective benefactor are very potent means of providing for the welfare and betterment of the Church. There is the added reason that such donations ward off from the Church the suspicion of avarice and conciliate the benevolence and

1 That is, one which can be legitimately disposed of by the donor.

2 Reiffenstuel, Lib. III, tit. 24, nn. 2, 3.

3 Cf. Reiffenstuel, *loc. cit.* and Schmalzgrueber: ". . . ut nomen hoc donatio aliqua mereatur, sufficit ut res donata non sit debita in jure seu justitia."—Lib. III, tit. 24, n. 15.

favor of men.[4] This is so true that in pre-Code law ecclesiastical administrators were permitted to make even donations of considerable importance for reasons of gratitude.[5]

Under present legislation only small donations are permitted. Diocesan statutes may determine further the limits of "small" donations. The field thus left open to the prudent judgment of individual Superiors and administrators is that of movable goods not implying great value. Such donations, for example, would be the alms given by a pastor or other ecclesiastical administrator to vagrants and others who come to him in search of assistance. Provided they do not exceed the limits of "small" donations, as determined by prudence or local prescriptions, they may be made freely even though they come from the church treasury. This faculty is contained in the text of the present canon. Consequently, a particular law prohibiting *all* small donations, of whatever amount, from church funds, would be against canon 1535 and thus would have no binding force.

Should a Superior give donations which cannot be termed *modicae* in the sense of the canon, but which nevertheless remain within the limits of his competence for alienation as fixed by canon 1532, his act will certainly be illicit. It will not, however, be invalid because he is acting within his powers. Because of the harm inflicted on the Church, his successor in office may revoke the donation. If, however, the amount of the donation exceeds the limits of the alienating powers of the Superior, the gift is null and void. Consequently, recourse can be had to the provisions of canon 1534, for application of the remedies against invalid alienation. Outside these cases, the amount or nature of the donation is left to the prudence of the Superior, since no general law can be established for all individual cases.[6]

4 ". . . quia per huiusmodi modicas donationes evitatur suspicio avaritiae, conservatur bona aestimatio et benevolentia hominum, indeque procuratur etiam Ecclesiae utilitas. Nec obstat, quod praelati non sint domini, sed tantum administratores; quia etiam saeculares administratores et curatores domini non sunt, et tamen modica donare possunt."—Reiffenstuel, Lib. III, tit. 24, n. 35.

5 Reiffenstuel, Lib. III, tit. 24, n. 44.

6 "Nihilominus licet dictis tutoribus et curatoribus *pro facultatibus, ac dignitate principalium,* proportionatas facere donationes remuneratorias pro meritis et servitiis principali collatis; item tales, quae *pro more et consuetudine* fieri solent."—Reiffenstuel, Lib. III, tit. 24, n. 24.

Thus it is seen that the present canon is very similar in content to n. XIII

The power to make moderate donations *inter vivos* for reasons of gratitude and the like, even though these donations come from church funds, does not imply liberty to make like donations *mortis causa* in last wills and testaments. Such an act cannot be construed as pertaining to ordinary administration. Should there be sufficient reasons for expressing gratitude to a given party, these reasons will be evident to the actual Superior who will be free to avail himself of the power accorded by this canon.[7]

Article 2. Gifts Made to Churches

Canon 1536

§1. Nisi contrarium probetur, praesumendum ea quae donantur rectoribus ecclesiarum, etiam religiosorum, esse ecclesiae donata.

§2. Donatio facta ecclesiae, ab eius rectore seu superiore repudiari nequit sine licentia Ordinarii.

§3. Repudiata illegitime donatione, ob damna quae inde obvenerint actio datur restitutionis in integrum vel indemnitatis.

§4. Donatio ecclesiae facta et ab eadem legitime acceptata, propter ingratum Praelati vel rectoris animum revocari nequit.

A) *General law*

Canon 1536, with its regulations on gifts made in favor of church organizations, opens up a much wider field than the preceding canon on gifts made by churches. Donations made to the Church are of much more frequent occurrence than those which are made by the Church. This is due to the fact that the usual means of support of the Church consists in the free-will offerings of the faithful. To insure her against

---

of the Instruction *Inter Ea* of the S. Congregation of Religious (30 July, 1909): "Donationes, etiam titulo eleemosynae vel subsidii, non fiant, nisi iuxta conditiones a Sancta Sede praescriptas, et iuxta mensuram in singulis constitutionibus ordinatam, vel a capitulis, et in eorum defectu, a Superioribus generalibus cum respectivis conciliis, legitime determinatam."—*Fontes,* n. 4394.

[7] The prohibition against disposing of ecclesiastical goods by will was clearly enunciated by Alexander III: ". . . clerici de mobilibus, quae per ecclesiam sunt adepti, de iure testari non possunt; viventes tamen et sui compotes moderate valent aliqua de bonis ipsis non ratione testamenti, sed eleemosynae intuitu erogare in aegritudine etiam constituti."—c. 8, X, *de testamentis et ultimis voluntatibus,* III, 26.

being defrauded of what is intended for her through donations is the purpose of the legislation contained in canon 1536.

Paragraph 1 of this canon lays down a general presumption regulating all donations made to the Church. Some guiding norm is necessary, since the intention of the donor, which is the fundamental source of information on the ultimate determination of the gift, is not always clear. Leaving aside the old distinction between donations made to a cleric by relatives and those made by non-relatives, the Code lays down the principle that, unless certain proof to the contrary is adduced, all donations made to rectors of churches are presumed to be made to the church itself rather than to the administrator. The faithful are considered as making these offerings for the spiritual welfare of their own souls rather than for the material welfare and comfort of the clergy.[8]

As Leo XIII points out in his Apostolic Constitution *Romanos Pontifices,* the presumption is all the more strongly in favor of the Church, and against the gift being personal, if the Church to which the cleric belongs is not well provided with temporalities. In all these cases the presumption is very decidedly in favor of the Church, unless the explicit will of the donor states otherwise:

> Namque receptum est hac in re spectari primum oportere *quid largitor voluerit;* quod si non appareat, placuit, parocho vel rectori Ecclesiae collatam donationem praesumi. . . . Praeterea si in parochum rectoremve, a quibus spiritualia adiumenta fideles accipiunt, haud inconcinne praesumi potest collata liberalitas, ubi Ecclesia praedita sit bonis, per quae religionis decori et ministrorum tuitioni prospiciatur, longe aliud iudicium esse debet ubi eam bonorum copiam Ecclesia non habeat, ac liberalitate fidelis populi unice aut potissimum sustentetur. Tunc enim largitores putandi forent voluisse consulere cultus divini splendori et religionis dignitati, ea ratione et modo quem ecclesiastica auctoritas decerneret.
>
> Ideo apud christianos primaevos lege cautum fuerat, ut pecunia omnis dono accepta, inter Ecclesiam, Episcopum, Clericos et egenos divideretur. Legis porro sese interponens auctoritas, si largitionum tempora et caussas praestituat, illud efficit quoque, ne fideles semper pro arbitrio possint modum et finem designare in quem oblatam stipem erogari oporteat; nequit enim facere privatorum voluntas, ut

[8] C. 3, C. XII, q. 3.

quod a legitima potestate in bonum commune praecipitur certo destituatur effectu.

Haec Nobis considerantibus visi sunt prudenter et opportune egisse Patres Concilii Provincialis Westmonasteriensis II, cum partim interpretantes piam et aequam donantium voluntatem, partim ea, quae Episcopis inest, utentes potestate imperandi pecuniae collationes decernendique quo tempore et qua de caussa conferri oporteat, statuerunt in capite *de bonis ecclesiasticis,* quid censendum sit intuitu missionis collatum. Jubet igitur ratio, itemque Nos constituimus, hac in re religiosos ad leges Westmonasteriensis Synodi sese affatim adcommodare oportere.[9]

According to the provisions of the Second Provincial Council of Westminster (1885), which are given apostolic approval in the abovementioned Constitution of Leo XIII, the following donations, and no others, may be considered as rightfully belonging to the priest personally.

a) articles intended for personal use, or even sacred objects given to the priest as a special token of affection or gratitude;

b) gifts made to the pastor or rector by families or friends who are particularly fond of him;

c) special gifts made usually at Christmas or Easter, on the occasion of Jubilees, etc.

B) *Particular Law for the United States*

The preceding paragraphs summarize the legislation of the Second Provincial Council of Westminster on the question of gifts made to pastors or rectors of churches. As has already been pointed out, the Holy Father, Leo XIII, confirmed these provisions and imposed them on both the secular and religious clergy at work in the English missions. On September 25, 1885, in answer to the request of the Fathers of the Third Plenary Council of Baltimore, His Holiness, through the S. Congregation of the Propagation of the Faith extended the prescriptions of the Constitution *Romanos Pontifices* to the United States.[10] In accord-

9 Leo XIII, const. "Romanos Pontifices," 8 maii 1881, §26—*Fontes,* n. 582.

10 Cf. S. C. de Prop. Fide, Decree—*Concilii Plenarii Baltimorensis III Acta et Decreta,* p. cv. The complete text of the Constitution can be found in the *Acta et Decreta* of the Third Plenary Council, pp. 212-230, or in the *Collectanea* of the S. Congregation of the Propagation of the Faith, n. 1552.

ance with the decree of the S. Consistorial Congregation (August 2, 1918)[11] this Constitution is still binding in those territories in which it was established as law, except for those details which may be in conflict with explicit provisions of the Code. All its provisions which are merely *praeter Codicem* still remain in force. Hence the Apostolic Constitution *Romanos Pontifices* not only affords safe norms for the application of its principles to the United States, but really constitutes special *particular law* for this country. It should be borne in mind that particular laws *praeter Codicem* are not abrogated by the Code.

In its legislation in favor of the Church on the question of church furnishings, the Third Plenary Council of Baltimore showed itself even more severe than the Second Provincial Council of Westminster. This latter had explicitly conceded to pastors and rectors, secular or religious, the right to receive gifts of church ornament as personal gifts, provided certain conditions were fulfilled. Number 276 of the decrees of the Third Plenary Council of Baltimore enacted that, unless the contrary intention of the donor was *clare et indubitanter* evident,[12] all gifts involving articles of church adornment were to be presumed as being in favor of the Church rather than to the pastor or rector personally.[13]

The very restricted field of what the pastor or rector can regard as

11 *AAS*, X (1918), 365.

12 In order to forestall all possible misunderstanding and difficulty n. 195 of the Second Plenary Council of Baltimore had reaffirmed the regulation established by the Seventh Provincial Council which required *written* proof of this contrary intention of the donor. "This documentary proof required by the Council seems to be *praeter Codicem* and, therefore, still of obligation."—Barrett, *A Comparative Study of the Councils of Baltimore and the Code of Canon Law*, Washington, 1932, p. 108.

13 ". . . Quia de quibusdam muneribus, ut quidam ex Nobis alia occasione prudenter notarunt, maxime rerum mobilium, ut supellectilis, ornamentorum sacerdotalium, vasorum aureorum argenteorumque, sive ab individuis fidelibus sive a sodalitatibus sponte ecclesiae rectori oblatis dubium sat frequenter oritur, utrum ad hunc pertineant an ad missionem vel ecclesiam: decernimus, nisi contrarium *explicite* fuerit a donatoribus declaratum, *res istas esse ecclesiae proprietatem*, atque ideo neque rectorem in discessu a missione, neque ejus haeredes post ipsius obitum, jus habere ad eas removendas vel vendendas. Servetur itaque regula statuta, ea scilicet quae ecclesiasticis usibus apta rectori missionario donantur, esse missioni donata, *nisi contrarium clare et indubitanter pateat*."—*Acta et Decreta*, p. 158.

personal property in the matter of gifts from the faithful is further evidence of the law's solicitude for the welfare of the Church. The rôle of mere administrator or steward rather than that of owner in those who handle ecclesiastical goods is very clearly emphasized in this legislation. The brief §1 of canon 1536 epitomizes the stand adopted in canon 6 of the Council of Agde (506) when it declared that it was only just for the Church to benefit by what is given to the priest, since the priest always profits by what is donated to the Church.[14]

These regulations were intended to obviate the danger of clerics enriching themselves at the expense of the Church. Clerics who, penniless at the time of their ordination, but who had since acquired money or fields, provoked from the Third Council of Carthage (397) the following reproof: ". . . tamquam rerum dominicarum invasionis crimine teneantur."[15] They were free, however, to dispose at will of whatever "liberalitate alicujus, uel successione cognationis euenerit."[16]

C) *Caution in accepting donations*

In accepting donations for the Church, especially if they be of considerable value, ecclesiastical administrators should emphasize to the donors the fact that their benefaction implies no right of patronage or supervision over the use of the donation. The civil law will recognize this exclusion of the donor from the administration or control of his gift once it has been accepted by the Church.[17] Many misunderstand-

14 "Pontifices, quibus in summo sacerdotio constitutis, aliquid ab extraneis aut cum ecclesia, aut sequestratim dimittitur, aut donatur (quia hoc ille, qui donat, pro redemptione animae suae, non pro commodo sacerdotis offerre probatur), non quasi suum proprium, sed quasi dimissum ecclesiae inter facultates ecclesiae conputabunt, quia justum est ut sicut sacerdos habet quod ecclesiae dimissum est, ita et ecclesia habeat quod relinquitur sacerdoti."—C. 3, C. XII, q. 3. Cf. also Mansi, *Sacrorum Conciliorum . . . Collectio,* VIII, 325.

15 C. 1, C. XII, q. 3.

16 *Loc. cit.*

17 ". . . money actually contributed to it (the church) will be vested in the church even against the assignee in bankruptcy of the donor or though the donation consisted in paying bills for the church or incurring large expenditures for it, and will not give the donors any control over the property purchased or maintained with it. Where, therefore, land is purchased by a religious corporation with money contributed by people outside the church, the donors will be considered as donors merely of the money and hence will not be permitted to impose restrictions on the land."—Zollmann, *American Church Law,* §433.

ings and much ill feeling may be avoided if this is made clear to the benefactors particularly before the donation is accepted.

It is likewise highly advisable that careful consideration be given to any conditions which benefactors may wish to impose in making their donation. Unless careful supervision is exercised on this point, the Church may find herself obligated by the civil courts to the observance of certain conditions at variance with her own juridical principles. The courts will not always decide according to the norms of Canon Law, and this makes judicious weighing of the implications and consequences of all conditions an imperative necessity.[18]

The first paragraph of canon 1536, with its regulations on the question of donations, has a wide field of application in the United States. The well-known generosity of the American faithful prompts them to make gifts to their priests, particularly on certain special occasions. The provisions of the Code and of Leo XIII's Constitution *Romanos Pontifices,* with its particular laws for the United States, may be easily forgotten. This forgetfulness may even go so far as to establish the opposite presumption, namely, that all gifts made to the priest are personal donations unless the contrary has been explicitly declared by the donor.

That insistence on the opposite principle is necessary to safeguard the best interests of the Church is shown by the fact that the provisions of the Constitution *Romanos Pontifices* were embodied in the particular legislation of various dioceses in the United States. The Fourth Provincial Council of New York (1883), for example, decreed that all gifts unless the contrary were clearly demonstrated, were presumed to have been given to the priest *as pastor,* and therefore were to be regarded as the property of the Church.[19] This same provision was repeated by the

[18] For instance, the United States Supreme Court upheld the legal right of the donors of a college to make as a condition of the donation that all ecclesiastical missionaries, and ministers of any sort, should be excluded from holding any station of duty in the college or even visiting the same. The validity of the devise was attacked on the grounds that the appended condition was contrary to the Christian religion. The court, however, declared that the condition was only negatively derogatory to the Christian religion and hence did not make the devise for the college void.—Fenelon v. Girard, 2 Howard, 127; 11 L. Ed. 205. A condition such as the one upheld in this decision would certainly be against the prescriptions of Canon Law, but compliance with it could not be avoided in the civil forum if it had been once accepted.

[19] *Conc. Prov. Neo-Eboracen. IV* (1883), cap. XVI, *de bonis eccles.,* art. IV, p. 77.

Fifth Diocesan Synod of New York (1886),[20] and by the First Synod of Chicago, (1887).[21]

Article 3. The Refusal and the Revocation of Donations

A) *The Refusal of Donations:* The absence of any indication of sources for this and the two following paragraphs of canon 1536 evidences the presence of new legislation. In fact, the older authors generally concurred in asserting that a refusal of donations was not forbidden.[22] In defending this position, however, they were viewing the refusal of donations in the light of its connection with alienation. When they claimed that a donation could be refused without violation of the law, they had in mind the specific laws on alienation. They were just as unanimous in holding that a Superior acting thus would really inflict harm on his church and in so doing would be violating the sacred trust assumed with his office. The Code here safeguards the Church by outlawing such a repudiation of gifts, independently of its lack of connection with alienation.

The Ordinary whose authorization is required to legitimize the refusal of donations is, according to the context of the canon, the local Ordinary. Vromant holds that his permission must be obtained in this instance even by non-exempt religious, since there is no other Ordinary to whom they can have recourse.[23]

B) *The Revocation of Donations:* Even though absolute irrevocability would evidently redound to the material welfare of ecclesiastical organizations, still the Code does not make all donations unconditionally irrevocable. It is not to be excluded that by retaining a donation once lawfully made to and accepted by the Church, ecclesiastical Su-

20 *Synodus Dioecesana Neo-Eboracen. V* (1886), tit. XX, n. 251; p. 62.

21 *Synodus Dioecesana Chicagien. I* (1887), tit. XX, *de bonis ecclesiasticis,* n. 245.

22 Cf., for example, Reiffenstuel, *De Regulis Juris,* R. J. 76, ad 4.

23 "Quamvis vi can. 618, §2, 1°, per se non liceat *Ordinario loci* in religionibus non exemptis *juris pontificii,* 'de re oeconomica cognoscere,' praesenti tamen praescripto particulari c. 1536, §2, *derogatur* normae generali c. 618, §2, 1°, eique applicanda videtur Regula Juris 34 in VI°: *generi per speciem derogatur.* Religiosi enim non exempti per se nullum habent Ordinarium proprium praeter *Ordinarium loci.*"—*De Bonis Ecclesiae Temporalibus,* n. 325.

periors might occasion harm to third parties. The solicitude which she manifests in other parts of the Code to avoid encroaching upon the rights of others, even when she might legitimately do so, motivates the legislation of this paragraph.

Among the reasons justifying the revocation of donations the old authors generally mentioned three as being the most forceful:

a) the fact that the donor becomes the parent of children;

b) the fact that a donation was made against the duties of charity or affection;

c) the fact that the donee showed himself ungrateful, or exposed the donor to danger of life or limb.[24]

Even though a donation had been made in favor of the Church, any one of these three reasons could be invoked before a court of law to obtain the voiding of the gift. The Code, while implicitly admitting the force of the first two motives, as being consonant with the natural obligation of love and affection for others, rules out the third, by legislating that no donation made to the Church may be revoked because of ingratitude on the part of the pastor or rector.

This provision is but a logical corollary of §1 of canon 1536. If benefactions to pastors and rectors of churches are presumed to be in favor of the Church rather than for the personal benefit of the individual priests, it follows that the Church should not be made to suffer for the deed of an ungrateful administrator. The ecclesiastical juridical person has rights which cannot be made subject to the whims of the physical person who acts as its guardian and administrator. Consequently, should the civil law of a particular state sanction the revocation of donations to the Church on the grounds of ingratitude, this provision would be oulawed by canon 1529 as contrary to an explicit prescription of Canon Law.[25] This fact, however, would have no practical effect on the necessity of compliance with such a statute in the external forum of the civil law.

24 Reiffenstuel, Lib. III, tit. 24, nn. 50-59; Schmalzgrueber, Lib. III, tit. 24, nn. 55-88.

25 Vromant, *De Bonis Ecclesiae Temporalibus,* n. 327.

Article 4. Remedies Against Illicit Repudiation of Gifts

After stating the law which prohibits the refusal of donations the Code specifies what remedies can be invoked in case a gift or bequest has been actually repudiated by the representative of an ecclesiastical juristic person. There can be no declaration of the nullity of the act, since the prohibition embodied in §4 of canon 1536 does not concern the validity of such a renunciation. Consequently, the only remedy available is that of voidability of the act, or restoring the individual church to the status it previously enjoyed, and thus enabling it to provide for its own welfare by now accepting the benefaction already refused.

This remedy can be adopted only in case the Church has suffered some harm from the refusal of the donation: *ob damna quae inde obvenerint.* This harm would have to be positive; the bare fact of non-acquisition of the benefaction would not be sufficient to constitute a genuine *damnum.* Thus the simple fact of repudiation of a gift affords no right for an appeal to restore the Church to its former status, nor does it furnish grounds for claiming damages. Although §2 forbids all refusals of gifts without authorization from the Ordinary, only those repudiations can be prosecuted with legal sanction which entail loss or harm to the Church.

CHAPTER XI.

MORTGAGES AND DEBTS

Canon 1538

§1. Si ecclesiae bona, legitima interveniente causa, oppignoranda vel hypothecae nomine obliganda sint, vel agatur de aere alieno contrahendo, legitimus superior, qui ad normam can. 1532 licentiam dare debet, exigat ut antea omnes, quorum interest, audiantur, et curet ut, cum primum fieri poterit, aes alienum solvatur.

§2. Hac de causa annuae ratae ab eodem Ordinario praefiniantur quae exstinguendo debito sint destinatae.

Article 1. Mortgages

A) *The Nature of Mortgages:* Chapter VIII has already discussed in detail the difference between general and special mortgages. Since, as was there pointed out, general mortgages do not fall under the laws restricting alienation and cannot be classified with those contracts which resemble alienation, only the transaction known as *special* mortgage need be considered here.

A special mortgage is a consensual contract by which the creditor acquires, as security for the settlement of a debt, a real right *(ius in re)* over a specifically determined piece of property. The reality of the right thus acquired by the creditor is emphasized very graphically in American law, which requires the debtor to hand over to the creditor the title to the mortgaged property. To this conveyance of title, which is absolute in its form, there is attached a defeasance clause, whereby the conveyance is declared to be inoperative when the debt is fully repaid. Should the debtor default, the creditor can assert his right of possession, subject to such rights of redemption as the debtor may possess. If the debtor continue in default throughout the period allowed for the redemption of his title,[1] the creditor may then institute foreclosure pro-

[1] This redemption period varies considerably in the different states.

ceedings to make his possession definite; he cannot acquire unqualified possession automatically from the simple fact of default.

The close connection of the power to mortgage with the corporate life of church bodies is well pointed out by Zollmann when he says that it is next in importance to the power to sell, and gives church property a usefulness which it would otherwise not have, by making it a means of bettering the financial or general property status of ecclesiastical corporations.[2] This power to mortgage, however, is held within certain well-defined limits; it can be exercised only in strict accord with the charter, by-laws or constitutions of the society concerned; otherwise the transaction will not be ratified by a court of law.[3] Irregular acts may become binding, none the less, if they are later approved in a lawful manner by the governing or administrative body of the corporation.[4]

If local statutes require previous permission of the court for contracting a legal mortgage, this permission must be obtained, in order to safeguard the validity of the contract in the eyes of the civil courts.[5] Since the power to mortgage is inherent in the corporation for its own welfare, not for that of the individual members, no member of the corporation, not even its Superior, can execute a valid mortgage on its property in order to furnish security for his own personal debts. This has been explicitly declared by the court in regard to the property held in trust by a bishop for a specific congregation.[6] It is expressly forbidden likewise for any church corporation with mortgaged property to set up a

2 *American Church Law,* §185.

3 In re First, 106, N.Y., 251; 12 N.E., 626; Wiswell v. First, 14 Ohio st., 31.

4 Civil enactments on this point must yield in the forum of conscience to the canonical provision that no Superior under the Roman Pontiff has the power to sanate transactions which are invalid for want of the necessary authorization. Cf. *supra,* page 145.

5 In re First, N.Y., 106., 251; 12 N.E., 626. Compliance with this prescription would be necessary only to safeguard the legality of the transaction before the civil authorities. Such a requirement would have no canonical binding force in conscience since it interferes with the natural right of the Church to dispose of her property with untrammeled freedom, and independently of any coaction on the part of lay authorities.

6 O'Donnell v. Holden, 21 *Weekly Law Bulletin,* 254.

trust for this property and place it in the custody of a third party, in order thus to safeguard it against seizure. The courts have rightly ruled that such a mortgage can be foreclosed like any other, notwithstanding the fictitious trust thus created. Thus, even in this case, the mortgagee on foreclosure will acquire free title after the redemption period has elapsed.[7] This provision would naturally have the full sanction of Canon Law, since it aims to forestall the possibility of any corporation evading its natural obligation of paying debts, by having recourse to legal technicalities devoid of juridical foundation. Within the scope of such limited restrictions, capacity to mortgage property is consequent upon capacity to own and administer. For this reason, as a Michigan court has decreed, this power can be exercised in every case where there is no contrary legislation forbidding it.[8] The binding force of any such prohibitions as may exist will depend entirely on their foundation in the natural law, and on their lack of conflict with the positive prescriptions of church law.

Mortgages do not constitute alienation in the strict sense of the term, because they do not involve an absolute and unconditional transfer of ownership. This notwithstanding, they fall within the scope of canon 1533, which is the basis of canon 1538, since they are drawn up in legal form and give as security some specific portion of property belonging to the stable capital of an ecclesiastical organization. In virtue of the mortgage, a determined piece of church property can be seized in case of default. This makes the holding of a mortgage the equivalent of possessing a real right against ecclesiastical property, and thus exposes the Church to the danger of diminution of her stable capital.

These conditions are not fulfilled in the case of money obtained by means of a mortgage taken out on buildings *to be constructed*. In this particular case no risk is taken on goods already belonging to the Church; the buildings affected by the mortgage are acquired only imperfectly. They cannot be called *bona ecclesiastica,* because they will not become the full property of the Church until the mortgage has been completely paid off. This method of raising money involves no risk on property which the Church already possesses as her own. Hence, since there is no jeopardizing of stable capital, there is no occasion to apply

7 Zollmann, *American Church Law,* §185.

8 Walworth v. Camel, 28 Mich., 111.

canon 1533, with its regulations on contracts whereby *conditio Ecclesiae peior fieri possit.*[9]

The application of this same principle solves the case in which an ecclesiastical corporation acquires property already burdened with a debt or mortgage, and continues to retain this obligation. The fact that this is an instance of *imperfect acquisition* without diminution of property already owned, safeguards the juristic person against diminution of its fixed capital. For the same reason a religious society may incur a debt on the strength of future incorporation, and then later, after incorporation, may take charge of the property thus burdened. The corporation thus assumes the debt,[10] but this fact implies neither alienation nor resemblance with alienation.

B) *Pawning:* In connection with mortgages, canon 1538, §1, mentions also the transaction known as *pawning (oppignoratio)*. Between pawning and mortgaging there is only an accidental difference. The dis-

9 Speaking of these "purchase-money mortgages," McManus (*The Administration of Temporal Goods in Religious Institutes,* p. 125, note 22) seems hesitant. He says: "However, this opinion (that is, permitting these mortgages without dependence on the legislation of the Code) seems to neglect the fact that money paid by the religious moral person on the mortgage, either as interest or as part payment of the principal, may possibly be lost, if the mortgage has to be foreclosed. Individual cases should be examined cautiously before applying this opinion." — It is always true that there is the possibility of a deficiency judgment being entered against the church body in case of default before the full repayment of the mortgage. Still, money thus paid out, either as interest or as part payment on the principal, will not be governed by canons 1530-1533 unless it is taken from the *stable capital* of the church. In the circumstances in which these mortgages are used, there is no stable capital belonging to the organization involved; otherwise they would not be obliged to have recourse to this particular type of mortgage. The principle still remains true that money taken from current resources is not subject to the regulations on alienation and contracts resembling it.

10 This has been upheld by the civil law: Eager v. Inhabitants, 10 Mass., 430. But a mortgagee who has foreclosed at loss against an unincorporated church society cannot legally enter a deficiency claim against this same society after incorporation. St. Patrick's v. Daly, 116., Ill., 76; 4 N.E., 211. — This exemption by the civil law, however, will not affect the forum of conscience. Legal incorporation brings about no change in the intrinsic juridical personality of the organization incorporated. Hence it remains bound in conscience to satisfy its debts, and meet all its obligations, even though it might be able to evade them before the law by having recourse to a legal technicality.

tinction consists, not in the nature of the transaction, but only in the nature of the goods given as security and in the length of time for which the transaction holds. A mortgage will almost always deal exclusively with immovable property and will run for a considerable length of time. Pawning, on the contrary, usually deals with movable goods,[11] and is restricted to a noticeably shorter period. For this reason such a transaction will rarely, if ever, touch upon the stable capital of a church corporation unless the object given in security is, for instance, a precious work of art. This circumstance would bring the contract within the scope of canon 1532, §1, 1°, requiring the permission of the Holy See.

Article 2. Debts

A) *Nature and Kinds of Debts:* Contracting a debt is a contractual engagement to repay a given sum of money within a specified period of time or to furnish its equivalent.[12] The canonical aspects of debts are much more involved than those of mortgages. This is due to the various kinds of debts which may arise in the course of temporal administration. Dom Bastien, at the beginning of his treatment of debts and other financial obligations mentions explicitly that the Instruction of the S. Congregation of Religious, *Inter Ea,* of September 15, 1909, which is reproduced substantially in canons 534-537, refers only to debts *which burden the patrimony of religious communities.*[13] Since the legislation of the Code on debts is practically the same in substance for both religious and ecclesiastical corporations, it seems legitimate to reaffirm here the conclusion aldready developed at length in Chapter VIII, that the restrictions of Canon Law apply only where there is a financial burden supported by legal sanction and involving risk for the safety of the ecclesiastical corporation's permanent assets.

The debts which burden an ecclesiastical or religious organization can be of three kinds: a) *current debts,* for ordinary expenses, provided for in the regular budget; b) debts consequent upon *borrowing money,*

[11] This is so true that the older authors found the etymology of *pignus* in the word *pugnus,* fist, as though the very name signified that it dealt exclusively with movable property which could be carried in the hand.

[12] Bastien, *Directoire Canonique,* n. 336.

[13] ". . . la S.C. des Religieux promulgua . . . un decret relatif aux dettes et autres obligations *qui grèvent le patrimoine des Instituts ou des communautés religieuses.*"—*Directoire Canonique,* n. 352.

with or without interest; c) debts contracted by *legal act,* e.g. by mortgage. This last species of debt has already been discussed. The first kind certainly does not fall within the prescriptions of canon 1538, §1, otherwise an almost insupportable burden would be placed upon all ecclesiastical and religious corporations. This explains why authors allow such organizations even to borrow money to meet the expenses of the current year, for example, when experience has shown that the gross receipts of the year will make it possible to repay this debt within a very short time. The second category of debts, namely those arising from borrowing money, will, upon the verification of certain conditions, fall within the restrictions on contracts resembling alienation. It is important, consequently, to determine precisely what modes of borrowing money in the United States are governed by canons 1530-1533, as implying for the Church the legal risk of losing ownership of all or part of its stable capital. Since the obtaining of a loan on the strength of a mortgage has already beeen treated, this discussion can be limited to the methods of obtaining money through promissory notes, the acceptance of annuity obligations, and borrowing on general credit.

a) *Promissory notes*

A promissory note is a written obligation whereby one party binds himself to pay to another a specified sum of money at a fixed future time in a stated place. Like mortgages, promissory notes can be issued by corporations only in accordance with their borrowing powers and their customary corporate procedure.[14] The civil law generally disqualifies the trustees of a corporation from issuing notes if the said trustees have in the particular transaction an interest adverse to the interests of the other members of the corporation.[15] For any notes not authorized by the charter and by-laws of a corporation, the issuers themselves, not the organization, are responsible before the civil law.[16]

Promissory notes given as legal evidence of a promise to repay a

14 Catron v. First, 46, Ia., 106; People v. St. Anthony's, 109, N.Y., 512; 17 N.E., 408; MacLaury v. Hart, 121 N.Y., 636; 24 N.E. 1013.

15 San Antonio v. Adams, 87 Tex., 125; S.W., 1040; Hill v. Rich, 119 Mo., 9; 24 S.W., 223.

16 Hewitt v. Wheeler, 22 Conn., 557; Devos v. Gray, 22 Ohio, 159; Klopp v. Moore, 6 Kan., 27; Neil v. Spencer, 5 Ill. App. 461; United v. Vandusen, 27 Wis., 54. Cf. also Canon 536.

loan are of two kinds: *secured* and *unsecured*. As the name itself implies, a secured note is one which is backed by some kind of collateral offered as security, for example, negotiable securities for the amount of the loan plus a mutually satisfactory margin, or pieces of movable or immovable property and the like. The primary difference between this kind of note and a mortgage is in the length of time which elapses before maturity,[17] and in the procedure required for taking possession of the property or of the proceeds therefrom.

An *unsecured* note, on the other hand, is simply a legally recognized promise of repayment without any security being offered in support of this promise. This engagement to repay the loan can be enforced by legal sanction, but no specifically determined piece of property can be seized or retained in settlement for the debt. In case of favorable court action satisfaction for the plaintiff can be taken from whatever assets the defendant may possess, but repayment will first be sought out of current assets. Only when these are not available will there be any seizure of what belongs to the stable capital.

In applying the principles enunciated in the commentary on canon 1533 to these cases it will be seen that there is an evident difference between these two methods of obligating one's self to pay a debt. Provided the requisite legal formalities have been fully complied with, all promissory notes, whether secured or unsecured, are contracts with juridical sanction which can be legally urged before the civil law. They thus fulfil the first condition required to bring them under the restrictions imposed by canon 1533 of the Code.

Nevertheless, not all these notes verify the second condition, according to which the contract in question must expose the Church to the danger of losing part or all of her patrimony. From the explanation of the nature of a secured note it is clear that it will or will not come within the field of application of canon 1533, in accordance with the nature of the collateral. If the security furnished with the note is taken from the fixed assets of the corporation, canon 1533 must be complied with, and the authorization of the competent Superior must be obtained, according to the prescriptions of canon 1532. Should the security offered for

[17] A promise to pay backed by collateral is customarily called a secured note if it matures within ten years; if any longer period of time is to elapse before maturity, it is known as a mortgage. Thus a thirty-year mortgage obligation would be tantamount to a secured note in the last ten years before maturity.

the debt come from the organization's current assets, or from a reserve fund not yet incorporated into the stable capital, the risks which canon 1533 aims to forestall will not be present. Consequently there will be no application of the restrictions provided by Canon Law. Limitations will be established by particular laws, charters and constitutions.

This is even more true when there is question of an unsecured note. Here there is legal responsibility arising from a contract, but without risk to stable capital. In case of default, claim will first be laid to current assets; the permanent assets are jeopardized only indirectly. The creditor acquires over them not the *ius in re,* which is the equivalent of ownership, but only a *ius ad rem,* which merely establishes a claim against the person of the owner, not against the property itself.

a) *Annuity Obligations*

Because of the great vogue they now enjoy in American ecclesiastical and religious organizations faced with the necessity of raising funds for various good works, annuity obligations call for special consideration in connection with debts.

As they are known and practised today, annuity agreements have no exact counterpart in old ecclesiastical law. They are commonly said to be a form of the contract known as *census,* whereby a person acquires in certain circumstances a right to a fixed income from a portion of ecclesiastical property. The principal of annuity funds, however, usually does not become the full property of the ecclesiastical corporation until the death of the annuitant, or with the expiration of the period of time agreed upon. Annuity agreements also have something in common with the old contract called *precaria,* which consisted in donations to the Church with the reservation that the usufruct of these donations was to go to the donor for a stipulated time or for life, and that the entire gross sum was then to become the full property of the Church. Nevertheless, although this is perhaps the closest approach to annuity agreements as they are known today, there is not a strict parallel, since it was commonly admitted that the laws against usury forbade such donations if they consisted of sums of money.[18] The simplest solution seems to be

[18] "Imo in numerata pecunia precariam constitui negat ratio; quia plerumque ex precariis subitur pensio, et finito tempore res ipsa integre restituitur; quod fieri in pecunia sine vitio usurae nequit."—Schmalzgrueber, Lib. III, tit. 14, n. 27.

to regard the acceptance of annuity obligations as the acceptance of a trust.

An annuity agreement can be defined as a bilateral contract whereby one party agrees to pay another a fixed sum at specific periods in return for a gross amount of money or equivalent property received. The contract is called an *annuity contingent* if it covers a certain number of years, e.g. until the annuitant marries, etc.; it is known as an *annuity certain* if it is entered into for a stipulated period of time, or a *life annuity* if it is to cease only at the death of the annuitant. The gross sum deposited by the annuitant usually does not become the property of the party paying the annuity until the death of the annuitant. In the meantime, as has been already observed, it resembles a sum held in trust.[19]

The acceptance of annuity obligations does not fall within the category of strict alienation. Nor, considered in itself, must it necessarily be placed among those legally recognized contracts whereby the stable capital of an ecclesiastical corporation is jeopardized before the civil courts. The risks involved in these agreements arise rather from the circumstances in which they are generally made, than from the intrinsic nature of the contracts in themselves. If an ecclesiastical organization had sufficient reserve or current resources to assure the discharge of its obligations without drawing on its stable capital, annuity contracts would not be affected by the restrictions of canon 1533. But the contrary is almost always the case.

In fact, annuity agreements are most commonly accepted, and even solicited, precisely by those ecclesiastical or religious bodies which are in need of current resources, and which are backed by little or no stable assets whence these resources can be derived through income. Finding themselves under the necessity of providing themselves with some sort of regular income, they readily accept amounts of money which they invest with the obligation of repaying a certain percentage of the interest to the annuitants. In order to pay a representative amount of interest to the annuitants, while at the same time assuring themselves of a proportionate share of the income from the investment, the religious or ecclesiastical organizations accepting annuities are obliged to put their money into investments which will pay a comparatively high rate of interest.

19 It is not, however, a trust in the strict sense of American law unless the religious Institute has legal title for the benefit of the donor; if the donor retains the legal title, the religious Institute is only administrator.

Such investments are seldom of the safest or most reliable kind, whatever may be the subjective mentality of the interested parties. Financial crisis could easily ruin all such placements of money, and consequently could entail the complete collapse of the entire organization in its efforts to meet its obligations. This is the danger which the law intends to forestall. Since most organizations which engage in the practise of accepting annuity obligations do so precisely because of their lack of stable capital for their enterprises, the law governing annuities and their acceptance must be a general law. If in some particular instance this danger did not exist, the law would nevertheless oblige there as in other cases, by virtue of canon 21. In this case the Holy See would very probably grant an indult authorizing the acceptance of these annuity obligations over a specified period of time.

The principal on which the annuities are paid partakes of the nature of a trust fund which is administered by the individual church body in favor of the annuitant for the amount of income agreed upon. It is on the grounds of abuse of trust or of maladministration, as circumstances may demand, that the annuitant can bring suit against the ecclesiastical organization in case of default. For this reason, as is stressed very emphatically in the Letter of the Apostolic Delegate to religious Superiors in the United States, on November 13, 1936: "In order to avoid the serious inconveniences when religious Institutes imprudently contract obligations under annuity agreements and later are not in a position to satisfy the annuity requirements, it is strictly and formally forbidden to use all or any part of the capital annuity fund which should remain intact as long as the annuitant is living."[20] Thus the Church insists that the principal of annuity funds remain in its integrity until all the accompanying obligations have been complied with.

On the same principle the church body violates its trust if it uses part of the principal to buy from a finance company an annual income to cover the obligation of the annuity to be paid to the annuitant. This procedure violates the rule enforcing preservation of the principal, and is likewise a frustration of the will of the benefactor, who naturally wishes *all* his money to benefit the pious cause to which he has contributed it.

The accumulation of annuity obligations and its relation to the limits

20 *Letter of the Apostolic Delegate,* §V—Bouscaren, *Canon Law Digest, Supplement 1938,* p. 21.

of competence set down in canon 1532 will be governed by the ordinary rules of moral theology on coalescence. The intention of amassing a considerable amount through the acceptance of these obligations will usually be sufficient to unify them to the extent of making the law applicable to them.[21]

c) *Borrowing on General Credits:* After the treatment of the method of borrowing money on unsecured notes, as given in an earlier section of this present chapter, little remains to be said of loans negotiated on the strength of general credit. Such loans involve no contracts resembling alienation because there is no conveyance of title *(ius in re)* to a particular portion of ecclesiastical property to secure the loan. Consequently, the legal status of the Church is in no way jeopardized before the civil courts. The Church is thus greatly assisted in her growth and development, without assuming any of the juridical risks and responsibilities which would require the application of canon 1533.

Article 3. Provisions of the Canon

Whether it be question of mortgages or debts to be contracted, canon 1538, §1, lays down the prescriptions dictated by the rules of prudent administration. In the first place it provides that all the parties interested in the transaction be consulted. Anyone whose interests are involved in the mortgage or loan in question has a right to be heard, and the competent Superior is empowered to see to it that this right is respected. Since allowing a mortgage on church property or contracting a debt is a business operation not unlike alienation in its consequences, a parallel might be drawn between those whose consent must be obtained by the Ordinary in certain cases of alienation, according to canon 1532, and those who must be consulted in the present case. Thus the interested parties would be the Board of Diocesan Consultors, the Diocesan Council of Administration, the Administrator, Trustees or Councillors of the juridical person carrying on the transaction, and others whose advice might be usefully asked in an individual case.[22]

21 *Letter of the Apostolic Delegate,* §V—Bouscaren, *Canon Law Digest, Supplement 1938,* p. 21.

22 This brief mention of the necessity of consulting the interested parties presupposes compliance with all the other formalities prescribed by canons 1530-1532.

The application of the rules of moral theology which govern the coalescence of individual actions to the accumulation of debts seems justifiable. It is altogether true that there is no perfect parallel between, for example, the accumulation of debts and the accumulation of goods through distinct thefts. In the latter case there is a question of incurring the guilt of serious sin, while in the former the concern of the law is to prevent church bodies from exposing themselves to the danger of legal financial jeopardy. At first sight this particular aim would seem to be concerned only with the attainment of a certain fixed sum, without any attention to the manner in which this particular sum was reached.

The difference between the two cases, however, does not appear to prevent the application of the same principle of calculation. Besides, there is the explicit assurance given by a response in *Periodica,* which applies these identical principles of coalescence to various distinct acts of alienation.[23]

This analogy would appear to have some value. In fact, particular transactions below the sum permitted according to the competence of individual Superiors stand before the law as individual units. In each particular instance the contract has been made under the supervision of the ecclesiastical Superior who was determined by the amount involved. He is thus enabled to view the general financial situation of the corporation over which he presides, and in this way he is enabled to formulate his judgment as to when it is advisable to prevent the organization from contracting further obligations. Only in the case an individual transaction surpasses the limit allowed by the law without recourse to Rome will the approbation of the Holy See be required. In other instances the individual contracts remain acts of ordinary administration, which are not regulated by the Code.[24]

This conclusion would seem to be confirmed by a consideration of

23 *Quaeres* utrum summa 30.000 francorum seu libellarum, pro cujus alienatione requiritur beneplacitum Apostolicum computanda sit attentis singulis contractibus, an simul additis pactionibus?

Resp. Dummodo vere sint distinctae pactiones, et non agatur in fraudem legis, solus separatus valor singularum pactionum vel susceptarum obligationum considerari debet.—XI (1923), (158).

24 "Quid si pluries successive debitum 25.000 libellarum contrahendum sit? Dummodo causae vere distinctae sint et absit fraudulenta calliditas, debita ista sine beneplacito Apostolico contrahi posse videntur."—Vermeersch-Creusen, *Epitome,* II, n. 658.

the almost impossible situation which would be created if an ecclesiastical organization, already in debt for more than six thousand dollars, were obliged to have recourse to Rome for every individual instance of further indebtedness, of no matter what proportions. It would not seem to be the intention of the law to subject ecclesiastical or religious corporations to such restrictions as would make it practically impossible for them to lead a normal corporative life. This impossibility would be verified if they were obliged to consider the Holy See as having sole and exclusive competence to approve the incurring of any and all indebtedness which adds to an already existing debt of six thousand dollars.

The second paragraph of canon 1538 explicitly indicates the manner in which the competent Superior will take care that the debt be paid off as promptly as possible, according to the concluding provision of §1. This will insure a regularly acquitted amortization of the debt in due time. According to the Instruction of the S. Congregation for the Propagation of the Faith to the Patriarch of the Armenians, the Ordinary could set aside a certain portion of church revenues for this purpose. This income was to be invested prudently or at least placed in the custody of some reliable person until such time as investment might prudently be made. Given the silence of the Code, these prescriptions no longer have the force of law. They are, however, indications of measures which the local Ordinary has the power to make, according to §2 of canon 1538.

Canon 1538 makes no mention of the necessity of declaring already existing debts, as is required for the contracting of debts by religious, according to the prescriptions of canon 534, §1.[25]

25 In view of the limitations established by the Code for the contracting of debts, according to the provisions of Canon 1532, it may be interesting to note the restrictions placed on expenditures in connection with church property by some of the earlier diocesan synods in the United States. Thus, for instance, the Diocesan Constitutions formulated in the First Synod of Chicago (1887) (tit. XX, *de bonis ecclesiasticis,* n. 241), forbade rectors to contract debts beyond two hundred dollars without the express authorization of the Ordinary. Likewise the Rules and Regulations of the Diocese of Grand Rapids, drawn up in the First Diocesan Synod (1903), prescribed that no expenses whatsoever not foreseen in the budget for the current year were to be incurred without the express and written permission of the bishop (n. 12). The fourth decree of the Third Provincial Council of Cincinnati (1861), following the tenor of the seventh decree of the Provincial Council of New York, held in June of that same year (1861), forbade the trustees of any parish to expend more than three hundred dollars, beyond the ordinary expenditures, on any particular

The stringency of the restrictions adopted by canons 1532 and 1538 show the seriousness with which the Church regards all debts burdening ecclesiastical or religious institutions. It is for this reasosn that the law prescribes such close control over all Superiors when there is question of assuming financial burdens which can involve risk to the corporation which they direct. The Holy See, however, readily recognizes that in some circumstances it may be advisable, or even necessary, to burden a church organization with debts, within the bounds of prudence; this is especially so when the temporary inconvenience of a debt will enable the church body to avoid serious partial or even total loss of property. This explains why the S. Congregation of the Council, in the decision which is one of the sources of canon 1538,[26] recommended, in place of authorization to sell, that a particular church should borrow money for necessary repairs to an adjoining building, so that the building could be sold for its full price rather than suffer considerable loss by selling it in a deteriorated condition.

This principle of administration is even more applicable when parishes and other ecclesiastical juridical persons are still in the stage of evolution and development. This consideration was clearly set forth in the Pastoral Letter addressed by the Hierarchy to the faithful of the United States after the Third Plenary Council of Baltimore:

> In the discharge of this duty (of administration) it often becomes necessary to contract church debts. Where the multiplication of the Catholic population has been so rapid, rapid work had to be done in erecting churches and schools. And if, under such circumstances, pastors had to wait till all the means were collected before beginning the work, a generation would have been left without necessary spiritual aids, and might be lost to the Church and to God. We fully recognize, Beloved Brethren, how strictly we are

---

work without the written authorization of the archbishop. The Fourth Provincial Council of Cincinnati (1882), (tit. III, cap. II, *de ratione reddenda*), required that the date of the bishop's permission for each individual instance be mentioned in the annual parish report. The Third Provincial Council of Cincinnati (1861) had limited expenditures on either church or school to one hundred dollars without the written permission of the Ordinary. In addition, the greater portion of the sum needed had to be already collected, at least in pledges.

26 S. C. Conc. *Romana,* 5 apr., 17 maii 1851; *Fontes,* n. 4118.

> bound to prevent the contracting of debts without real necessity; and this we have endeavored to effect by careful legislation. Still, despite all our efforts, it must inevitably happen that the burden imposed on us by our gigantic task of providing for the spiritual wants of the present and the rising generation will always be heavy, and will weigh upon us all.

Then, to provide means for the extinction of debts as promptly as possible, the Council Fathers declared in the conclusion of the Letter's section on pastoral rights:

> It is our earnest wish that existing debts should be liquidated as soon as possible in order that the money now spent in paying interest may be employed in the great improvements still to be made, and especially in helping on the glorious work of Christian education.[27]

In the decrees of the Council on the duties of rectors of churches, it was declared most emphatically:

> Igitur strictissime prohibemus, vetmus et interdicimus, ne quis rector, sacerdos et pii loci Curator, sive Ecclesiae sive missionis sive Episcopi nomine ecclesiam suam vel locum aere alieno gravare quocumque titulo vel colore audeat, sine expressa et scriptis exarata licentia Ordinarii.[28]

It may be observed that the provisions of canon 1538 relative to the prompt extinction of debts do not bind necessarily as a hard and fast rule in every individual instance. In fact, the more general and more fundamental principle of always safeguarding the best interests of the Church may make it advisable to keep ecclesiastical property in some instances always burdened with mortgages or debts. Although the circumstances which Vromant brings up — mortgages or debts being guarantees against seizure or grounds for lower tax-rates — will not be verified in the United States, still the general principle which he invokes from the traditional Rules of Law can be used to advantage in solving particular cases which may arise: *Quod ob gratiam alicuius conceditur, non est in eius dispendium retorquendum.*[29]

27 *Concilii Plenarii Baltimorensis III Acta et Decreta,* p. lxxxii.

28 *Acta et Decreta,* n. 279.

29 *De Bonis Ecclesiae Temporalibus,* n. 330, 4.

CHAPTER XII.

THE SALE AND EXCHANGE OF ECCLESIASTICAL GOODS

Canon 1539

§1. In venditione aut permutatione rerum sacrarum nulla ratio consecrationis vel benedictionis in pretii aestimatione habeatur.

§2. Administratores possunt *titulos ad latorem,* quos vocant, commutare in alios titulos magis aut saltem aeque tutos ac frugiferos, exclusa qualibet commercii vel negotiationis specie, ac de consensu Ordinarii, dioecesani Consilii administrationis aliorumque quorum intersit.

ARTICLE 1. GENERAL NOTIONS

Sale is a consensual, bilateral contract whereby one of the parties transfers or agrees to transfer the ownership of a thing for the consideration of a price which the other party obligates himself to pay.[1] Sale usually refers to an *actual* transfer of ownership, while a contract regarding a future transfer of dominion is generally called an *executory sale.* The presence of a pecuniary consideration differentiates the contract of sale from the somewhat similar contracts of barter and exchange. Because the conveyance of title is absolute, a sale differs from a mortgage, since this latter is conditioned by a defeasance clause.

Civil laws vary in the precise determination of the moment when the transfer of ownership takes place in a contract of sale. Roman Law and European law generally have stipulated that the conveyance of title takes place at the moment the object of the sale is delivered to the purchaser. English and American law prefer to leave the arrangement of this detail to the will of the contracting parties. Since this will is rarely, if ever, explicitly expressed, it is to be gathered from the intention of the contracting parties. This intention, in turn, is to be judged according to their actions. In this connection it may be noted that the fact of simple deliv-

[1] Cleary, *Canonical Restrictions on the Alienation of Church Property,* p. 88.

ery of the object of the contract is not, in itself, always equivalent to transfer of title, since goods are not infrequently delivered on approval. Delivery plus acceptance by the purchaser will generally effect transfer of ownership,[2] without prejudice to the right of the interested parties to reach other agreements and stipulate conditions of their own.

Article 2. The Sale of Consecrated Objects

Canons 1539, §1, and 1540, like the preceding canon 1538, lay down further norms for the application of canons 1530-1533. The legislation embodied in these two canons regulates contracts which involve the sale or exchange of ecclesiastical goods. The cross-reference made by the sources of canon 1539, §1, to canon 730, draws attention to the ever-present danger of simony in all such transactions. It is evident that exacting a higher price for an object in view of its consecration or blessing would involve simony *iuris divini,* as is explicitly stated by canon 727, §1. The prescrption of canon 1539, however, is not to be understood as constituting a prohibition against the sale of all consecrated objects, to avoid the danger of simony. Such articles can be legitimately sold for whatever price is in keeping with their material or artistic value. This would be a case for the application of canon 730, since there would be sale of a material or temporal object to which is attached something spiritual, namely, consecration. Nevertheless, such articles may not be set up for *public* sale or auction without losing their consecration or blessing, as the case may be.[3] This will be the case even though the price of the object has not been raised in view of the consecration or blessing. In case an object has already lost its consecration or blessing for any of the reasons enumerated in canon 1305, it may be used for profane purposes, provided they be not of a sordid nature.[4]

Article 3. The Exchange of Securities

One of the most common methods used by ecclesiastical corporations for the investment of their stable capital is that of buying bearer-bonds.

[2] The separation of goods from stock to the account of a purchaser is delivery under the Uniform Sales Act. This Act, however, is not applied in all its details throughout the entire country.

[3] Canon 1305, §1, 2°.

[4] Canon 1510, §1.

These bonds are usually issued by the national government, by local municipalities or by reliable business corporations. Their great advantage over other kinds of securities is in the fact that they are not payable to any particular individual, but to the bearer. Hence mere change of hands suffices to effect change of ownership. This fact evidently facilitates the transfer of such securities, particularly in cases wherein prompt action is a highly desirable factor.

The legislation embodied in §2 of canon 1539 takes into consideration the requirements and possible contingencies of financial transactions in the modern business world. The provisions of this paragraph reaffirm what was at one time, on the testimony of Vermeersch, a very general usage in ecclesiastical corporations as well as in secular business organizations.[5] This general usage had been set aside by the decision of the S. Congregation of the Council, issued on February 17, 1906.[6]

According to this response of the S. Congregation, the Holy See declared that only the sale, but likewise the exchange of these securities fell within the restrictions governing the alienation of immovable property and precious goods. Consequently, apostolic approbation was required in every individual instance except in case of extreme urgency, when recourse to the Holy See would be difficult and delay would entail danger of loss.

In his commentary on the decision just referred to, Vermeersch suggests that the motive underlying the severity of the stand thus adopted by the S. Congregation may have been to emphasize the fact that ecclesiasical funds were not to be lightly handled or invested without all due precautions. It is not hard to see how insistence on this rigorous answer of the S. Congregation of the Council would impose severe hardships on ecclesiastical organizations by requiring recourse to Rome for acts which, in the common estimation of present-day businessmen, do not exceed the bounds of ordinary administration. This response of the S. Congregation no longer binds, since the Code reverts to the general usage in vogue prior to the decision of 1906. Consequently, it leaves ec-

5 *Periodica,* II (1914), 74.

6 S. C. Conc. *Romana et aliarum,* 17 feb. 1906, ad 2—*Fontes,* n. 4328, and *Thesaurus Resolutionum,* CLXV, 236-239.

clesiastical administrators free to exchange one species of bonds for others which are at least equally safe and income-bearing.

It would not seem that this last condition, namely that the new investments be *equally safe and lucrative,* should be regarded as referring to mathematical equality. It is not hard to conceive of a case in which a prudent administrator would find it advisable to change investments from one kind to another and to accept a lower rate of interest rather than retain a higher rate of interest with risk of partial or total loss. In such circumstances the decrease in income would seem to be legitimately counterbalanced by the increase in security, and this would preserve the balance and proportion required by the canon for a lawful change of investments.

Even in these necessary or useful transactions, ecclesiastical administrators are not to forget that pecuniary profit cannot lawfully be their primary aim. To this end the last part of canon 1539 insists that such transfers be kept free from all taint of money-seeking or playing the stock-market. This is only a specific application of the general prescription formulated in canon 142 against the *negotiatio* which is forbidden to clerics. The exclusion of even the semblance of trafficking, as required in the present canon, does not, however, forbid church administrators to avail themselves of legitimate opportunities for financial betterment of their situation. It would hardly be consonant with the general principles of ecclesiastical administration to hold that the Code forbids church administrators to sell their securities at a profit when the occasion presents itself. The prohibition of the canon is intended to forestall the abuse of acquiring securities with the avowed intention of selling them when the price increases. This would evidently be engaging in *negotiatio.*

In the exchange of securities there are precautions to be observed. The Code does not wish even this apparently routine operation to be left to the judgment of one individual. In order to provide for prudent control in such matters, canon 1539, §2, requires that for each individual instance the permission of the Ordinary be obtained, as also the consent of the Diocesan Council of Administration, and of all parties whose interests may be involved in the proposed transfer. This provision is very similar to the one contained in canon 1532, §3, which provides that the Ordinary may not authorize certain contracts of alienation without the consent of the Diocesan Consultors, the Council of Administration and the interested parties.

Lastly, in view of the conclusions reached by a study of the nature of alienation and its relationship with stable capital,[7] it is hardly necessary to remark that the restrictions on these transfers of securities do not affect those assets which have not yet been incorporated into the stable capital of the ecclesiastical organization engaged in the transfer. It is necessary to observe also, that not all surplus funds held in reserve are necessarily to be considered as forming part of the fixed capital.

The context of canon 1539, §2, as Vromant points out,[8] shows that its prescriptions do not apply to religious as such. They will, nevertheless, be bound by the enactments of this canon as often as they engage in the administration of property which belongs to the diocese but which is entrusted to their care, as in a parish or mission station.

Article 4. Limitations on the Sale and Rental of Ecclesiastical Property

Canon 1540

Bona ecclesiae immobilia propriis administratoribus eorumque coniunctis in primo aut secundo consanguinitatis aut affinitatis gradu non sunt vendenda aut locanda sine speciali Ordinarii loci licentia.

This present canon formulates a very specific rule on the disposal of the immovable property of an ecclesiastical corporation. According to canon 1531, §2, church property is to be disposed of through public auction to assure the Church of the greatest possible profit in all her financial operations. To avoid even the slightest suspicion of collusion in injustice or favoritism dictated by considerations of friendship or relationship, any individual interested in a given transaction has an equal right with all the others to offer his bid. The danger of loss to the Church entailed by considerations of merely private or personal interest can be seen in a study of some of the cases presented to the Holy See for consideration.[9]

7 Chapter V, *Alienation and its Requisite Conditions.*

8 *De Bonis Ecclesiae Temporalibus*, n. 333, 3).

9 Cf. especially S. C. Ep. et Reg. *Catacen. Super edictorum affixione in locationibus bonorum Ecclesiae*, 11 maii 1743—*Collectanea* S. C. Ep. et Reg., p. 363.

This explains the precaution established in canon 1540. According to this provision immovable ecclesiastical property may not be sold or rented to the administrators thereof, nor to their relatives in the first or second degree of consanguinity or affinity without a *special* authorization from the local Ordinary. Hence the local Ordinary's permission to sell or rent church goods within his field of competence will have to be supplemented by additional specific authorization if there is question of selling or renting to the parties just mentioned. This is a new provision in Canon Law and is intended to obviate a recurrence of the ever-threatening danger of favoritism or nepotism. Since the canon refers only to the sale or rental of *immovable* goods, there is no restriction other than that of prudence if there is question of movable property. The reason for the distinction would be that contracts involving movable property would not deprive the Church of the free use of her goods for so long a period as would be entailed in the sale or rental of immovable possessions.

CHAPTER XIII

THE RENTAL, LEASING, AND LENDING OF ECCLESIASTICAL PROPERTY

Canon 1541

§1. Contractus locationis alicuius fundi ecclesiastici ne fiant, nisi ad normam can. 1531, §2; et in iis addantur semper conditiones de limitibus custodiendis, de bona cultione, de rite solvendo canone, de opportuna cautela pro conditionibus implendis.

§2. Pro locatione bonorum ecclesiasticorum, servato praescripto can. 1479:

1°. Si valor locationis excedat triginta millia libellarum seu francorum et locatio sit ultra novennium, requiritur beneplacitum apostolicum; si locatio non sit ultra novennium, servari debet praescriptum can. 1532, §3;

2°. Si valor contineatur intra mille libellas et triginta millia libellarum seu francorum et locatio sit ultra novennium, servari debet praescriptum eiusdem canonis 1532, §3; si locatio non sit ultra novennium, praescriptum eiusdem can. 1532, §2;

3°. Si valor non excedat mille libellas seu francos et locatio sit ultra novennium, servari debet praescriptum can. 1532, §2; si locatio non sit ultra novennium, fieri potest a legitimis administratoribus, monito Ordinario.

Article 1. Contracts of Rental

A) *General Observations*

Contracts of rental, leasing and lending are discussed in the same chapter because of their great similarity. The particular elements differentiating each from the other will be pointed out in the commentary on each type of contract. This commentary will deal only with an explanation of the particular points emphasized in the Code, which itself singles out only a few specific aspects for special consideration. In keeping with canon 1529 and its principle of adaptation to civil law within certain well-defined limits, the Code leaves the determination of further details to the prevailing civil law. Detailed statutes on contracts of rental may vary greatly in different States. The considerations of Canon Law, consequently, will have to be supplemented by recourse to a study of the civil law in force in given localities.

In connection with the civil law on rental contracts, the parties to a contract of rental of ecclesiastical property will be subject to all legal provisions which are consonant with the Church's liberty. For instance, the law which states that rent becomes due in the first minute of the stipulated day and is in arrears from the first minute of the following day will have the explicit sanction of Canon Law.[1] Likewise canon 1529 accepts the provisions of the various States determining whether in case of default of payment the landlord may apply the Law of Distress or is restricted to recourse to the ordinary means of collecting a debt or evicting the tenant.[2] Other details, such as the specification of what goods may be seized in distress, or regarding the continuation of the obligation of payment even though, for instance, a check for payment has gone astray in the mails, will have canonical binding force. The foregoing are only examples. For a complete understanding of all the legal aspects of the matter, it will be necessary to seek out expert advice in particular instances in order to prevent the Church from running afoul of the civil law.

The contract of rental is a consensual contract whereby a determined price is paid for the use or enjoyment of a determined piece of property. This contract is called *rental (locatio)* on the part of the owner who thus disposes of his property, and is known as *hire (conductio)* on the part of the individual or the organization which thus acquires the use of the property. Because the contract of rental is a bilateral obligation, the Latin authors always specify these two different aspects just as they do for the element of sale and purchase in what is ordinarily called simply sale: contractus *locationis conductionis,* contractus *emptionis venditionis.* In English usage the specific mention of one element implies the presence of the other. In legal parlance, however, the two aspects of the individual contracts are very specifically mentioned by name or in the equivalent of the name.

The indication of a decision of the S. Congregation of Bishops and Regulars as far back as 1597 as a source of this canon[3] shows with what solicitude the Holy See has always guarded against even a diminution of the rights of the Church over her rightfully acquired property. The

1 Canon 33, §2.

2 Most of the states provide for the application of the Law of Distress.

3 S. C. Ep. et Reg. *Ianuen. et Parmen.* 12 feb. 1597—*Fontes,* n. 1564, and *Collectanea S. C. Ep. et Reg.,* p. 240.

well-defined jurisprudence of the S. Roman Rota, as indicated in the above-mentioned decision, considered as null and void all alienation or acquisition of church property without due regard for the formalities of ecclesiastical law. The continuity of this viewpoint is borne out by a later decision of the same Congregation of Bishops and Regulars, insisting that without papal approval all contracts of rental of ecclesiastical property which were to be considered as automatically renewed at the end of three years if no formal revocation of the contract was intimated to the parties, were in reality null and void from the beginning and caused the contracting parties to incur the penalties reserved by law for the irregular alienation of church property.[4]

The faculties now accorded to ecclesiastical Superiors and administrators by Canon 1541 are much more generous than those which existed under pre-Code legislation. In virtue of canon 1543, canon 1541 requires conformity with all the provisions of canons 1530-1532. In other words, the restrictions of canon 1541 will apply only when there is question of renting in due legal form a piece of property pertaining to the ecclesiastical juristic person's stable capital. This will almost always be the case, since rental usually deals exclusively with immovable property, and immovable property most generally belongs to the fixed capital of an organization.

Every precaution is to be taken to insure the permanence of the property under the dominion of the Church and in the most favorable condition possible. But even prescinding from the restrictions imposed now by canon 1541, present-day Superiors have much more ample faculties than were enjoyed previously, when, for example, no contracts of rental could go beyond three years without recourse to the Holy See. The nine-year period now allowed by the Code represents the time-limit which the Instruction to the Patriarch of the Armenians allowed as the extreme permitted by special faculties.[5]

B) *Competence of Various Ecclesiastical Superiors:* At the beginning of the paragraph on the limits within which individual Superiors may authorize contracts of rental, §2 reiterates expressly the provision of canon 1479, which forbids the anticipation of the collection of rent on

4 S. C. Ep. et Reg. *Viterbien. Locationis*, 28 nov. 1783—*Collectanea S. C. Ep. et Reg.*, p. 39.

5 S. C. Prop. Fide Instruct. (ad Patriarch. Armen.) 30 iul. 1867, n. 6 —*Collectanea S. C. de Prop. Fide*, n. 1310, and *Fontes*, n. 4867.

benefice property by more than six months, without the explicit consent of the Ordinary. This is something of a mitigating departure from previous law, since the above-quoted Instruction to the Patriarich of the Armenians applied this restriction to the rental of all ecclesiastical property without restriction. The purpose of the prohibition, as evidenced in the precautions to be taken by the Ordinary in permitting these anticipated collections of rent,[6] is to protect future incumbents of the benefice from danger of reduction or even complete suppression of their income over a protracted period of time.

In the following schematic presentation of canonical regulations on the renting of church property it will be noticed that the provisions of canon 1541 follow very closely those of canon 1532 on contracts of strict alienation. The standard of sum-limits used for determining the fields of authority of respective Superiors is the same as for alienation, because the amount of rental paid indicates the extent of rights over church property conferred on another through the contract. This explains why the sums given in canon 1541 represent, not the value of the property rented, but the amount received in payment of the rental. These amounts are to be computed year by year. It should be remembered that in determining the competence of various Superiors the time element and the amount of rent involved must be verified *cumulatively*, not disjunctively. The following outline shows these fields of competence:

SUM	TIME-LIMIT	COMPETENT SUPERIOR	CONSENT REQUIRED	ADVICE REQUIRED
Not over $200.00	Not more than nine years	Administrator	——	After notifying Ordinary
Not over $200.00	For more than nine years	Local Ordinary	Interested parties	Council of Administration
Between $200.00 and $6000.00	For not more than nine years	Local Ordinary	Interested parties	Council of Administration
Between $200.00 and $6000.00	For more than nine years	Local Ordinary	Diocesan Consultors Council of Administration Interested parties	——
Over $6000.00	For not more than nine years	Local Ordinary	Diocesan Consultors Council of Administration Interested parties	——
Over $6000.00	For more than nine years	Holy See	Cf. terms of the indult	Cf. terms of the indult

[6] Canon 1479.

ARTICLE 2. CONTRACTS OF LEASE

Canon 1542

§1. In emphyteusi bonorum ecclesiasticorum emphyteuta nequit canonem redimere sine licentia legitimi Superioris ecclesiastici de quo in can. 1532; quod si redemerit, eam saltem pecuniae vim ecclesiae dare debet, quae canoni respondeat.

§2. Ab emphyteuta congrua exigatur cautio pro solutione canonis et conditionibus implendis; in ipso instrumento pacti emphyteutici forum ecclesiasticum arbiter statuatur ad dirimendas controversias inter partes forte exorituras, et expresse declaretur meliorationes solo cedere.

A) *General Observations:* A lease implies a more far-reaching hold on church property than mere rental. It usually confers on the lessee the practical equivalent of property rights without any actual transfer of direct ownership. Leases likewise generally extend over a much longer period of time than ordinary contracts of rental. The contract of *emphyteusis* which is discussed explicitly in this present canon really belongs to the general category of leases even though it has no exact counterpart in English or American law.[7] The rights conferred by a contract of emphyteusis were not necessarily restricted to one individual party, but were transferable by inheritance or by will. Property thus affected usually reverted to the Church automatically after the third generation of the first lessee had enjoyed the use of it. In view of the time element in this contract and the possibility of its conveyance to heirs or legatees, its closest parallel in American law would be a ninety-nine year lease.[8]

Leaving the general regulation of the details of lease-contracts to

[7] It is defined by Reiffenstuel: "Contractus . . . quo res immobilis cum translatione dominii utilis, retento dominio directo, seu proprietate, alteri fruenda et colenda, pro annua pensione in recognitionem dominii directi praestanda conceditur vel in perpetuum, vel ad alicuius vel plurium vitam, vel ad certum tempus." — Lib. III, tit. 17, n. 119. Thus it is really an indefinite lease, or the practical equivalent of an actual transfer of title without going to the extent of a juridical transfer.

[8] Cleary, *Canonical Restrictions on the Alienation of Church Property*, p. 96; Bouscaren, *Canon Law Digest*, I, 733; Leage, *Private Roman Law*, p. 189.

the local civil law,[9] according to the principle laid down in canon 1529, canon 1542 legislates on only a few points which are more closely connected with safeguarding the best interests of the Church. The first prescription of §1 provides that the lessee who wishes to buy the rental cannot do so without the authorization of the competent Superior. The Superior, in turn, is limited in his powers by the prescriptions of canon 1532, since the "redemption of the canon" really implies acquisition of the title to the property, as is well observed by Cleary[10] and Bouscaren.[11] "The redemption of the rental," says this latter, "is almost equivalent to the exercise by the lessee of an option of purchase which, upon payment of a lump sum, transfers to him the full legal title and relieves him of the obligations of further annual payments of rental."[12]

The conclusion of §1 of canon 1542 states the manner of compensating the Church for the purchase of the rental. The lessee must hand over to the Church *at least* a sum of money corresponding to the sum-total of the rent for the unexpired term. The words *at least* show that the competent Superior is perfectly within his rights if he requires some additional consideration beyond the total of the rent for the remaining period, if the general welfare of the Church so demands.[13]

The use of the specific term *pecunia* in the canon would seem to indicate that such redemption of the rental must be conmpensated for

9 The civil law will determine, for instance, whether the contract must be oral or written; a written contract is generally required for leases extending over more than a year. It also legislates on the remedies available to the lessor in case of default: seizure of lessee's goods by distress or customary action at law for recovering payment, as well as on the mutual extinction of rights and obligations in case one party fails in the performance of the stipulated covenants. The courts will also take action if a lessee, even with power to re-lease, attempts to do so for a period exceeding the duration of his own contract. The original lease of realty or land must always be in writing; it is automatically renewed at the end of the year by the acceptance of rent.

10 Cleary, *Canonical Restrictions on the Alienation of Church Property,* p. 97.

11 *Canon Law Digest,* I, 733.

12 *Loc. cit.*

13 Usually in our courts this sum will be much less than the total rent. The courts argue that since such a lump sum can be made fruitful the revenue accruing therefrom will, when added to the principal, equal the aggregate that would have been paid in rent.

in legal tender rather than in negotiable securities. If, however, the competent Superior deems it to be to the interest of the Church to accept securities such as government bonds, and the like, he must see to it that, if the bonds are not negotiable at their face value, compensation in cash be provided for the difference between the nominal and the actual value of such securities. In all cases cash transactions are to be preferred. Inconvenience and financial embarrassment easily arise when securities are not easily negotiable or when they are not redeemable at their face value. Even if the civil law permits payment of obligations in money or securities at their nominal value, despite the possible disparity between this value and the actual value, this provision of civil law must yield to the specific prescription of Canon Law. This would be required by the nattural law obliging all ecclesiastical Superiors to protect the general economic welfare of the church corporations entrusted to them.[41]

B) *Requisite Conditions for Leases:* To insure the Church against possible fraud or deception, and also against unforeseen financial embarrassment of the lessee, §2 of canon 1542 exacts the fulfilment of several conditions in all contracts of lease. In addition to the special conditions prescribed in canon 1541, §1, for contracts of rental, canon 1542 requires the lessee to furnish security to insure the payment of the rent and compliance with the other conditions which may be imposed by the Superior. The Instruction of the Congregation for the Propagation of the Faith to the Patriarch of the Armenians exacted that the contractual document be accompanied by a map or plan of the property in order to insure proper preservation of the boundaries. As security for the payment of the rent, the same Instruction required a mortgage in favor of the Church on some property already fully owned by the lessee; the Code is satisfied with any reasonable security. Since leased property remains under the dominion of the Church, an express stipulation shall designate an ecclesiastical court as competent arbiter in the event of future disputes. For the same reason there shall be an express understanding that any and all improvements made on the property will benefit the property itself rather than the lessee personally.[15]

14 *Jus Pontificium,* III (1923), 179.

15 This is the usual principle of civil law. It has also been explicitly upheld by the S. Congregation of the Council, *Resolutio,* Romana et aliarum, 12 dec. 1931, in answer to a *dubium* on the profits accruing from the exploitation of mines and quarries on property belonging to a benefice. — *AAS,* XXIV (1932), 147. Cf. comments by Vermeersch, *Periodica,* XXI (1932), 195.

Article 3. Contracts of Loan

Canon 1543

Si res fungibilis ita alicui detur ut eius fiat et postea tantundem in eodem genere restituatur, nihil lucri, ratione ipsius contractus, percipi potest; sed in praestatione rei fungibilis non est per se illicitum de lucro legali pacisci, nisi constet ipsum esse immoderatum, aut etiam de lucro maiore, si iustus ac proportionatus titulus suffragetur.

A) *Loans for consumption:* The loans here considered are those which an ecclesiastical organization makes to another party, not loans which it receives from others. These active loans thus differ from the passive loans for which regulations are found in the commentary on canon 1538.[16] According to the particular nature of the transaction a loan will be either strict alienation or will merely resemble alienation.

The Latin authors distinguish between two kinds of loans: *mutuum* and *commodatum.* The first involves the conveyance to another of something which is consumable at first use. The person to whom the loan is made thus acquires full dominion over what he receives. He is bound to restore to the lender, not the object loaned in the first place, but another of the same kind or in the same quantity. This relinquishment of ownership puts a *mutuum,* or loan for consumption, in the category of alienation strictly so called and subjects it to all the prescriptions of canons 1530-1532.

The traditional stand of the Church against usury and its inevitable abuses has motivated the prescription of canon 1543, forbidding any financial profit by reason of a contract to loan to another a fungible object. This does not outlaw the exaction of the usual legal rate of interest payable on money loaned, but excludes only that profit which might be required from the simple fact of making the loan. The text of canon 1543 makes this clear: *ratione ipsius contractus.* It goes even farther and provides that higher interest than the legal rate may be legitimately agreed upon, provided this higher rate is justified by a proportionately grave reason. Hence the seriousness of the reason will vary according to circumstances.

16 Cf. *supra,* Chapter XI, *Mortgages and Debts.*

B) *Loans for use:* The *commodatum* of the commentators corresponds to the English term *loan for use.* As its name implies, it cedes to another the use of a thing without renouncing ownership over it. The person to whom the loan is made is under obligation to restore the identical object at the stipulated time. Consequently, since there is no strict alienation involved, a loan for use will be governed by the regulations of canon 1533. By its very nature, a loan for use is a gratuitous contract. If remuneration enters into the transaction, the intention to loan thus becomes an intention to rent, subject to the respective regulations of canon 1541.

Article 4. The Loaning of Sacred Objects

Canon 1537

Res sacrae ne commodentur ad usum qui earundem naturae repugnet.

The Code does not prohibit unconditionally the loaning of sacred objects. It lays down only certain precautions to safeguard the respect and reverence due to consecrated things.

Because real and direct dominion over sacred objects remains in the Church when these objects are loaned to another, there is no question of alienation in such transactions. The Code merely insists that these articles be not put to uses which are not in accord with their sacred character; the loan should, of course, be regulated by canon 1541. This canon presents but another manner of stating the principle enunciated in canon 1150 and in Number 51 of the Rules of Law, where it is declared that *semel Deo dicatum non est ad usus humanos ulterius transferendum.*

As an example of the improper use of sacred objects, Vromant, quoting Génicot-Salsmans, mentions the loan of blessed or consecrated articles for use in a theatrical performance.[17] Provided all due safeguards are taken to insure respect and becoming reverence, there would be no objection to loaning sacred objects of artistic or historical value for use in an exposition, etc.

[17] *De Bonis Ecclesiae Temporalibus*, n. 328. Cf. also Reiffenstuel: "Nam res sacrae Ecclesiae applicare ad usus profanos continet irreverentiam, et speciem sacrilegii."—Lib. III, tit. 15, n. 11.

CHAPTER XIV

THE DISPOSAL OF CHURCH PROPERTY IN CASE OF THE EXTINCTION OR DISMEMBERMENT OF ECCLESIASTICAL CORPORATIONS

Article 1. General Observations

The preceding chapters have dealt with the precautions with which the Church safeguards the patrimony of the individual units of her organization in the course of their corporate existence. The fundamental principle underlying all this detailed legislation on alienation and on contracts resembling it has been that inferior ecclesiastical juristic persons are rightly understood only when viewed as units in the great structure of the Church as a whole. This same principle now comes into play in the consideration of the provisions which the Code has made to preserve church property in ecclesiastical hands even after an individual unit of ecclesiastical life and organization has been divided or has even passed out of existence.

The Church in its general organization is perennial; the individual units composing it are not endowed with this prerogative of perpetuity. As the Church expands in certain localities, the increasing needs of the faithful call for the establishment of new centers of Catholic life: dioceses, parishes, and the other subsequent units which are indicative of spiritual and corporate vitality. This development entails the division of church corporations already constituted. Likewise certain unfavorable elements of other kinds may make for the suppression of various church bodies: v.g., the extinction of a parish or a diocese which no longer serves its purpose because of shifting population. Or general apathy may allow an ecclesiastical society, like a confraternity, to lapse into inactivity and even into non-existence over a determined period of time. Such events in the life of the Church could very easily give rise to much misunderstanding and bitterness, were there not well defined rules regulating the disposition of property in all these instances. Besides, such events in the life of the Church might be the occasion for the intrusion of outsiders and the subsequent seizure of what formerly belonged to the Church.

This is not the place to discuss the motives which authorize the dismemberment or the extinction of juridical persons in the Church, nor to comment on the procedure to be followed in individual cases. A summary indication of both these points can be obtained from a perusal of the canons referred to in the footnote.[1] The purpose of the present chapter is to point out briefly the manner in which the Code provides for the distribution of property in such instances, in the light of canons 1500-1501, with particular attention to any phases of the problem which may have special application to the United States.

Article 2. The Division of an Ecclesiastical Corporation

Canon 1500

Diviso territorio personae moralis ecclesiasticae ita ut vel illius pars alii personae morali uniatur, vel distincta persona moralis pro parte dismembrata erigatur, etiam bona communia quae in commodum totius territorii erant destinata, et aes alienum quod pro toto territorio contractum fuerat, ab auctoritate ecclesiastica, cui divisio competat, cum debita proportione ex bono et aequo dividi debent, salvis piorum fundatorum seu oblatorum voluntatibus, iuribus legitime quaesitis, ac legibus particularibus, quibus persona moralis regitur.

The ecclesiastical juridical persons whose division is provided for in this canon are dioceses, vicariates and prefectures apostolic, ecclesiastical provinces, parishes and quasi-parishes, confraternities and other canonically erected associations. In the case of religious communities, the division would be verified in the establishment of new provinces or the modification of provinces already existing.

In the execution of this division there may be two alternatives. Either the portion separated from a previously constituted juridical person is annexed to another church organization, as, for instance, when

[1] For the *division* of an ecclesiastical corporation: cf. canons 215, §1; 248, §2; 252, §1; 255; 260, §1; 494, §1; 1427; 1428. For the *extinction* of such juristic persons: cf. canons 102, §§1, 2; 252; 255; 493; 494, §1; 488, 5°; 498; 674; 699, §§1, 2; 1422; 1494; 1514; 1517; 2292.

part of one diocese or parish is joined with another diocese or parish; or, in the second place, the portion thus separated may be erected into a distinct juristic person. The procedure for the apportionment of property is the same in both cases. The Code requires that there be a division of the common property destined for the welfare of the territory entrusted to the previous legal person, as also the apportionment of the debts already contracted for that same purpose.

This division of assets and liabilities is not necessarily to be made according to the principles of strict justice. It may, as the Code expressly provides, be carried out *ex bono et aequo*. This is to insure an equitable assignment of both advantages and liabilities arising from the division, even though one of the church bodies involved might in strict justice be awarded more property or be assigned a greater portion of the indebtedness. Thus, in keeping with this canon, the bishop might very well *ex bono et aequo,* according to the principles of equity, assign to one of the bodies a larger portion of the common indebtedness and a smaller share of the common assets, if this particular body were destined to have better financial backing because of its more numerous or more affluent membership. In any arrangement adopted, the mother church must always be assured of sufficient income for honorable and fitting maintenance. The text of the canon states explicitly that the ecclesiastical authority which makes this apportionment of assets and liabilities is the Superior competent to authorize the division. According to circumstances determined for individual cases, this will be either the local Ordinary or the Holy See.

The property which is to be equitably distributed is that which remains, *even after the division,* destined for the welfare of the entire territory formerly existing prior to the dismemberment. For example, if a trust fund had been established to care for the Catholic poor of a county or town, or district once served by one parish, a new parish erected within the same county, town, or district will be entitled to a fair share of this fund for its own poor. The new parish, however, would have no claim on any donations or legacies which had been made specifically in favor of the mother church even when it was the only church in the territory.

The same principle applies to the distribution of debts already contracted. The new juristic person arising from dismemberment will be proportionately liable for the satisfaction of debts incurred by the previous organization for the welfare of the entire territory. But it will not be bound, for example, to pay a share of the debt burdening the mother church alone, since this debt is no longer in favor of the whole territory; the mother church no longer has any juridical connection with this new legal person coming from the division. On the same principle the new ecclesiastical organization arising from dismemberment will be exclusively responsible for its own debts, with no claim for these against the mother church.

At the same time canon 1500 provides some restrictions in the regulations just enunciated. First of all, the pious wishes of founders or donors are to be religiously respected. Hence, for example, if the express wish of the benefactor stipulates that his donation or foundation is for the benefit of a determined and specifically named school or hospital, income from this fund cannot be diverted to a new organization erected within this same territory, even though it have the same general end of charity or beneficence. This provision is a direct application of canon 1493.

Secondly, all vested rights already acquired are to be scrupulously honored. As examples of these vested rights, Vromant mentions the cases in which a benefactor would have reserved to himself the usufruct of his foundation for a period not yet expired, or in which a division would take place at the expiration of one year of a legally contracted nine-year lease. The lessee would have a vested right to the full term of his lease, even though his lease deals with property which should normally be divided in favor of the new ecclesiastical juristic person.[2]

Lastly, the particular provisions of the charter or constitutions of the organization involved in the division are to be respected. These have the character of particular or local laws which the Code wishes to be honored in the circumstances, since they provide special rulings for particular needs.

It is hardly necessary to remark that the prescriptions of this canon envisage only the legitimate division of an ecclesiastical legal person. No provision is or can be made in church law for the unlawful division which would result from schism. By the very fact of their separation from the body of the Church the schismatics lose all claim to any share in or benefit from ecclesiastical property. Generally considered, only dis-

2 *De Bonis Ecclesiae Temporalibus*, n. 52, 4, b.

putes arising from a schismatical division within the Church will be brought to the civil courts for adjudication. The verdicts in such cases will be along the lines of the principles of civil law already explained in Chapter IV, on *The Relationship of Canon Law with Civil Law.*

The norm followed in such cases will usually be the charter or constitution of the organization as it existed before the division:

> The title to the church property of a divided corporation is in that part of it which is acting in harmony with its own laws, and the ecclesiastical laws, usages, customs and principles, which were accepted among them before the dispute began, are the standard for determining which party is right.[3]

In 1902 the State of New York adopted an amendment to its Constitution, which dealt specifically with the legal status of the property of Roman Catholic church corporations in case of division by the competent Superiors of the Church. The text of this amendment is as follows:

> *Division of Roman Catholic Parish; Disposition of Property* — Wherever a Roman Catholic parish has been heretofore or shall hereafter be duly divided by the Roman Catholic bishop having jurisdiction over said parish, and the original Roman Catholic church corporation is given one part of the old parish, and a new or second Roman Catholic church corporation is given the remaining part of the old parish, and it further appears that by reason of the said division the original Roman Catholic Church corporation holds title to real property situate within the part of the old parish that was given to the new or second Roman Catholic church corporation, then the said Roman Catholic bishop or his successor shall have the right and power, of himself, independently of any action or consent on the part of the trustees of the original Roman

[3] Zollman, *American Church Law,* §285. The general acceptance of this sound principle which safeguards the objective rights of the Church is evidenced by the number of decisions which it has motivated in the courts. Cf., among others, Smith v. Pedigo, 145, Ind., 361, 375; 33 N.E., 777; 44 N.E., 363; 19 L.R.A., 433; 32 L.R.A., 838; True Reformed Dutch Church v. Iserman, 64 N.J., Law, 506; 45 Atl. 771; Roshi's Appeal, 69 Pa. (19 P. F. Smith), 462; 8 Am. Rep., 275; Appeal of First M.E. Church of Scranton, 16 W.N.C., 245 Pa.; see Barton v. Fitzgerald, 65 So., 390 (Ala.); Philomath College v. Wyatt, 27 Ore., 390; Whitelick Quarterly Meeting v. Whitelick Quarterly Meeting, 89 Ind., 136.

> Catholic church corporation to transfer the title of the said real property, with or without valuable consideration, to the said new or second Roman Catholic church corporation. Said transfer shall be made by the said Roman Catholic bishop or his successor after having complied with the requirements of the code of civil procedure in the same manner as the trustees of any religious corporation are compelled to do before making a transfer of church property. If a valuable consideration is paid for the transfer the same shall be received by the said Roman Catholic bishop or his successor, and distributed between the said original Roman Catholic church corporation and the new or second Roman Catholic church corporation, in such proportions as in the discretion of the said bishop or his successor may seem proper.[4]

Many court decisions dealing with disputed ownership of property in case of division of church corporations have been very noticeably along the lines of what is prescribed in the present canon. Thus, for example, a Pennsylvania court has decided that where a sum of money had been bequeathed to a parish (Lutheran) in a certain town at a time when it was the only parish, and another parish was subsequently erected, the old church continued vested with the title to the property and all its funds.[5] This decision harmonizes with the prescriptions of canon 1500. After the division, the property and other goods of the previous parish were no longer destined for the well-being and sipiritual upkeep of the entire territory. In most cases involving mere internal disputes as to division, as has been already pointed out, the courts will decide, as a Connecticut court has done, that in case of division in a denomination by the secession of some members from the mother church, the legislature has no authority to divide its funds and give a part to the seceding division of the corporation.[6] Likewise, on the matter of debts, a change effected in the personal constitution of a church by a

4 The text of this amendment is taken from the *AER*, XLV (1911), 597. It will be remembered that the S. Congregation of the Council, in its decree of 1911, recommended that church property in the United States be incorporated with the precautions and safeguards guaranteed by the State of New York. This text shows an added reason for this preference of the Holy See. With slight variations these provisions are now in force in practically all the states.

5 App. v. Lutheran, 6 Pa. St., 201.

6 Second v. First, 23 Conn., 255.

division of its members will not affect obligations incurred prior to the division.[7]

Article 3. The Extinction of Ecclesiastical Corporations

Canon 1501

Exstincta persona morali ecclesiastica, eius bona fiunt personae moralis ecclesiasticae immediate superioris, salvis semper fundatorum seu oblatorum voluntatibus, iuribus legitime quaesitis atque legibus particularibus, quibus persona moralis regatur.

As in canon 1500, a consideration of the place of individual corporations in the life of the Church furnishes the foundation for a correct understanding of the prescriptions of canon 1501. In the event that an ecclesiastical juristic person automatically becomes extinct with the lapse of time, or is suppressed by competent authority, its property is thereby incorporated into the patrimony of the juridical person immediately above it in the order of hierarchical precedence. The property does not revert to the person, physical or juridical, who is competent to effect the suppression or to declare it already accomplished. The Code is explicit on this point.

In the light of the general juridical principles of church government, the *persona moralis ecclesiastica immediate superior* can be determined as follows for individual cases:

a) the *Holy See* for the suppression of an ecclesiastical province, of a diocese, of a vicariate or of a prefecture apostolic;[8]

b) the *Holy See* also usually reserves to itself the disposition of property in case of the extinction of a Pontifical National College in Rome;[9]

[7] West v. Ottesen, 80 Wis., 62; 49 N.W., 24.

[8] An ecclesiastical province will have no right to the property of a suppressed diocese since it is not the Superior of the diocese in the sense of having real jurisdiction over it.

[9] The following provision is found in the Apostolic Constitution whereby Pope Pius XI erected the Pontifical College for the Netherlands: "VII. Si quavis ex causa Pontificium Collegium Neerlandicum Pianum esse desierit, omnes eius possessiones, res mobiles, se moventes et quae moveri non possunt, pecuniae, reditus aliaque huiusmodi ad Sanctam Sedem devolventur, ut ab eadem, quantum fieri poterit, ad alumnos e Neerlandiae diocesibus ecclesiasticis altioris ordinis disciplinis instituendos erogentur."—*AAS*, XXIII (1931), 23.

c) the *diocese* in case of the suppression of a parish, or of a non-collegiate juridical person, as a hospital, orphanage, etc.;

d) the *vicariate* or *prefecture apostolic,* for the suppression of a quasi-parish or of a non-collegiate ecclesiastical institute existing in the territory, as in c);

e) the *religious province* if an individual house of an Institute of pontifical right is closed;

f) the *religious Institute,* if one of its provinces is suppressed; the property will be disposed of in accordance with the provisions of its particular constitutions;

g) the *Holy See* in case a religious Institute, even if it be only of diocesan approval, or in case a community without vows, ceases to exist by action of legitimate authority;[10]

h) if a pious association of the faithful, for instance, a confraternity, is suppressed, the more probable opinion assigns the property of the association to the *diocese,* vicariate or prefecture apostolic, rather than to the parish or quasi-parish in which it was erected. The same principle can be invoked as in a). The parish or quasi-parish is not a genuine *persona moralis ecclesiastica immediate superior,* in the sense of this present canon, since it lacks *jurisdiction* over the confraternity which is suppressed."[11]

The Code qualifies the provisions of canon 1501 with the same restrictions as those found in the preceding canon. The wishes of the founders or donors of the property of an extinct church organization are to be strictly complied with. Consequently, if a donation had been made with the specific clause that in case the corporation ever ceased to exist the money or property should revert to the donor or his heirs or be transmitted to some other pious ecclesiastical work, this prescription would take precedence over the regulations of canon 1501. The

10 A religious Institute on the verge of extinction, for whatever reason, may not turn over its common property even to another Institute having the same founder, without papal approval.

11 Cf. Vermeersch-Creusen, *Epitome,* II, n. 822, III. De Meester (*Compendium Iuris Canonici et Iuris Canonico-Civilis,* Lib. III, pars VI, n. 1451), also supports this opinion.

ecclesiastical corporation receiving the property of an extinct juridical person within the Church would be bound to fulfil all the obligations attached thereto, such as acquitting the obligations of Masses, allowing leases already made to run their full time, etc. This would prevent violations of the vested rights already acquired by third parties. The Code also leaves intact the legitimate constitutions and regulations proper to particular organizations, in so far as they determine the disposition of property in case of dissolution. Since these particular laws of the extinct legal person were approved by competent ecclesiastical authority, they cannot be left at the mercy of subsequent individual Superiors.

CONCLUSIONS

A study of alienation in the light of canonical tradition brings out the following general conclusions:

1) The *Canon Law* on alienation applies *only* to those contracts the observance of which can be urged before the *civil* law.

2) Alienation in the strict sense of the term is verified only in operations which affect the *stable capital* of an ecclesiastical juristic person.

3) Alienation in the broad sense, or contracts *quibus conditio Ecclesiae peior fieri possit* (canon 1533), are *only* those which, supported by juridical sanction, expose the Church to the proximate danger of losing all or part of her fixed assets or patrimony.

4) Likewise, transactions involving the transfer (sale, exchange, donation, or loan for consumption), or the diminution (rental, leasing, loans for use) of property rights, will fall within the prescriptions of Canon Law only in so far as they affect the status of the church corporation's *permanent assets.*

5) The contracting of debts or the allowing of mortgages is regulated by Canon Law in the degree in which these financial operations jeopardize the security of an ecclesiastical organization's stable capital.

6) In the light of these general conclusions, many of the financial transactions commonly carried on in the United States do not come under the law as it actually stands, because, a) either they do not touch upon the field of stable capital, or b) they do not imperil the security of the church corporation before the civil courts.

BIBLIOGRAPHY

Sources

Acta Apostolicae Sedis, Romae, 1909.

Acta et Decreta Concilii Provincialis Portlandensis in Oregon IV; Portland, 1932.

Acta Sanctae Sedis, 41 vols., Romae, 1865-1908.

Codex Iuris Canonici, Pii X Pontificis Maximi iussu digestus, Benedicti Papae XV auctoritate promulgatus, Romae, 1918.

Codicis Iuris Canonici Fontes, cura E.mi Petri Card. Gasparri et E.mi Iustiniani Card. Serédi editi, 9 vols., Romae, 1922-1940.

Collectanea in usum Secretariae Sacrae Congregationis Episcoporum et Regularium, ed. Bizzarri, Romae, 1885.

Collectanea Sacrae Congregationis de Propaganda Fide, 2 vols. Romae, 1907.

Concilia Provincialia Baltimori habita ab anno 1829 usque ad annum 1849, Baltimore, 1853.

Concilii Plenarii Baltimorensis II Acta et Decreta, Baltimorae, 1868.

Concilii Plenarii Baltimorensis III Acta et Decreta, Baltimorae, 1886.

Concilii Provincialis Neo-Eboracensis IV Acta et Decreta, New York, 1886.

Concilium Provinciale Neo-Eboracense III anno 1861 celebratum, Neo-Eboraci, 1862.

Constitutiones Diocesanae Neo-Eboracenses, New York, 1890.

Corpus Iuris Canonici, editio Lipsiensis secunda post Aemilii Richteri curas . . . instruxit Aemilius Friedberg, 2 vols., Lipsiae, 1922.

Corpus Iuris Civilis, vol. I, *Institutiones*—recognovit P. Krueger; vol. II, *Codex Iustinianus*—recognovit et retractavit P. Krueger; vol. III, *Novellae Constitutiones*—R. Schoell; opus Schoelli morte interceptum absolvit G. Kroll, Berolini, 1928-1929.

Decreta Quatuor Conciliorum Provincialium Cincinnatensium, Cincinnati, 1886.

Encyclical Letter to the Bishops of North America, Pius IX, January 21, 1861.

Letter to Religious Superiors, Apostolic Delegate to the United States, November 13, 1936.

Litterae Apostolicae, "Quo longius," Leo XII, August 16, 1828.

Litterae Apostolicae, "Non sine magno," Pius VII, August 24, 1822.

Mansi, *Sacrorum Conciliorum Nova et Amplissima Collectio;* Venice, 1727.

Statuta Dioecesis Sanctae Mariae (Sault Ste. Marie), Cincinnati, 1856.

Synodus Cincinnatensis III, Cincinnati, 1898.

Synodus Dioecesana Chicagiensis I, Chicago, 1887.

Synodus Dioecesana Denveriensis IV, Las Vegas, 1907.

Synodus Grandormensis I, Big Rapids, 1903.

Synodus Dioecesana Neo-Eboracensis V, New York, 1886.

Synodus Dioecesana Trentonensis II, Trenton, 1897.

Synodus Dioecesana Wayne Castrensis, Notre Dame, Indiana, 1903.

Synodus Dioecesana Wayne Castrensis, 1926.

Thesaurus Resolutionum Sacrae Congregationis Concilii, 167 vols., Romae, 1718-1908.

Authors

Aichner, *Compendium Juris Canonici*, Brixinae, 1887.

American Law Institute, *Restatement of the Law on Contracts* (Four pamphlets), St. Paul, 1933.

André, Abbé, *Cours Alphabétique et Méthodique de Droit Canon*, 2 vols., Paris, 1844.

d'Annibale, J., *Summula Theologiae Moralis*, 5 ed., Romae, 1908.

Ayrinhac, H. A., *Administrative Legislation in the New Code of Canon Law*, New York, 1930.

(Bachofen) Charles Augustine, O.S.B., *A Commentary on the New Code of Canon Law*, 8 vols., St. Louis, 1918-1921.

(Bachofen), Charles Augustine, O.S.B., *The Canonical and Civil Status of Catholic Parishes in the U.S.A.*, St. Louis, B. Herder Book Co., 1926.

Barbosa, Aug., *Jus Ecclesiasticum Universum*, Lugduni, 1660.

Bargilliat, M., *Praelectiones Juris Canonici*, ed. 25, Parisiis, 1909.

Barrett, J., *A Comparative Study of the Councils of Baltimore and the Code of Canon Law*, Washington, 1932.

Bartlett, C., *The Tenure of Parochial Property in the United States of America*, Washington, 1926.

Bastien, O.S.B., Dom Pierre, *Directoire Canonique*, 4 ed., Paris, Bloud et Gay, 1933.

Bastien, O.S.B., Dom Pierre, *Les Censures qui atteignent la liquidation des biens ecclésiastiques et des Congrégations religieuses*, Collection "Science et Religion," Paris, Bloud.

Baumgartner, Reinhardus, *Conclusiones ex V Libris Decretalium*, Romae, 1759.

Blat, A., *Commentarium Textus Codicis Iuris Canonici*, 5 vols., Romae, 1921-1927.

Bogert, G. G., *The Law of Trusts and Trustees*, 7 vols., St. Paul, 1935.

Bouix, *De Jure Regularium*, 2 vols., Paris, 1857.

Bouscaren, S. J., T. Lincoln, *The Canon Law Digest*, 2 vols., (1934-1937) with supplements for 1938; Bruce Publishing Co., Milwaukee, 1938.

Brown, B. *The Canonical Juristic Personality with Special Reference to its Status in the United States of America*, Washington, 1927.

Bucceroni, J. *Institutiones Theologiae Moralis*, 2 ed., Romae, 1893.

Cance, A., *Le Code de Droit Canonique*, 2 ed., 3 vols., Paris, 1929.

Chelodi, J., *Ius de Personis*, 2 ed., Tridenti, 1927.

Cicognani, A. G., *Canon Law*, Philadelphia, 1934.

Claeys-Bouaert, Simenon, *Manuale Iuris Canonici*, 2 ed., 3 vols., Wattern, 1926.

Cleary, Joseph F., *Canonical Limitations on the Alienation of Church Property*, Washington, 1936.

Cocchi, G., *Commentarium in Codicem Iuris Canonici*, 8 vols., Taurini, 1925-1930.

Coronata, Matthaeus a Conte, *Institutiones Iuris Canonici*, 5 vols., Taurini, Marietti, 1934.

Coronata, Matthaeus a Conte, *Compendium Iuris Canonici*, 2 vols., Taurini, 1937-1938.

De Lugo, Card. *Responsorum Moralium Libri VI., Opera Omnia*, ed. Vivès, vol. VIII.

De Meester, A., *Juris Canonici et Juris Canonico-Civilis Compendium*, 3 vols. in 4, Brugis, 1921-1928.

De Varceno, Fr. Gabriel, *Compendium Theologiae Moralis*, Augustae Taurinorum, 1889.

Devoti, J., *Ius Canonicum Universum*, 2 vols., Romae, 1837.

Dictionnaire de Droit Canonique, fasc. I-XV, 1928-1939, Paris.

Dignan, *History of Legal Incorporation of Catholic Church Property in the United States* (1784-1932), Washington, 1933.

Doheny, William J., C.S.C., *Church Property: Modes of Acquisition*, Washington, 1927.

Doheny, William J., C.S.C., *Practical Problems of Church Finance*, Milwaukee, Bruce Publishing Co., 1941.

Elbel, Benjamin, *Theologia Moralis Decalogalis*, Augustae Vindelicorum, 1743.

Fagnanus, Prosper, *Commentaria in quinque Libros Decretalium*, 4 vols., Venetiis, 1696.

Fanfani, Ludovicus, O.P., *De Iure Religiosorum*, Taurini, 1920.

Farricelli, Alessandro Rafaele, *Raccolta di opuscoli di giurisprudenza canonica e civile*, Roma, 1867.

Ferraris, L., *Bibliotheca Canonica, Juridica, Moralis, Theologica*, ed. novissima, 9 vols., Romae, 1885-1899.

Génicot-Salzmans, *Institutiones Theologiae Moralis*, 11 ed., 2 vols., Bruxellis, 1927.

Giraldi, Ubaldo, *Expositio Juris Pontificii*, Romae, 1829.

Grandclaude, E., *Jus Canonicum*, 3 vols., Parisiis, 1882.

Gudelinus, *De Jure Novissimo Libri Sex Commentariorum*, Florentiae, 1839.

Guilday, Peter K., *The National Pastorals of the American Hierarchy*, 1792-1919, N.C.W.C., Washington, 1923.

Guilday, Peter K., *The Life and Times of John Carroll,* New York, Encyclopedia Press, 1922.

Hannan, Jerome D., *The Canon Law of Wills;* Washington, 1934.

Hawks, *Contribution to the Ecclesiastical History of the United States.*

Hughes, S.J., Thomas, *History of the Society of Jesus in North America, Colonial and Federal,* 2 vols., with documents, New York, 1908.

Ives, Moss J., *The Ark and the Dove, New York,* Longmans, Green Co., 1936.

Kirlin, J. L., *Catholicity in Philadelphia,* 1909.

Lambing, A. A., *History of the Catholic Church in the Dioceses of Pittsburgh and Allegheny,* New York, 1880.

Laurentius, *Institutiones Juris Ecclesiastici,* Friburgi Brisgoviae, 1903.

Leage, R. W., *Roman Private Law,* 2 ed., London, 1930.

Manfried, Franciscus L. M., *Juris Canonici Universi Compendium,* Paris, 1863.

McManus, James Edward, C.SS.R., *The Administration of Temporal Goods in Religious Institutes,* Washington, 1937.

Meehan, A., *Compendium Juris Canonici,* Roffae, 1891.

Memorial Volume, *A History of the Third Plenary Council of Baltimore,* Baltimore, 1885.

Munerati, D. M., *Juris Ecclesiastici Publici et Privati Elementa,* Romae, 1926.

Navarrete, *Coleccion de Viages y Descubrimientos,* Madrid, 1829.

Navarrus, *Opera Omnia,* 6 vols., Venetiis, 1618.

Novarius, Joannes Antonius, *De Alienatione Rerum Regularium Prohibita,* in the "Summa Bullarum."

Oesterle, *Praelectiones Juris Canonici,* Romae, 1931.

Ojetti, B., *Commentarium in Codicem Juris Canonici,* 4 vols., Romae, 1927-1930.

Ojetti, B., *Synopsis Rerum Moralium et Juris Pontificii,* 3 vols., Romae, 1909.

Pallottini, *Collectio Resolutionum Sacrae Congregationis Concilii,* 17 vols., Romae, 1868.

Panormitanus, Abbas (Nicholaus de Tudescis), *Commentaria in quinque Libros Decretalium,* 8 vols., Venetiis, 1588.

Papi, Hector, S.J., *The Government of Religious Communities,* New York, 1919.

Pastoral Letter, The Second Plenary Council of Baltimore.

Peregrinus, *Compendium Privilegiorum Clericorum Regularium,* verb. "Alienatio."

Perry, *Papers Relating to the Church in Pennsylvania.*

Petra, Vincentius Card., *Commentaria ad Constitutiones Apostolicas,* Venetiis, 1729.

Pirhing, Henricus, *Jus Canonicum in quinque Libros Decretalium*, 4 vols., Venetiis, 1630.

Pirhing, Henricus, *SS. Canonum Doctrina*, Romae, 1849.

Pistocchi, M., *De Bonis Ecclesiae Temporalibus*, Taurini, 1932.

Pruemmer, O.P., *Manuale Iuris Canonici*, 5 ed. Friburgi-Brisgoviae, 1927.

Raus, J. B., *Institutiones Canonicae*, Parisiis, 1923.

Redoano, G., *De Alienationibus Rerum Ecclesiasticarum*, Placentiae, 1589.

Reiffenstuel, A., *Jus Canonicum Universum*, 7 vols. Venetiis, 1735.

Robinson, W., *Elementary Law*, Boston, 1910.

Rood, John R., *Wills*, Chicago, 1904.

Sanguineti, *Institutiones Juris Ecclesiastici Privati*, Romae, 1884.

Santi, F., *Praelectiones Juris Canonici*, 4 ed., 5 vols., Ratisbonae, 1886.

Scanlan, Charles U., *The Clergyman's Handbook of Law*, New York, 1909.

Scharf, Thomas J., *History of Maryland*, Baltimore, 1879.

Schmalzgrueber, F., *Jus Ecclesiasticum Universum*, 12 vols., Ingolstadii, 1728.

Scott, *The Civil Law*, Translation of the *Corpus Juris Civilis* of Justinian, 17 vols., Cincinnati, 1932.

Sebastianelli, Gulielmus, *Praelectiones Juris Canonici*, Romae, 1905.

Sédillot, *Le Drame des Monnaies*, Paris, 1937-1938.

Shea, John Gilmary, *The Catholic Church in Colonial Days*, New York, 1886.

Shea, John Gilmary, *Life and Times of the Most Reverend John Carroll*, New York, 1888.

Shea, John Gilmary, *History of the Catholic Church in the United States*, 4 vols., New York, 1886-1892.

Sherman, C. P., *Roman Law in the Modern World*, 3 ed., 3 vols., New Haven, 1922.

Sipos, Stephanus, *Enchiridion Iuris Canonici*, Pecs, 1926.

Smith, S. B., *Elements of Ecclesiastical Law*, 7 ed., 3 vols., New York, 1882.

Smith, S. B., *Notes on the Second Plenary Council of Baltimore*, New York, 1874.

Spalding, J. L., *The Life of the Most Rev. M. J. Spalding, D.D.*, New York, 1873.

Stutz, U., *Der Geist des Codex Iuris Canonici*, Stuttgart, 1918.

Suarez, *Defensio Fidei Catholicae Adversus Anglicanae Sectae Errores*, in vol. XXIV of *Opera Omnia*, ed. Vivès, Paris, 1869.

Suarez, *De Religione*, *ibi.*, vol. XV.

Thomassinus L. *Vetus et nova Ecclesiae Disciplina circa Beneficia et Beneficiarios*, 10 vols., Moguntini, 1786-1787.

Torricelli, J. D., *De Rebus Ecclesiae non Alienandis, ex sententiis Sacrae Romanae Rotae Tractatus*, Ferrariae, 1674.

Trombetta, Aloisius, *Praxeos Regulae circa Contractus Rerum Ecclesiasticarum.*

Van Espen, Zegerus Bernardus, *Jus Ecclesiasticum Universum,* Neapoli, 1766.

Vecchiotti, S., *Institutiones Canonicae,* 3 vols., Taurini, 1875.

Vermeersch, S., *De Religiosis Institutis ac Personis,* Brugis, 1907.

Vermeersch, A.,-Creusen, J., *Epitome Iuris Canonici,* 6 ed., 3 vols., Mechlinii, 1937.

Vromant, G., *De Bonis Ecclesiae Temporalibus,* Lovanii, 1934.

Vromant, G., *De Fidelium Associationibus,* Lovanii, 1932.

Washburn, Emory, *A Treatise on the American Law of Real Property,* 6 ed., 3 vols., Boston, 1902.

Waterman, T. W., *A Treatise on the Law of Corporations,* 2 vols., New York, 1888.

Wernz, F. X., *Ius Decretalium,* 3 vols., ed. 2, Romae, 1906-1908.

Wernz-Vidal, *Ius Canonicum,* 7 vols. in 8, Romae, 1923-1928.

Williston, Samuel, *The Law of Contracts,* 4 vols., New York, 1920.

Woerner, J. G., *American Law of Administration,* 2 ed., Boston, 1899.

Woywood, Stanislaus, O.F.M., *A Practical Commentary on the Code of Canon Law,* New York, Jos. F. Wagner Inc., 1925.

Zallinger, J. A., *Institutiones Juris Ecclesiastici,* 5 vols. Romae, 1823,

Zitelli, Z. *Apparatus Juris Ecclesiastici,* Romae, 1886.

Zollmann, Carl, *American Church Law,* St. Paul, West Publishing Co., 1933.

Periodicals

American Ecclesiastical Review (AER), Philadelphia, 1889-

Ami du Clergé, Langres, 1897-

Analecta Ecclesiastica, 1893-1911.

Apollinaris, Romae, 1928-

Catholic Historical Review, Washington, 1915-

Commentarium pro Religiosis (CpRM), Romae, 1920-

Ephemerides Theologicae Lovanienses, Lovanii, 1924-

Homiletic and Pastoral Review, The, New York, 1900-

Il Monitore Ecclesiastico, Roma, 1879-

Irish Ecclesiastical Record, Dublin, 1864-

Jurist, The, Washington, 1941-

Jus Pontificium, Romae, 1921-

Le Canoniste Contemporain, Paris, 1878-1926.

Nouvelle Revue Théologique, Louvain, 1869-

Periodica de re canonica et morali, Brugis, 1907; ab anno 1927: *Periodica de re canonica, morali, liturgica.*

Articles

Doheny, W. J., C.S.C., "Church Finance and Problems of Alienation," *The Jurist,* I (1941), 97-107.

Ellis, Adam, S.J., "Triginta millia libellarum seu francorum," *Periodica,* XXVII (1938), 348.

Guilday, Peter K., "The Appointment of Father John Carroll as Prefect Apostolic of the Church in the New Republic," *Catholic Historical Review,* VI (1921), 204.

Larraona, Arcadius, "Commentarium Codicis," *Commentarium pro Religiosis,* XIII (1932), 184-195, 353-362.

McCann, Sr. Mary Agnes, "The Most Reverend John Baptist Purcell," *Catholic Historical Review,* VI (1921), 172.

Meehan, A. B., "The Contracting of Debts by Religious," *American Ecclesiastical Review,* LIII (1915), 669.

White, Robert J., "Certain Aspects of the Legal Status of the Church in the United States," *The Jurist,* I (1941), 20.

ALPHABETICAL INDEX

BIOGRAPHICAL NOTE

Edward Louis Heston was born at Ravenna, Ohio, September 9, 1907. His primary education was received at St. Joseph's Parochial School, South Bend, Indiana. From there he entered Holy Cross Seminary, Notre Dame, Indiana, in 1921, and after completing his high school was admitted to the Novitiate of the Congregation of Holy Cross in 1925, and to temporary profession the following year. In 1928, after two years at Moreau Seminary Seminary, Notre Dame, Indiana, he was assigned to continue his studies in Rome. He obtained the degree of Doctor of Philosophy at the Pontifical Gregorian University in 1931. In 1936 he returned to the United States and for two years taught philosophy at Moreau Seminary, Notre Dame, and religion at Dujarié Institute. In 1938, on the publication of his dissertation entitled *The Spiritual Life and the Rôle of the Holy Ghost in the Sanctification of the Soul, as Expressed in the works of Didymus of Alexandria,* he was declared a Doctor of Sacred Theology by the Pontifical Gregorian University. That same year he returned to Rome as Assistant to the Congregation's Procurator General to the Holy See, and Assistant Superior of Holy Cross International College. At the same time he enrolled in the Faculty of Canon Law at the Pontifical Gregorian University, and after being awarded the degree of Bachelor in Canon Law in 1939, he received the Licentiate in Canon Law in 1940. In the summer of 1940 he returned to the United States because of the international situation, and was admitted to the School of Canon Law at the Catholic University of America in the fall of that same year.

CANON LAW STUDIES

1. Freriks, Rev. Celestine A., C.PP.S., J.C.D., Religious Congregations in Their External Relations, 121 pp., 1916.
2. Galliher, Rev. Daniel M., O.P., J.C.D., Canonical Elections, 117 pp., 1917.
3. Borkowski, Rev. Aurelius L., O.F.M., J.C.D., De Confraternitatibus Ecclesiasticis, 136 pp., 1918.
4. Castillo, Rev. Cayo, J.C.D., Disertacion Historico-Canonica sobre la Potestad del Cabildo en Sede Vacante o Impedida del Vicario Capitular, 99 pp., 1919 (1918).
5. Kukelbeck, Rev. William J., S.T.B., J.C.D., The Sacred Penitentiaria and Its Relation to Faculties of Ordinaries and Priests, 129 pp. 1918.
6. Petrovits, Rev. Joseph, J.C., S.T.D., J.C.D., The New Church Law on Matrimony, X-461 pp., 1919.
7. Hickey, Rev. John J., S.T.B., J.C.D., Irregularities and Simple Impediments in the New Code of Canon Law, 100 pp., 1920.
8. Klekotka, Rev. Peter J., S.T.B., J.C.D., Diocesan Consultors, 179 pp., 1920.
9. Wanenmacher, Rev. Francis, J.C.D., The Evidence in Ecclesiastical Procedure Affecting the Marriage Bond, 1920 (Printed 1935).
10. Golden, Rev. Henry Francis, J.C.D., Parochial Benefices in the New Code, IV-119 pp., 1921 (Printed 1925).
11. Koudelka, Rev. Charles J., J.C.D., Pastors, Their Rights and Duties According to the New Code of Canon Law, 211 pp., 1921.
12. Melo, Rev. Antonius, O.F.M., J.C.D., De Exemptione Regularium, X-188 pp., 1921.
13. Schaaf, Rev. Valentine Theodore, O.F.M., S.T.B., J.C.D., The Cloister, X-180 pp., 1921.
14. Burke, Rev. Thomas Joseph, S.T.D., J.C.D., Competence in Ecclesiastical Tribunals, IV-117 pp., 1922.
15. Leech, Rev. George Leo, J.C.D., A Comparative Study of the Constitution "Apostolicae Sedis" and the "Codex Juris Canonici," 179 pp., 1922.
16. Motry, Rev. Hubert Louis, S.T.D., J.C.D., Diocesan Faculties According to the Code of Canon Law, II-167 pp., 1922.
17. Murphy, Rev. George Lawrence, J.C.D., Delinquencies and Penalties in the Administration and the Reception of the Sacraments, IV-121 pp., 1923.
18. O'Reilly, Rev. John Anthony, S.T.B., J.C.D., Ecclesiastical Sepulture in the New Code of Canon Law, II-129 pp., 1923.

19. MICHALICKA, REV. WENCESLAS CYRIL, O.S.B., J.C.D., Judicial Procedure in Dismissal of Clerical Exempt Religious, 107 pp., 1923.
20. DARGIN, REV. EDWARD VINCENT, S.T.B. J.C.D., Reserved Cases According to the Code of Canon Law, IV-103 pp., 1924.
21. GODFREY, REV. JOHN A., S.T.B., J.C.D., The Right of Patronage According to the Code of Canon Law, 153 pp., 1924.
22. HAGEDORN, REV. FRANCIS EDWARD, J.C.D., General Legislation on Indulgences, II-154 pp., 1924.
23. KING, REV. JAMES IGNATIUS, J.C.D., The Administration of the Sacraments to Dying Non-Catholics, V-141 pp., 1924.
24. WINSLOW, REV. FRANCIS JOSEPH, M.M., J.C.D., Vicars and Prefects Apostolic, IV-149 pp., 1924.
25. CORREA, REV. JOSE SERVELION, S.T.L., J.C.D., La Potestad Legislativa de la Iglesia Catolica, IV-127 pp., 1925.
26. DUGAN, REV. HENRY FRANCIS, A.M., J.C.D., The Judiciary Department of the Diocesan Curia, 87 pp., 1925.
27. KELLER, REV. CHARLES FREDERICK, S.T.B., J.C.D., Mass Stipends, 167 pp., 1925.
28. PASCHANG, REV. JOHN LINUS, J.C.D., The Sacraments According to the Code of Canon Law, 129 pp., 1925.
29. POINTEK, REV. CYRILLUS, O.F.M., S.T.B., J.C.D., De Indulto Exclaustrationis necnon Saecularizationis, XIII-289 pp., 1925.
30. KEARNEY, REV. RICHARD JOSEPH, S.T.B., J.C.D., Sponsors at Baptism According to the Code of Canon Law, IV-127 pp., 1925.
31. BARTLETT, REV. CHESTER JOSEPH, A.M., LL.B., J.C.D., The Tenure of Parochial Property in the United States of America, V-108 pp., 1926.
32. KILKER, REV. ADRIAN JEROME, J.C.D., Extreme Unction, V-425 pp., 1926.
33. MCCORMICK, REV. ROBERT EMMETT, J.C.D., Confessors of Religious, VIII-266 pp., 1926.
34. MILLER, REV. NEWTON THOMAS, J.C.D., Founded Masses According to the Code of Canon Law, VII-93 pp., 1926.
35. ROELKER, REV. EDWARD G., S.T.D., J.C.D., Principles of Privilege According to the Code of Canon Law, XI-166 pp., 1926.
36. BAKALARCZYK, REV. RICHARDUS, M.I.C., J.U.D., De Novitiatu, VIII-208 pp., 1927.
37. PIZZUTI, REV. LAWRENCE, O.F.M., J.U.L., De Parochis Religiosis, 1927. (Not Printed.)
38. BLILEY, REV. NICHOLAS MARTIN, O.S.B., J.C.D., Altars According to the Code of Canon Law, XIX-132 pp., 1927.
39. BROWN MR. BRENDAN FRANCIS, A.B., LL.M., J.U.D., The Canonical Juristic Personality with Special Reference to its Status in the United States of America, V-212 pp., 1927.

40. CAVANAUGH, REV. WILLIAM THOMAS, C.P., J.U.D., The Reservation of the Blessed Sacrament, VIII-101 pp., 1927.

41. DOHENY, REV. WILLIAM J., C.S.C., A.B., J.U.D., Church Property: Modes of Acquisition, X-118 pp., 1927.

42. FELDHAUS, REV. ALOYSIUS H., C.PP.S., J.C.D., Oratories, IX-141 pp., 1927.

43. KELLY, REV. JAMES PATRICK, A.B., J.C.D., The Jurisdiction of the Simple Confessor, X-208 pp., 1927.

44. NEUBERGER, REV. NICHOLAS J., J.C.D., Canon 6 or the Relation of the Codex Juris Canonici to the Preceding Legislation, V-95 pp., 1927.

45. O'KEEFE, REV. GERALD MICHAEL, J.C.D., Matrimonial Dispensations, Powers of Bishops, Priests, and Confessors, VIII-232 pp., 1927.

46. QUIGLEY, REV. JOSEPH A. M., A.B., J.C.D., Condemned Societies, 139 pp., 1927.

47. ZAPLOTNIK, REV. JOHANNES LEO, J.C.D., De Vicariis Foraneis, X-142 pp., 1927.

48. DUSKIE, REV. JOHN ALOYSIUS, A.B., J.C.D., The Canonical Status of the Orientals in the United States, VIII-196 pp., 1928.

49. HYLAND, REV. FRANCIS EDWARD, J.C.D., Excommunication, Its Nature, Historical Development and Effects, VIII-181 pp., 1928.

50. REIMANN, REV. GERALD JOSEPH, O.M.C., J.C.D., The Tihrd Order Secular of Saint Francis, 201 pp., 1928.

51. SCHENK, REV. FRANCIS J., J.C.D., The Matrimonial Impediments of Mixed Religion and Disparity of Cult, XVI-318 pp., 1929.

52. COADY, REV. JOHN JOSEPH, S.T.D., J.U.D., A.M., The Appointment of Pastors, VIII-150 pp., 1929.

53. KAY, REV. THOMAS HENRY, J.C.D., Competence in Matrimonial Procedure, VIII-164 pp., 1929.

54. TURNER, REV. SIDNEY JOSEPH, C.P., J.U.D., The Vow of Poverty, XLIX-217 pp., 1929.

55. KEARNEY, REV. RAYMOND A., A.B., S.T.D., J.C.D., The Principles of Delegation, VII-149 pp., 1929.

56. CONRAN, REV. EDWARD JAMES, A.B., J.C.D., The Interdict, V-163 pp., 1930.

57. O'NEILL, REV. WILLIAM H., J.C.D., Papal Rescripts of Favor, VII-218 pp., 1930.

58. BASTNAGEL, REV. CLEMENT VINCENT, J.U.D., The Appointment of Parochial Adjutants and Assistants, XV-257 pp., 1940.

59. FERRY, REV. WILLIAM A., A.B., J.C.D., Stole Fees, V-136 pp., 1930.

60. COSTELLO, REV. JOHN MICHAEL, A.B., J.C.D., Domicile and Quasi-Domicile, VII-201 pp., 1930.

61. KREMER, REV. MICHAEL NICHOLAS, A.B., S.T.B., J.C.D., Church Support in the United States, VI-136 pp., 1930.
62. ANGULO, REV. LUIS, C.M., J.C.D., Legislation de la Iglesia sobre la intencion en la application de la Santa Misa, VII-104 pp., 1931.
63. FREY, REV. WOLFGANG NORBERT, O.S.B., A.B., J.C.D., The Act of Religious Profession, VIII-174 pp., 1931.
64. ROBERTS, REV. JAMES BRENDAN, A.B., J.C.D., The Banns of Marriage, XIV-140 pp., 1931.
65. RYDER, REV. RAYMOND ALOYSIUS, A.B., J.C.D., Simony, IX-151 pp., 1931.
66. CAMPAGNA, REV. ANGELO, PH.D., J.U.D., Il Vicario Generale del Vescovo, VII-205 pp., 1931.
67. COX, REV. JOSEPH GODFREY, A.B., J.C.D., The Administration of Seminaries, VI-124 pp., 1931.
68. GREGORY, REV. DONALD J., J.U.D., The Pauline Privilege, XV-165 pp., 1931.
69. DONOHUE, REV. JOHN F., J.C.D., The Impediment of Crime, VII-110 pp., 1931.
70. DOOLEY, REV. EUGENE A., O.M.I., J.C.D., Church Law on Sacred Relics, IX-143 pp., 1931.
71. ORTH, REV. CLEMENT RAYMOND, O.M.C., J.C.D., The Approbation of Religious Institutes, 171 pp., 1931.
72. PERNICONE, REV. JOSEPH M., A.B., J.C.D., The Ecclesiastical Prohibition of Books, XII-267 pp., 1932.
73. CLINTON, REV. CONNELL, A.B., J.C.D., The Paschal Precept, IX-108 pp., 1932.
74. DONNELLY, REV. FRANCIS B., A.M., S.T.L., J.C.D., The Diocesan Synod, VIII-125 pp., 1932.
75. TORRENTE, REV. CAMILO, C.M.F., J.C.D., Las Processiones Sagradas, V-145 pp., 1932.
76. MURPHY, REV. EDWIN J., C.PP.S., J.C.D., Suspension Ex Informata Conscientia, XI-122 pp., 1932.
77. MACKENZIE, REV. ERIC F., A.M., S.T.L., J.C.D., The Delicit of Heresy in Its Commission, Penalization, Absolution, VII-124 pp., 1932.
78. LYONS, REV. AVITUS E., S.T.B., J.C.D., The Collegiate Tribunal of First Instance, XI-147 pp., 1932.
79. CONNOLLY, REV. THOMAS A., J.C.D., Appeals, XI-195 pp., 1932.
80. SANGMEISTER, REV. JOSEPH V., A.B., J.C.D., Force and Fear as Precluding Matrimonial Consent, V-211 pp., 1932.
81. JAEGER, REV. LEO A., A.B., J.C.D., The Administration of Vacant and Quasi-Vacant Episcopal Sees in the United States, IX-229 pp., 1932.
82. RIMLINGER, REV. HERBERT T., J.C.D., Error Invalidating Matrimonial Consent, VII-79 pp., 1932.

83. BARRETT, REV. JOHN D. M., S.S., J.C.D., A Comparative Study of the Third Plenary Council of Baltimore and the Code, IX-221 pp., 1932.
84. CARBERRY, REV. JOHN J., PH.D., S.T.D., J.C.D., The Juridical Form of Marriage, X-177 pp., 1934.
85. DOLAN, REV. JOHN L., A.B., J.C.D., The Defensor Vinculi, XII-157 pp., 1934.
86. HANNAN, REV. JEROME D., A.M., S.T.D., LL.B., J.C.D., The Canon Law of Wills, IX-517 pp., 1934.
87. LEMIEUX, REV. DELISE A., A.M., J.C.D., The Sentence in Ecclesiastical Procedure, IX-131 pp., 1934.
88. O'ROURKE, REV. JAMES J., A.B., J.C.D., Parish Registers, VII-109 pp., 1934.
89. TIMLIN, REV. BARTHOLOMEW, O.F.M., A.M., J.C.D., Conditional Matrimonial Consent, X-381 pp., 1934.
90. WAHL, REV. FRANCIS X., A.B., J.C.D., The Matrimonial Impediments of Consanguinity and Affinity, VI-125 pp., 1934.
91. WHITE, REV. ROBERT J., A.B., LL.B., S.T.B., J.C.D., Canonical Ante-Nuptial Promises and the Civil Law, VI-152 pp., 1934.
92. HERRARA, REV. ANTONIO PARRA, O.C.D., J.C.D., Legislacion Ecclesiastica sobra el Ayuno y la Abstinencia, XI-191 pp., 1935.
93. KENNEDY, REV. EDWIN J., J.C.D., The Special Matrimonial Process in Cases of Evident Nullity, X-165 pp., 1935.
94. MANNING, REV. JOHN J., A.B., J.C.D., Presumption of Law in Matrimonial Procedure, XI-111 pp., 1935.
95. MOEDER, REV. JOHN M., J.C.D., The Proper Bishop for Ordination and Dimissorial Letters, VII-135 pp., 1935.
96. O'MARA, REV. WILLIAM A., A.B., J.C.D., Canonical Causes for Matrimonial Dispensations, IX-155 pp., 1935.
97. REILLY, REV. PETER, J.C.D., Residence of Pastors, IX-81 pp., 1935.
98. SMITH, REV. MARINER T., O.P., S.T.Lr., J.C.D., The Penal Law for Religious, VII-169 pp., 1935.
99. WHALEN, REV. DONALD W., A.M., J.C.D., The Values of Testimonial Evidence in Matrimonial Procedure,XIII-297 pp., 1935.
100. CLEARY, REV. JOSEPH F., J.C.D., Canonical Limitations on the Alienation of Church Property, VIII-141 pp., 1936.
101. GLYNN, REV. JOHN C., J.C.D., The Promoter of Justice, XX-337 pp., 1936.
102. BRENNAN, REV. JAMES H., S.S., M.A., S.T.B., J.C.D., The Simple Convalidation of Marriage, VI-135 pp., 1937.
103. BRUNINI, REV. JOSEPH BERNARD, J.C.D., The Clerical Obligations of Canons 139 and 142, X-121 pp., 1937.

104. Connor, Rev. Maurice, A.B., J.C.D., The Administrative Removal of Pastors, VIII-159 pp., 1937.

105. Guilfoyle, Rev. Merlin Joseph, J.C.D., Custom, XI-144 pp., 1937.

106. Hughes, Rev. James Austin, A.B., A.M., J.C.D., Witnesses in Criminal Trials of Clerics, IX-140 pp., 1937.

107. Jansen, Rev. Raymond J., A.B., S.T.L., J.C.D., Canonical Provisions for Catechetical Instruction, VII-153 pp., 1937.

108. Kealy, Rev. John James, A.B., J.C.D., The Introductory Libellus in Church Court Procedure, XI-121 pp., 1937.

109. McManus, Rev. James Edward, C.SS.R., J.C.D., The Administration of Temporal Goods in Religious Institutes, XVI-196 pp., 1937.

110. Moriarty, Rev. Eugene James, J.C.D., Oaths in Ecclesiastical Courts, X-115 pp., 1937.

111. Rainer, Rev. Eligius George, C.SS.R., J.C.D., Suspension of Clerics, XVII-249 pp., 1937.

112. Reilly, Rev. Thomas F., C.SS.R., J.C.D., Visitation of Religious, VI-195 pp., 1938.

113. Moriarity, Rev. Francis E., C.SS.R., J.C.D., The Extraordinary Absolution from Censures, XV-334 pp., 1938.

114. Connolly, Rev. Nicholas P., J.C.D., The Canonical Erection of Parishes, X-132 pp., 1938.

115. Donovan, Rev. James Joseph, J.C.D., The Pastor's Obligation in Prenuptial Investigation, XII-322 pp., 1938.

116. Harrigan, Rev. Robert J., M.A., S.T.B., J.C.D., The Radical Sanation of Invalid Marriages, VIII-208 pp., 1938.

117. Boffa, Rev. Conrad Humbert, J.C.D., Canonical Provisions for Catholic Schools, VII-211 pp., 1939.

118. Parsons, Rev. Anscar John, O.M.Cap., J.C.D., Canonical Elections, XII-236 pp., 1939.

119. Reilly, Rev. Edward Michael, A.B., J.C.D., The General Norms of Dispensation, XII-156 pp., 1939.

120. Ryan, Rev. Gerald Aloysius, A.B., J.C.D., Principles of Episcopal Jurisdiction, XII-172 pp., 1939.

121. Burton, Rev. Francis James, C.S.C., A.B., J.C.L., A Commentary on Canon 1125, X-222 pp., 1940.

122. Miaskiewicz, Rev. Francis Sigismund, J.C.L., Supplied Jurisdiction According to Canon 209, XII-340 pp., 1940.

123. Rice, Rev. Patrick William, A.B., J.C.L., Proof of Death in Pre-Nuptial Investigation, VIII-156 pp., 1940.

124. Anglin, Rev. Thomas Francis, M.S., J.C.L., The Eucharistic Fast.

125. Coleman, Rev. John Jerome, J.C.L., The Minister of Confirmation.

126. DOWNS, REV. JOHN EMMANUEL, A.B., J.C.L., The Concept of Immunity.
127. ESSWEIN, REV. ANTHONY ALBERT, J.C.L., Extrajudicial Penal Powers of Ecclesiastical Superiors.
128. FARELL, REV. BENJAMIN FRANCIS, M.A., S.T.L., J.C.L., The Rights and Duties of the Local Ordinary Regarding Congregations of Women Religious of Pontifical Approval.
129. FEENEY, REV. THOMAS JOHN, A.B., S.T.L., J.C.L., Restitutio in Integrum.
130. FINDLAY, REV. STEPHEN WILLIAM, O.S.B., A.B., J.C.L., Canonical Norms Governing the Deposition and Degradation of Clerics.
131. GOODWINE, REV. JOHN, A.B., S.T.L., J.C.L., The Right of the Church to Acquire Property.
132. HESTON, REV. EDWARD LOUIS, C.S.C., PH.D., S.T.D., J.C.L., The Alienation of Church Property in the United States.
133. HOGAN, REV. JAMES JOHN, S.T.L., J.C.L., Judicial Advocates and Procurators.
134. KEALY, REV. THOMAS M., A.B., Litt.B., J.C.L., Dowry of Women Religious.
135. KEENE, REV. MICHAEL JAMES, O.S.B., J.C.L., Religious Ordinaries and Canon 198.
136. KERIN, REV. CHARLES A., S.S., M.A., S.T.B., J.C.L., The Privation of Christian Burial.
137. LOUIS, REV. WILLIAM FRANCIS, M.A., J.C.L., Diocesan Archives.
138. MCDEVITT, REV. GILBERT JOSEPH, A.B., J.C.L., Legitimacy and Legitimation.
139. MCDONOUGH, REV. THOMAS JOSEPH, A.B., J.C.L., Apostolic Administrators.
140. MEIER, REV. CARL ANTHONY, A.B., J.C.L., Penal Administrative Procedure Against Negligent Pastors.
141. SCHMIDT, REV. JOHN ROGG, A.B., J.C.L., The Principles of Authentic Interpretation in Canon 17 of the Code of Canon Law.
142. SLAFKOWSKY, REV. ANDREW LEONARD, A.B., J.C.L., The Canonical Episcopal Visitation of the Diocese.
143. SWOBODA, REV. INNOCENT ROBERT, O.F.M., J.C.L., Ignorance in Relation to the Imputability of Delicts.
144. DUBÉ, REV. ARTHUR JOSEPH, A.B., J.C.L., The General Principles for the Reckoning of Time in Canon Law.
145. MCBRIDE, REV. JAMES T., A.B., J.C.L., Incardination and Excardination of Seculars.

www.ingramcontent.com/pod-product-compliance
Lightning Source LLC
LaVergne TN
LVHW050247080826
844660LV00012B/607

* 9 7 8 0 8 1 3 2 2 3 2 1 6 *